| DATE | | | |
|------|------|------|------|
|      |      |      |      |
|      |      |      |      |
|      |      |      |      |
|      |      |      |      |
|      |      |      |      |
|      |      |      |      |
|      |      |      |      |
|      |      |      |      |
|      |      |      |      |
|      |      |      |      |
|      |      |      |      |

# 60 MINUTES

THE POWER & THE POLITICS
OF AMERICA'S MOST
POPULAR TV NEWS SHOW

## ALSO BY AXEL MADSEN

# 60 MINUTES

## THE POWER & THE POLITICS OF AMERICA'S MOST POPULAR TV NEWS SHOW

## Axel Madsen

DODD, MEAD & COMPANY

NEW YORK

Published by Dodd, Mead & Company, Inc.
79 Madison Avenue, New York, N.Y. 10016

Distributed in Canada by
McClelland and Stewart Limited, Toronto

Manufactured in the United States of America

Designed by Berta Lewis

First Edition

Library of Congress Cataloging in Publication

Madsen, Axel.
  60 minutes.

  Bibliography: p.
  Includes index.
  1. 60 minutes (Television program).   2. Television
broadcasting of news—United States.   I. Title.
II. Title: Sixty minutes.
PN4888.T4M33   1984        791.45′72        84-10174
ISBN 0-396-08401-X

*To Jane Jordan Browne*

# Contents

# Acknowledgments

I could not thank all the people who took time to help me prepare this unauthorized story of the most famous newsmagazine—and not all would want their names to appear. Let me thank my editor, Jerry Gross; and, in television, Frank Goodman, David Schoenbrun, Sy Pearlman, William Leonard, Van Gordon Sauter, and staff members of the Columbia Graduate School of Journalism. In Los Angeles, I am indebted to Pierre Sauvage, Tom Thompson, Gerard Alcan, H. Hantford Brookings, and Yale Udoff. In Washington, there are Hodding Carter, Roger Mudd, and Vernita Grimes; in Chicago, William O. Petersen and family; in Polo, Illinois, Eric Gubelman; and in Indianapolis, Paul Shriver.

I would have liked to be able to acknowledge the cooperation of key members of the *60 Minutes* staff in allowing me to be the proverbial fly-on-the-wall observer from inception to airing of a story of their choice. This, however, was denied me.

# Introduction

This book is about a program that is a vital example of the phenomenon it covers—television news. It tells the story of a national institution that is both at the height of its power and at a crossroads in its evolution.

I have worked in television as a writer, a director, and as an associate producer, a job that requires persuading reluctant people to appear on camera and signing for the crew's hotel rooms. I have never worked for CBS News, however, and am not in any sense beholden to the network. Nor have I any axe to grind. My interest in *60 Minutes*—its power and its politics—is focused on news and information, the one area where a growing number of Americans watch more, not less, network television.

Conventional wisdom has it that the nature of television is such that it makes audiences lazy, that we are not used to thinking while watching the tube. Glutted on a diet of game shows, sitcoms, and shoot-em-ups that require little more than our distracted attention, we are not supposed to be interested in sober and even accusatory nonfiction programming demanding a degree of concentration. Yet the latest industry surveys find that it is in news and news coverage that a majority of people think television is improving. Television news conveys information and insights and, more than entertainment fare, remains a matter of *content*. This book is a searching look at the foremost of the newsmagazines with, for comparison, a side glance at the "opposition" on ABC and NBC. It is about content and credibility and what they mean to all of us.

To write about *60 Minutes* I approached the subject not as a sometime television hand but as an inquiring journalist with a writer's license to talk to anyone and to travel everywhere. In concept and execution the book parallels in many ways the work methods of the famous CBS pro-

gram it examines and purports to judge. *60 Minutes* stories that promised to reveal the power and the politics of the newsmagazine were isolated, first on tape and then reexamined in the field. The research took
me from the CBS headquarters in Manhattan to small towns in North
Carolina and Illinois; from courthouses in Newark and Akron to the
campuses of Columbia and Princeton universities; from the state prison
for women in Indianapolis to an investigating journalists' collective in
Los Angeles; from beneficiaries to victims of the power of *60 Minutes*
to spotlight and to influence.

My major purpose was to seek answers regarding the how and why
of the program's success from the people whose lives were spotlighted
and influenced by it, rather than soliciting the views of Don Hewitt,
founding father and executive producer of *60 Minutes,* and his four ad-
venturous correspondents. Sunday, November 26, 1978, was the momentous day when *60 Minutes* first reached the top of the ratings. In the
fearfully competitive and imitative medium of TV, this is the only regularly scheduled news and public affairs program to reach this enviable
position, which has made the program a powerful voice in the society it
tries to explain.

To reach for the ratings brass ring that makes everything possible,
*60 Minutes* turns events, emotions, issues, and trends into stories. The
story is the big bang in the beginning of all mass media success, the
bedrock of all pop entertainment. Storytelling relies on good guys and
bad guys, on the clash between them and, not too incidentally, on the
*thrill* of getting to know the bad guys. When public affairs are shaped
into such story form on a television program that has the means and the
clout to be fearlessly provocative and controversial, we get the other guy's
point of view, the enemy's side, in startlingly new "global village" ways
that politicians cannot quite accept. Four months into the Iranian hostage crisis, the Carter White House tried desperately to have a *60 Minutes* background segment suppressed, and the Reagan administration was
startled to see *60 Minutes* air Syrian foreign minister Abdel Halim
Khaddam's perspective and minimal requirements for a lasting solution
to Lebanon four days after Damascus released downed flier Robert O.
Goodman.

Being Number One invites criticism. The newsmagazine has been
accused of every sin—of being biased, sensational, superficial, and of
invading people's privacy and then walking off without regard to the
pains and chaos left behind. Many complaints have less to do with the
accuracy or fairness of the stories than with the techniques used to get

them. At one time or another the program has been guilty of virtually every serious charge leveled against it, yet the overriding conclusion of this book is that *60 Minutes* is the most informative, most entertaining prime time information show on the air. Any criticism of the show— and it is a "show"—must include ourselves as viewers, as consumers of reprocessed images. In an entertainment industry where longevity is often measured only in months and seldom in years, it is our decision to watch that has kept *60 Minutes* growing and going for more than a decade and a half. Our tuning in year after year is tacit approval of the broadcast's storytelling style; it is facts as stories with plot lines, facts as thirteen-minute playlets. Astonish us! we ask of the show each week. Amuse us, inform us, influence us.

The *60 Minutes* high command on Manhattan's West 57th Street finds outside criticism uninformed and beside the point. Yet CBS News has begun to question the program's journalistic practices, both out of the public eye and, more intriguingly, on the air. One *60 Minutes* season opener was devoted to such ethical questions as whether reporters should confront reluctant witnesses, whether it is more honest to *say* this is what happened or to *show* it happen, even if the showing is a reconstruction, a restaging of the event. Is it fair for investigating reporters to set up their own "sting"—a bar, a clinic—and in effect lure unsuspecting people before the cameras? Don Hewitt is keenly aware of the news program's inordinate influence and of the fact that people talk about *60 Minutes*. CBS News is aware of its newsmagazine's sometimes controversial techniques. And so are the courts.

This book examines various legal scuffles of *60 Minutes*, including a much-publicized defamation suit that it won—but barely—in a California Superior Court. In the hundreds of interviews I conducted for the book, I found people almost equally divided into "get-the-bastards-Mike" fans and enemies of the program with an almost visceral wish to see Mike Wallace and cohorts cut down to size. The changing social and political climate may have something to do with this. In the mid-1970s Bob Woodward and Carl Bernstein became folk heroes, while less than ten years later people often saw journalists as arrogant, amoral cynics. The image of the Lone Ranger journalist cornering a villain with an interview is giving way to a news business primarily interested in its own profits, ready to believe the worst, hungry for blood and status. It can easily be argued that *60 Minutes'* finest hours belong to the post-Watergate years when reporters were seen as irreverent but dedicated seekers of truth and that the program has been coasting ever since. But each era has its challenges, obsessions, and fantasies. The standards by which we judge ourselves and the purveyors of our entertainment and information cannot remain immutable. If I were to offer a piece of advice to the talented makers of *60 Minutes,* it would be: People are smarter than you think. More and more of us have had the experience of being interviewed or of being at an event that has been covered, and we know that what we see on the television screen is not the way it was, that real life is not so neat and its confrontations rarely as conclusive. News watching is now a generation-old habit, and audiences have more savvy than newspeople often give them credit for. A lot of us out there in TV land can see the manipulation, the con coming. But we can also appreciate the special appeal of high-wire TV journalism, of reality retold and reshaped with punch, glamor, and excitement.

Power is fleeting. Governments are voted out of office; dictators are toppled. Going into its seventeenth season, *60 Minutes* is being challenged by ABC and NBC newsmagazines bristling with talent and lusting for a chance to take on the aging leader. When I started writing this book, Sunday evenings in the 1984–85 season seemed destined to be the time for the biggest showdown in nonfiction television. Before the book was in galleys, NBC's challenge, *First Camera,* had been cancelled for being the lowest-rated broadcast on network television, and a new newsmagazine was being developed.

*60 Minutes* has had an extraordinary hold on one hour of prime time since the mid-1970s, a hammerlock on popular attention that no one in news has ever had before. Its distinctive confrontation style, its provocative fare, leavened with wit and showbiz flair, have guaranteed its continued presence. Yet like everyone else in the consumer arts and entertainment business, Hewitt and his angels—as the band of celebrity correspondents and worker bees are called on 57th Street—must top themselves. The broadcasts can be so much better, say the more perceptive industry insiders, who are also among the program's sincerest fans. Hewitt and his angels must guard against trivializing their own success. They have the freedom and the money to go wherever they want, the clout to get access, the talent to do any story they want, and that great big audience just sitting there waiting for them every Sunday.

This book is offered as a challenge to the makers of *60 Minutes* to top themselves and to the rest of us to recognize their reaching for the brass ring. The book's aim is to examine the ethics, morals, and techniques of *60 Minutes,* to stimulate discussion, and to retell some of its watershed episodes. It is a look at how—for better or for worse—the program uses its power, and it offers an in-depth look at the complex politics that lay behind the choice and editing of its stories. The book will have succeeded if the reader finds it to be a progress report, a sharing of notes on one of the most influential and controversial programs we have on television.

Axel Madsen
*April 1984*

# 1

# Afterburn

## *Polo, Illinois. A "60 Minutes"*
## *story retraced*

It is hard to catch Mayor Saunders. The best bet, says town clerk Noralee Gray down at the municipal office, is to try his business up on Jefferson Street. Can't miss it, the farm machinery place. But Bill Saunders isn't there. "He's in and out," says his wife, still holding the office phone. Parts for pipes and tractors sit on the cement floor, waybills and invoices neatly tucked under them. Off to the side of the office by the big store window overlooking the parking lot and the Illinois Central track is a kid's table and chair, a toy refrigerator, and freshly abandoned crayons. Pat Saunders and her four-year-old daughter spend a lot of time in the shop while Bill is out in the pickup. This afternoon the girl went with her father. Harvest time is busy in farm machinery, Pat explains.

Polo is in western Illinois, twelve miles of gentle, straight-plowed hills west of Oregon, the Ogle County seat. Ogle County consistently ranks among the fifty leading U.S. counties in the value of all farm products sold. Polo makes lawn spreaders, air conditioning coils, and relay switches. Three industries in a town of 2,600 is pretty good for these parts, but that doesn't mean the recession didn't hurt. If you need jeans or jackets these days, you drive twelve miles down to Dixon. The

1

retail clothing store on Mason Street closed. Families are smaller, and everybody knows someone who left. True grit in the heartland, they say over at the *Tri-County Press,* Ogle County's weekly newspaper. The real Polo, like the real America, just won't fit the stereotypes, they add, a little defensively. Besides, this is Reagan country. Down in Dixon, the highway department put up green road markers pointing to the President's home. Those years Ronald Reagan spent in California and other places don't count here.

It was just before harvest time in 1982 that William Willson and Mike Wallace piled out of a van with smoked windows and came in asking for Bill Saunders. Mike Wallace! Pat had to tell them her husband wasn't in right now. They conferred, and Pat heard them say in that case they'd shoot the street stuff first. "We'll be back," Mike Wallace said, smiling. Pat smiled back, to show she knew who he was. Pat Saunders is thirty-two. She has a way of showing her gapping teeth and touching her glasses when she smiles. She watched Mike Wallace and Bill Willson, who had identified himself as the producer, climb into the van. It didn't have the CBS eye or anything on the side, she noticed before calling Noralee down at the office. Noralee knew everything. Sure was *60 Minutes;* in town to do a story about public assistance. You mean the Stitzel case? That's what it looked like. This morning, Mike Wallace and crew had been over in Oregon filming Stewart Stitzel appearing in circuit court on behalf of his eleven-year-old daughter. Later in the day Mike Wallace would try to interview Dorothy Clothier. In fact, that guy Willson had been in Polo three weeks ago. He'd come into Dorothy's office and, without saying who he was, asked for the forms you fill out when you want township assistance. Pat didn't know the Stitzels.

Stewart and Trudy Stitzel were relatively newcomers in town. They had four children, including little Susan who was severely handicapped. One of the boys worked at the supermarket after school, the father worked at Ludwig's Dairy down in Dixon, but they all kind of kept to themselves. Pastor William Penn said they rejected friendship and were quick to sue or threaten to sue. Pastor Penn's First Baptist Church wasn't the only congregation that had tried to help.

Stewart Stitzel was suing city officials for turning off the water for ten hours last January 15 because of nonpayment of a $672 water bill and for denying the family general assistance. County Supervisor Dorothy Clothier said the township believed it had followed Illinois state standards in denying the assistance. Stitzel made $19,000 a year at the dairy, and little Susan's basic social security and Medicaid benefit for 1981 had come to just over $4,000. In circuit court this morning of August 25, Judge Alan W. Cargerman had called Susan profoundly disabled and, pending trial, granted Stitzel's request that his daughter's eligibility be maintained even if he couldn't prove that he and his family spend $579 a month toward her medical expenses. "With due deference to Illinois taxpayers," Judge Cargerman ruled, continuing Susan's eligibility for a month or two seems justified by her severe condition. She had been in a vegetative state since suffering measles encephalitis at fifteen months, he said. "She weighs but thirty-five pounds at age eleven and can neither walk nor attend to her needs for food and elimination. Her mental development and speech have been severely retarded, and she requires frequent broncholidation and suctioning to keep her lungs clear of fluid."

Outside Daws' drugstore over on Mason, Mike Wallace interviewed Joe Eichholz. Joe sat in his wheelchair and listened to the questions Mike Wallace read to him from a typed crib sheet. Did Joe know the Stewart Stitzel family? Did he feel the city would be better off if they left? Did he feel the township was wrong in denying aid, in cutting off the water? Would he have cut off their water if he had been mayor? Did he believe the Stitzels were exploiting their handicapped child for financial gain? Joe said he didn't really know the Stitzel family, but that the township had been good to him and helped him financially for a long time. Jim Kavanaugh, too. Kavanaugh was a newcomer, a man with eight kids. His son had been in a bad accident. People had taken care of the seven Kavanaugh children and even raised $1,000 to help with the medical bills. Joe has a speech impediment, as everyone knows, but he didn't hesitate too much on camera. In fact, he was better than Gary Daws, the pharmacist, who fidgeted with his glasses when it was his turn. Doris Weaver was next, telling Mike Wallace she had a grandson who had leukemia and that she herself had raised two handicapped children and had been able to pay her bills, that Polo had been nothing but good to her and her family. Mike Wallace kept his jacket on. Newspeople do that, even on a hot August day like this.

After the street interviews, Wallace put his questions to Bill Shaw, the publisher of the *Tri-County Press,* which proudly announces it has published in Polo for 125 years. Everybody calls it the *Tri-County* or just the *TCP*. Mike Wallace asked Shaw if he felt the paper should have covered the plight of the Stitzel girl, if he felt he should have urged town officials to provide aid. The publisher answered that he felt the Stitzels might not qualify for any financial aid, that he believed the township was doing its best to allocate emergency funds and protect the taxpayers' interest. No, *Tri-County* had not done a story on the Stitzels because Trudy Stitzel hadn't wanted to talk about her family's problem to the newspaper.

Willson, Wallace, and crew got to the mayor late that afternoon when the Saunders' thirteen-year-old son was home from school and could watch his father being interviewed. Before they started filming, Bill Saunders explained he couldn't talk much because of the lawsuit. The interview lasted an hour. Yes, it was true the town had cut off the water, but only after trying for one year to collect the Stitzels' water bill. Yes, it was unfortunate that Susan was severely retarded and suffering. Did he know she needed water to run a suction machine, that she needed several baths a day to control her temperature? Bill Saunders answered by asking what kind of parents would jeopardize their suffering child by making no effort to pay the water bill or tell the city why they couldn't? No, he had never visited the family, but . . . Mike Wallace asked a lot of questions, and Bill came away thinking the famous reporter was trying to get all the facts. When they were through and the crew was packing up, Pat Saunders asked how they had gotten wind of the Stitzel story. They weren't very forthright, but she gathered the Stitzels' lawyer in Chicago had put CBS onto it. When she asked when the program would air, Willson told her probably around Thanksgiving, if at all.

Dorothy Clothier caused the *60 Minutes* crew some difficulty. She remembered Willson coming into her office three weeks earlier and asking for the forms you fill out if you want assistance. She had asked who he was. It was for a friend in the township, he had answered. Dorothy is an energetic lady, an upright person who tells it like it is. Randy Reese, the lawyer defending the township in the Stitzel suit, didn't think it was a good idea for Dorothy to grant an interview. But Mike Wallace persuaded Reese to check with Judge Stanley Roszkowski. After all, the Stitzels had spoken at length on camera and disclosed medical and financial details about themselves. Why couldn't Miss Clothier? She did. There were Stewart Stitzel's $19,000 salary and the boy's earnings at the supermarket, which brought the family total to $21,000. There were Susan's basic social security income, her Medicaid benefits, and the Ogle County public aid. In 1981, the township had approved $557 in assistance so Commonwealth Edison would not cut off the Stitzels' electricity. And the Catholic and Lutheran churches in town had helped pay the family's fuel bill for each of the three years the Stitzels had lived in Polo. General assistance was discontinued in 1982, however, when the family refused to submit the correct eligibility forms. "I asked them to come in and prove to me that they were still eligible for assistance," Dorothy told Wallace. "They had to bring in their pay stubs. I could never get them to cooperate.'' Wallace also interviewed Donna Mann, the home economist adviser who had helped pull the financial details together for Judge Cargerman. Now she did it for the television people. ''The money just wasn't there,'' she said on camera.

The *60 Minutes* crew left Polo the next afternoon. The following week, the *Tri-County* ran Mike Wallace's questions on page three and asked readers to send in their answers, which would be forwarded to the newsmagazine. Do you know the Stewart Stitzel family? Do you feel the city would be better off if they left? To Wallace's eight questions, the paper added a few of its own.* Do you read the *Tri-County Press* regularly? Do you feel the *TCP* should have covered the plight of the Stitzel child better and urged officials to provide aid? Do you believe *60 Minutes* will fairly portray the Stitzel situation in Polo? Being interviewed by Mike Wallace, publisher Shaw wrote in his weekly column, was ''like David meeting Goliath's bigger brother.'' On September 26, one month after *60 Minutes* had left town, little Susan Stitzel died. The family buried her in Chicago on the 30th. A CBS crew filmed the funeral. The following Sunday, October 3, 1982, *Small Town, USA* was the lead-in story on the *60 Minutes* broadcast.

Correspondent Morley Safer introduced the segment, describing Polo as ''the kind of place that would put out a welcome mat.'' But that was not what the Stitzel family experienced during their four years in Polo. ''We have to move—there's no two ways about it,'' said Stewart Stitzel. ''For my family and for our own self-respect, we're going to have to move.''

There was Mike Wallace, walking down Mason and telling the camera how the Stitzels ran up a $672 water bill the previous winter and how they had their water cut off January 15 in temperatures below zero. The water was cut off, Wallace explained, even though Mayor Saunders knew that Susan Stizel, because of her condition, required extra water. The program said the mayor also knew of the budget analysis by Donna Mann, which showed that, after expenses, the Stitzel family had ''a meager $46.75 to feed and clothe their family of six.'' Wallace described how the water had been turned back on later that January day after the city made Stitzel sign an agreement to come up with $25 a week in back

*The other six were: Do you feel the township was wrong in denying aid? Do you think the city should have cut off their water? Would you have cut off their water if you were mayor? Do you believe the Stitzels are exploiting their handicapped child for financial gain? Do you believe it would be wrong to order and pay for cable TV and not pay a water bill? Do you watch the TV show *60 Minutes* regularly?

payments. "The circumstances were forced upon us and what happened was totally unreal," Stitzel told Wallace. "We have a daughter we feel that indirectly, if not directly, caught pneumonia because of this. And her life was endangered." When Stitzel couldn't pay the $25 a week, the city threatened to turn the water off again. This time the family went to court and sued Polo. Judge Cargerman ordered the Stitzels to pay $5 a week on the back bill and restrained the city from turning off the water.

Dorothy Clothier was next, agreeing with Mike Wallace's suggestion that the Stitzels "are bent on bilking the township of Polo or the welfare people." She claimed the family refused to submit the correct eligibility forms and were eventually ruled ineligible because they didn't meet income guidelines. And there was the *Tri-County* poll results. Two hundred and fifty people had answered the survey, and 91 percent of them said the city was right in shutting off the Stitzels' water, and 80 percent thought the community would be better off if the family left town. None of the other questions were broadcast. After talk of institutionalizing Susan and what it would cost the state of Illinois, Trudy Stitzel said of her daughter, "She's not taking anything away from us. If anything she's giving us an awful lot." There was footage of Susan, and the story ended with shots of her funeral that previous Thursday.

The fire storm began before *Small Town, USA* was over and built through the evening as viewers in the western time zones began to watch *60 Minutes*. The Saunders had planned to go bowling after the program. Pat got the first phone threat from someone in Tampa, Florida, who said he'd come to Polo and when he'd be through with the mayor, hizzoner's hospital bill would be more than $2,600, an apparently garbled reference to the amount the Stitzels had paid in medical care for their daughter. Tillie Monks, who was on the police switchboard that Sunday evening, got hold of Chief Tim Goodson, who came down to help with the phones. Many callers believed Susan Stitzel had died the day after the water had been cut off. Some made threats of bodily harm to Bill Saunders and other town officials. Some wanted to blow up Polo. And it was not a night to be named Shaw in Ogle County. The publisher, who was on a previously scheduled trip, called home and learned that his wife had received calls. And the wife of another Bill Shaw received abusive calls from nine states.

Chief Goodson had watched *60 Minutes* at home and thought the reaction would be vehement, but he was taken aback by the obscenities. He advised Bill and Pat to take the kids and spend the night somewhere else. Gunshots were fired in the vicinity of the Saunders' home and there were sporadic, but false, reports to police that the home was on fire. By

11 P.M., more than two hundred calls had been logged at the police station. Goodson called officer Gary Schultz from vacation and put the rest of the department on extended shifts. The calls continued until after 2:30 Monday morning, resumed later in the day, and ran on into the early afternoon. At times, both phones at the township office were busy. At the *Tri-County* office over on Franklin, other dozens rang in, most calling the residents of Polo heartless monsters.

More than twenty mailgrams were delivered to Noralee's office. All but four expressed outrage at Polo's handling of the Stitzels and disgust toward the town's residents. "You all stink," said the shortest mailgram, from Cincinnati. "The people of Polo we heard on *60 Minutes* made us so ashamed we cried," wrote a couple in Wilsonville, Oregon. A mailgram from Olympia, Washington, said, "May God forgive you. I cannot." "We are shocked, appalled, and ashamed to share this country with people like you," wired a couple in Madison, Wisconsin, a sentiment echoed in a Brooklyn, New York, family's message: "My family witnessed what you people did to that little girl and feel that you, Mayor Saunders, and your townspeople are a disgrace to our country." The most drastic suggestion came from a couple in Arvada, Colorado: "After watching Mike Wallace on *60 Minutes* this evening we have decided your town would be the perfect spot for the next nuclear test site. Never have we seen so much hate come from so many ugly people. Aren't you relieved your problem died last week? Bless you. God knows you need it." A man in Stone Mountain, Georgia, said, in part, "Go to hell" and repeated the suggestion in a second mailgram to the *Tri-County Press.* A message from a woman in San Francisco said, "Can one small town have so much hatred for a sick child? Does an unpaid water bill of $755 seem worth a child's life?"

Bill Saunders got a round of applause from a packed gallery at a council meeting the Monday night after the show. Bill is a former Jaycee member—older folks think of him as a nice young man—but at the council meeting that night the thirty-four-year-old mayor was angry. Polo had been ripped apart by *60 Minutes,* he said, and the town had no choice now but to "hang together." Representatives from the Chamber of Commerce asked what they could do to help repair the town's good name. Council member Dave Wagner wasn't sure the community had lost its good name. "I love this town," he said. He called Mike Wallace "a son of a gun," and, noting the microphone held by a reporter from WDSR, Dixon, said he'd like to get Wallace there and talk to him in front of a microphone. Arlene Bloom suggested from the audience that everybody write to CBS. "Tell them we're caring people—they make us out like monsters." Noralee Gray told the meeting she got a call from a minister in Las Vegas who claimed he would be coming to Polo with 5,000 to 10,000 people "to save your souls." Callers ranged from Canada to Hawaii, and many calls were religious in nature, she said. A person claiming to be from Moody Engineering in Boston said the firm planned to boycott Polo, and one anonymous caller hoped everyone in Polo would die of thirst. Publisher Shaw said he got a call from one woman who said she planned "to win a free trip to Polo to see what kind of horses' asses lived there." Dorothy Clothier said the program had only aired the very end of the long interview she had given Mike Wallace.

The mayor got up again and told how *his* interview had lasted one hour. Sure Mike Wallace had asked if he had visited the Stitzels, if he knew of the girl's condition and how important water was for her. Bill had answered yes to all three questions, and Mike Wallace had said, "And yet it was you, Mr. Mayor, as I understand it, who authorized that their water be turned off because of that unpaid bill. Isn't that a fact?" "That's correct," Bill had answered and proceeded to explain. On the air, his explanation disappeared. Somebody wanted to know why Mike Wallace had portrayed the family as too hard up to pay their water bill without mentioning that the Stitzels had enough money to subscribe to Rock Valley Cablevision, that they maintained three cars, all of them admittedly old.

The meeting turned to the Stitzels' lawsuit. Marv Ripley, who defended the town, Mayor Saunders, Dorothy Clothier, water superintendent George Salter, and former township supervisor Larry Lannen, told the meeting several days of court time would be taken up to present the facts, something that couldn't be done in twelve minutes of television air time. At the trial, all the facts would be put on the table. Maybe *60 Minutes* would be back then to do a follow-up and, Ripley suggested, when the final story is told, we believe the city will be vindicated. The Chamber of Commerce voted to set up a committee to deal with the hate mail because Polo was a decent place and every letter would be answered. Former supervisor Lannen and Noralee were named to the committee.

Before letters began arriving—there were to be 643 one week later when the Saunders quietly moved back into their home—reporters from channel 8 in Moline and channels 4, 6, and 23 up in Rockford climbed out of vans at Jefferson and Dixon and came in, cameras and recorders drawn. If Bill was out in the pickup, they interviewed Pat. When they spotted the Saunders girl with her crayons in the corner of the shop by the window, they wanted to film her. "*You*'ve got a daughter," they told Pat. A couple of times Pat felt they thought they were Mike Wallace and the crew of *60 Minutes*.

The Stitzels moved to Sterling, thirteen miles west of Dixon, that year. The eldest son had continued in Polo Community High School, where principal Leroy Hooks overheard him telling classmates the family had received $7,000 from *60 Minutes* watchers across the country. Hooks wouldn't say the Stitzels had been run out of town, but there were some hard feelings. Ron Clark, the Stitzels' Chicago attorney, characterized the family's life in Polo following the broadcast as "miserable." No one would speak to the Stitzels or acknowledge their presence in public. "They never received an ounce of charity from Polo following the *60 Minutes* broadcast," Clark said, adding that a couple of Polo residents sent letters of support to the family but that these were anonymous. The children suffered in school, the lawyer said, taunted by their classmates. Chief Goodson confirmed the Stitzels had reported harassing calls, and County State Attorney Dennis Schumacher sent a notice to the area newspapers and radio stations advising that his office had placed taps on telephones in Ogle County to catch those making threatening or obscene calls. Several ministers tried to verify the existence of the Las Vegas preacher who had said he would lead a crusade to save Polo's soul.

The committee answered the hate mail, and the *Tri-County Press* ran a photo of Noralee sitting with a sample of the 643 letters. Some of the letters contained money to cover the Stitzels' water bill. There was a one-dollar bill from a correspondent who directed the money be given to the city "to help it get back on its feet again." Noralee was contacted by WBBM, the CBS owned and operated station in Chicago; by UPI; by the *Quad City Times,* and was interviewed live by WBBF Radio in Rochester, New York. Mike Mooney of the *Rockford Register-Star,* the area's daily, did a piece of investigative journalism of his own. "This is the best place a handicapped person could live," Joe Eichholz told Mooney. Joe was obviously the best advertisement for Polo, but when Mooney called *60 Minutes* in New York, he was told the interview with Joe Eichholz hadn't been used out of regard for Joe's speech impediment. Eric Gubelman, the new *Tri-County Press* editor, was the new man in town, a twenty-four-year-old journalist from Robinson in eastern Illinois. He had started working a few days before *Small Town, USA* aired and didn't know what to think. To begin at the beginning, he tooled the thirty-nine miles up to Rockford and read the Stitzels' court depositions. He came away feeling Stewart Stitzel just wasn't plugged into modern money matters. The man didn't have a bank account.

In January 1983, seven of the fourteen counts in the Stitzels' suit against the city and township, Mayor Saunders, Dorothy Clothier, Larry Lannen, and George Salter were dismissed in U.S. District Court in Rockford. Judge Stanley Roszkowski didn't rule on the merits but on whether there was legal sufficiency in the way the charges were framed. Thrown out were the family's charges that the city and its officials discriminated against the handicapped by turning off the water, that the city acted arbitrarily and capriciously, violating the equal protection clause of the Constitution, that the city breached a contract by not supplying uninterrupted water service, and that the city intentionally inflicted emotional stress on the Stitzels. Another count thrown out—one that may not be amended—was a claim that since the city allowed the Stitzels to pay their water bill in installments, it in effect granted them credit, making them subject to federal Truth in Lending Act laws. Allowed to stand and go to trial were the family's claim that the city denied due process by turning off the water without notice, their allegation that the city violated state law by inflicting emotional stress, their claim that they should not have to pay back their unpaid water bill because a written agreement made with the city the night the water was turned back on was not made of Stewart Stitzel's free will, and the family's right to seek punitive damages for violation of due process.

Clark, the Stitzels' lawyer, credited Judge Roszkowski with persuading Stewart and Trudy to settle by talking frankly to them about the benefits of putting the past and its hardship behind them and continuing with their life. "He was very persuasive," said Clark of the judge. What persuaded the town and the township to lean toward an out-of-court settlement was the realization by Mayor Saunders and his council that defending the lawsuit would be expensive. Clark could amend the plaintiffs' charges, which meant Polo and the township could challenge the amended charges, thereby delaying a trial date, but the legal fees would keep rising. Emotionally, Bill and Pat Saunders would want their day in court, but it wasn't their money that was on the line. "Bill gets $1,000 a year of being mayor, probably what Mike Wallace makes an hour," Pat said after reading in *Newsweek* that his new CBS contract would give Wallace $1 million a year. Like Eric Gubelman, Leroy Hooks, and Noralee Gray, Pat couldn't help thinking it was Susan Stitzel's death that had made the story for *60 Minutes*. Bill Willson had told her the story would air, if at all, around Thanksgiving. And then three days after they buried little Susan, *Small Town, USA* was broadcast. "Who was exploiting whom?" she asked defiantly.

By spring 1983, the attorneys fees for Marv Ripley and Randy Reese, the lawyers representing Polo and the township, were topping $12,000. Going to trial would bring the legal defense costs to at least $40,000, not counting the settlement a jury might award. No one was happy, when in open session the council voted, 6 to 0, to give Ripley authority to make an offer. The $450,000 the Stitzels demanded in their lawsuit came down to $150,000, an amount Ripley termed "totally ludicrous." The Stitzels came down again to $75,000, and in a topsy-turvy April week of postponed and cancelled court dates up in Rockford, to $60,000.

Television intruded one more time. Saunders, Ripley, and everybody else in Polo learned on the Rockford evening news that the city and township had settled for $60,000. The surprise disclosure angered Saunders and Ripley, and, back in his Chicago office, Clark tried to explain. The announcement had been a "miscommunication," he said. He thought all parties knew there was a $60,000 settlement at the conclusion of a conference call he had attended in Rockford. When he left the courtroom, television cameras had been waiting. Said Ripley, "I sure would have liked to have been advised before Mike Wallace."

*Small Town, USA* is typical of high-powered broadcast reporting. Conflict makes for exciting television, and exciting television achieves the top ratings. *60 Minutes* segments are not John LeCarré set pieces of moral ambiguity, exploring the gray areas of good and evil in an increasingly complex society. The *60 Minutes* format cannot accommodate too many "but on the other hand" qualifiers, too much time spent on dark and tortured moral frontiers. Stories are shaped into allegorical dramas, and such thirteen-minute playlets demand a good guys-bad guys cast, clear plot, and dramatic buildup. Once the Stitzels' lawyer alerted the newsmagazine to a possible gothic piece about small minds in a small town and producer Willson had shown up in Dorothy Clothier's office to confirm the bare essentials, Polo never had a chance.

On that cold January morning when the water had been cut off, frail little Susan had become a victim, and Polo was damned as a town of heartless monsters. That was the story. Willson couldn't phone executive producer Don Hewitt in New York and say this was a sad tale of misunderstanding between a struggling, somewhat bitter family on the social edge and a small town trying to manage its resources in a recession. No doubt there were decent folk in Polo, but their testimony could not be considered. While Joe Eichholz might stammer on about how well the community had treated him over the years, both Willson and Wallace knew his declarations wouldn't be used (Joe's speech impediment proved a nice excuse), but they stood there on Mason Street in the August heat and let him rattle on. The price of goodwill. When they moved on to the Saunders' farm machinery shop and Wallace asked Bill if it wasn't true he had authorized the water shutoff and the mayor said, "That's correct," his subsequent explanation became irrelevant. Of the local newspaper's poll, only the results that made the community hang itself were used. Never mentioned was the fact that even those who were sympathetic to the Stitzels' plight—and there were many—could not understand why the family thought it was entitled to a cash windfall because the water was turned off for ten hours. The July 1983 rerun, introduced by Wallace himself, mentioned the out-of-court settlement, but not that it had resulted in higher taxes for Polo. Of the two day's interviews that Willson and crew filmed in Polo, only the lines that accommodated the plot line became part of the broadcast.

Such is the power and the politics of the most widely watched nonentertainment series in television history.

# 2

# From There
# to Here

## *The newsmagazine in overview*

*60 Minutes* made its debut September 24, 1968, as a twice-a-month, Tuesday-night-at-ten, news hour. Murder and riots, along with an unpopular war and fizzled peace moves, shaped the incredible U.S. election year that saw President Johnson challenged and withdrawing as the Democratic Party candidate and succeeded by a man many had come to regard as an easy-to-beat loser. The lead story featured Richard Nixon and Vice President Hubert Humphrey in their hotel suites the night they were nominated at their respective conventions. It was followed by a segment called *Cops,* a topic very much in the news a month after the tumultuous Democratic Convention in Chicago, a commentary by Art Buchwald that reviewers thought was below the humorist's par, and ex-cerpts from *Why Man Creates,* a film made for Kaiser Aluminum by Hollywood's master of screen credit sequences, Saul Bass.

The segments were reported by Harry Reasoner and Mike Wallace. Reasoner kind of owed one to producer Don Hewitt and that summer had agreed to do the sample pilot. The bosses hadn't been impressed, but they had suggested the multiformat magazine might work if Hewitt had *two* on-camera reporters and especially if the second guy had a style

13

different from Reasoner's. The correspondent in the CBS News pool *least* like Reasoner was probably Mike Wallace and, after the Democratic Convention and between covering the Nixon campaign, Wallace did a second demo reel with Reasoner.

From the beginning, the idea was not to have hosts sitting in a studio but reporters out doing their stuff. On too many news stories, the camera crew covered the event, and the correspondent merely provided the captions. The *60 Minutes* approach was: If you're doing a story about aircraft carriers, show your correspondent on the deck of a flattop with jets screeching off behind him. If you're doing a profile on a tennis star, have your man try to smack a ball across the net to the pro. Show your reporter confronting someone suspected of having something to hide. Let people *see* the give and take. People are not interested in issues; they are interested in people. As a very young television director of several episodes of the legendary Edward R. Murrow series *See It Now*, Hewitt had noticed that audiences weren't so much interested in the story as in Murrow and what Murrow found out. Viewers, Hewitt believed, will identify with the reporter asking the questions *they* would ask. The criteria for a story on the new *60 Minutes* were that it tell something new and have a national dimension; that it would lend itself to simple and concrete pictures and argument, preferably a confrontation of people and issues; and that it could be told in just thirteen minutes.

That this could be a winning proposition was apparent to very few people at CBS in 1968. The newsmagazine bumped along in the lower depths of the Nielsen ratings. The network had so little confidence that it preempted *60 Minutes* many times. As a result, the program was never seen two fortnights in a row until December 1969. The following year *60 Minutes* lost Reasoner and his writer chum Andy Rooney, who for years had written the lighter stuff Harry was so good at. Morley Safer, who headed the London bureau of CBS News, agreed to become Reasoner's replacement on condition that he could have the London job back if the program was cancelled. NBC came up with a once-a-month imitation called *First Tuesday*, but on Tuesday nights at ten, viewers were engrossed in a show about a fatherly doctor who still made house calls and half the time seemed to forget to charge his patients. ABC's *Marcus Welby, M.D.* was such a success that NBC shifted *First Tuesday* to Fridays and weighed in with a sitcom, *Marriage Can Be Fun*. CBS cancelled *60 Minutes* as a regular every-other-Tuesday offering and pitted *Cannon*, a chubby private eye, against the good Dr. Welby.

But 1970 was the year of the "access rule," when the Federal Communications Commission decided television stations in the top fifty markets would have to give up a half hour of prime time programming on weekdays and one hour on Sundays. The FCC's noble intention was to increase the diversity of TV fare by making it necessary for stations to program those periods on their own initiative. Local sponsors, however, could not or would not buy time on locally made half-hour programs, and syndicated Hollywood product proved to be a lot cheaper. Soon an exception to the access rule was made for children's specials, documentaries, and public affairs programs on Sunday. *60 Minutes* found new life on Sunday evenings from six to seven.

Morley Safer was perfectly happy doing stylish, urbane, and finely honed "soft" pieces to complement the more muscular exposés and prosecutorial interviews that his senior partner did (Wallace: "I'll take a question as far as it can go"). The times were confrontational. The Nixon administration felt increasingly under siege and mounted an unprecedented assault on broadcast journalism. Within months, Safer was also turning out tough stories and pithy profiles. Don Hewitt's energy and instinct for drama and angle, the legwork of his producers, and the deft styles of Wallace—incisive, inquisitional—and Safer—persistent, prodding—were behind a harrowing look at cluster bombs and the Minneapolis blue chip company making them; a profile of columnist Jack Anderson, who was the prime White House suspect of increasingly embarrassing leaks; a long look at the South Vietnamese army; examinations of women and marriage laws; and of amnesty for draft evaders in Canada. There was southern gothic in a report on the shenanigans in a Georgia company town, and reports on conflict in Nigeria, the Middle East, and Northern Ireland. There were interviews with Vice President Spiro Agnew, POW wives, Clifford Irving of the fake Howard Hughes biography caper, and, on the lighter side, profiles of Federico Fellini, and a ninety-one-year-old Irish lady who had bought a Rolls-Royce in 1927 and kept it for forty-four years. There were stories on what it was like to be middle class and poor in Seattle, and to be stuck in an Italian traffic jam. There were reports on stolen credit cards and the auto repair racket. In fact, 20 percent of the stories dealt with one swindle or another, something that moved Safer to observe that no con man thought he'd made it until he had been on *60 Minutes*. The program was the first network news show to ask for feedback, to have a "Letters from Our Viewers" desk. It also had exchanges of opinion between James J. Kilpatrick, conservative pundit on *The Washington Star,* and Nicholas von Hoffman, liberal columnist for *The Washington Post.* They found each other hopelessly muddleheaded. Von Hoffman's liberal torch was handed to former *Life* magazine writer Shana Alexander, who got herself fired in 1979 when she demanded two and a half times what Kilpatrick earned for their three-minute on-air disquisitions. Andy Rooney, who had returned to CBS after a brief stint with PBS and ABC, slipped into the back of *60 Minutes* as a summer replacement for Alexander and Kilpatrick.

Dan Rather joined Wallace and Safer as the third reporter in December 1975 just as the newsmagazine began to soar in the ratings. There are two schools of thought as to why *60 Minutes* in three short years became the first regularly scheduled news or public affairs program to reach the top. The time slot school believes the network decision in 1975 to move the newsmagazine back one hour was momentous. Whatever program goes into the seven-to-eight time slot is expected to have "leadership," to pull the rest of the Sunday evening schedule onwards and upwards. The crucial new time gave *60 Minutes* clout with the CBS programming people who, in turn, began to promote this one exception (but also to cut it short when Sunday football ran into overtime in the Eastern time zone). The chicken-before-the-egg school is convinced *60 Minutes* got network respect because it was beginning to have power and clout.

In January 1975, Safer did a piece on handguns, showing how revolvers, purchased legally in South Carolina, were sold illegally on the streets of New York. Within months, the South Carolina legislature passed the state's first restrictive handgun law. A week later, Morley reported a real estate scam in Arizona, a piece that capped months of undercover digging and led to a federal crime strike force to hand down indictments. A story Rather did on the pesticide Kepone resulted in 153 indictments and a $13 million fine against Allied Chemical Corporation for its part in contaminating Virginia's James River. Four months later, *60 Minutes* ran a piece on Representative Robert L. F. Sikes of Florida, who had got entangled in grievous conflicts of interest as head of the House Military Construction Appropriations Committee. Common Cause, the reform group, had prodded the House to investigate Sikes, but the House Committee on Standards of Official Conduct had refused to move, and House members were not eager to pursue the case. Then Rather went on the air with a scorching exposé of the congressman, and the House was deluged with mail. The House reprimanded Sikes for financial misconduct, and the Democratic caucus stripped him of the committee chairmanship. After a segment exploring the risk of thyroid cancer among people who had undergone massive radiation treatment in the neck years earlier, thousands of former patients thronged doctors' offices for checkups. A piece Mike Wallace did on Syrian Jews so offended the American Jewish Congress that its president made a formal complaint to CBS. Others quick to object following various stories were the National Council of Churches, the National Rifle Association, the Irish Republican Army, and the government of South Africa. A probe of such journalistic practices as press junkets had Walter Cronkite hopping mad in 1974. Six years later, *60 Minutes* turned its cameras on itself and devoted an entire hour to examining its own ethics.

The protracted Watergate hearings, the closing tragedy in Vietnam, the high drama of Richard Nixon's resignation, the attempted assassination of President Ford—caught by news cameras—kept an ever-growing number of Americans glued to breaking news, panel discussions, investigative reports, magazine broadcasts, specials, and the expanded local news hours. Still, the battle was uphill. *60 Minutes* finished the 1975–76 season in fifty-second prime time place, but by the fall of 1976 was climbing so fast it was allowed to "bump the network." That is, it would be shown in its entirety in the Eastern time zone whenever football finished and the rest of the Sunday night schedule was simply bumped back. In 1975, a thirty-second spot sold for $17,000 to $27,000 on the newsmagazine, depending on the time of year (rates are highest from mid-October to December). A year later, the rates for half a minute jumped to $30,000 to $50,000, which was comparable to what advertisers paid on such hits as *Tony Orlando and Dawn* and *Barnaby Jones*. In 1977, CBS tried a first spin-off called *Who's Who* with Dan Rather as anchor and chief reporter. Harry Reasoner returned to CBS and became a fourth correspondent in time for the tenth anniversary in September 1979. Two months later, *60 Minutes* climbed—for one triumphant week—to the top of the ratings. Toward the end of 1979, the newsmagazine's only competitor for the Number One spot was CBS's own *Dallas*. A commercial minute on *60 Minutes* sold for a record $230,000. By 1982, the newsmagazine commanded the highest advertising rate on prime time for a thirty-second ad: $175,000. The program rode the crest of "reality programming" and the new public fascination with ongoing events.

Uncovering the hypocrisy, foibles, and scandals of politics and government is in the best muckraking tradition, and *60 Minutes* cheerfully investigated and exposed the boondoggles and Catch 22s of the Environmental Protection Agency and a good deal more of the federal alphabet soup from the FDA to the IRS and the NRC. It went after the Defense Department on so many embarrassing occasions that the Pentagon has a standing order of no cooperation; had fun with liberal big shots in Washington, who on Capitol Hill pushed busing while making sure their own children went to private schools; and, to the chagrin of right-of-center politicians, took up the Immigration and Naturalization Service and its treatment of illegal aliens, subsidies to agrobusiness, and *Fortune 500* chemical polluters.

Charges of exploitation have always swirled around the program. Producer Steve Glauber and Dan Rather had an easy time denying that their 1979 look at teenage gang warfare in Los Angeles was staged and rehearsed. Some of the Mexican-American youngsters featured in the story claimed they had been lied to by Glauber and Rather, that anything positive they had said and done was systematically eliminated. The L.A. Sheriff's Department, however, concluded that the allegations were unfounded. Another L.A. story Glauber and Rather did that year on faked injuries from car accidents blew up in their faces in a 1983 trial that was not *60 Minutes'* finest hour, although CBS won the suit. The court ordered the network to hand over the outtakes (sound and picture footage that had been edited out of the broadcast segment), which Dr. Carl A. Galloway claimed showed the Rather team coaxing witnesses, staging a confrontation, and repeating questions until it got the most vividly phrased answers.

But along with the distinctive confrontational style and the controversy that brought ratings, prestige, and clout came also the power to do good. Victims of miscarriage of justice walked out of prisons after their stories were aired, and professionals in difficult areas of medicine and social services earned nationwide recognition and support of a kind that publicity could never buy. When *60 Minutes* began calling local and state officials in Orange, New Jersey about the thirty-year sentence handed down in 1978 against a black high school teacher for a kidnapping that never took place, authorities soon began calling the newsmagazine back to say the convicted teacher was being considered for parole. Before his story was aired, he was back teaching in his classroom. Five years later, a black engineer who was given a life sentence for an armed robbery prosecutors later said he didn't commit walked out of a Texas prison eleven days after a *60 Minutes* investigation questioned the case. The story of a twenty-year-old girl who ended up pregnant by a prison guard and had her baby in a Florida prison while serving seven and a half years for stealing five dollars provoked such an outrage that the parole board released mother and baby a few weeks after the broadcast. Doctors working with Alzheimer's disease, Reye's syndrome, chorea, and electronic prostheses that will make the lame walk, express nothing but gratitude for the exposure they and their research received. A hospice for children dying of cancer in surburban San Francisco received tremendous support following a 1979 segment called *Helping,* a story Morley Safer said he and producer Al Wasserman approached with some hesitation: "We don't want to be voyeurs at someone's private agony," said Safer. Enrollment doubled at a Houston drug abuse program for teenagers after *60 Minutes* exposure. The newsmagazine not only publicized the problem of runaway kids but practically invented the expression "throwaways" to describe youngsters fleeing the wreckage of their families, the neglect, abuse, and abandonment of home.

For *60 Minutes,* Dan Rather disguised himself as an Afghan tribesman and made a theatrical foray into rebel territory from Pakistan. A story on health spas featured Wallace soaking in the bathing parlor of Marienbad, Czechoslovakia. Reasoner has reported on bleak alcoholism among Greenland's Eskimos and Safer on the discreet qualms of white South African bourgeois in sinful Bophuthatswana.

Mere interest by the newsmagazine provokes reaction. Violence flared anew in a year-long strike against Phelps Dodge Corporation when two *60 Minutes* producers showed up at the Clifton, Arizona copper mine in 1984 to look into the possibility of doing a story on what had become the bitterest labor confrontation in the country. Desperate to keep the strike alive after the company hired hundreds of out-of-work people, including some laid-off and once striking workers, labor leaders called out strikers to taunt the carloads of strikebreakers speeding to and from round-the-clock shifts at the mine. The demonstration staged to impress the two producers culminated in stone-throwing incidents, the arrest of eighteen individuals, and the imposition of a nighttime curfew in the mining town 140 miles northeast of Tucson. The *60 Minutes* crew interviewed Dr. Jorge O'Leary, a forty-three-year-old physician who had become the strikers' rallying point but filmed nothing. They told O'Leary they didn't like the strikers' pitch for national publicity. *First Camera* and the Los Angeles based TV newsmagazine *Newsscope,* however, found the copper miners' bid for attention compelling enough to do stories on the strike.

Van Gordon Sauter became CBS News president in 1981, and there was persistent talk that he wanted a woman opposite Wallace, Safer, and Reasoner when he moved Dan Rather to replace Walter Cronkite as the evening news anchor. When the dust settled, however, Ed Bradley became the fourth member of the exalted men's club. When Rather had joined *60 Minutes,* the mail had indicated that viewers found him too pugnacious, too controversial, and Bradley was keenly aware that if the

ratings were to slip he would be blamed. The show was by now something of a national habit, and the audience had no difficulty accepting
this seasoned foreign correspondent, political reporter, and sometime
*Sunday Evening News* anchor. Bradley has sipped the best cru of the
Baron de Rothschild's vintage Bordeaux and probed the mysterious
hanging under London's Blackfriars Bridge of Vatican banker Robert
Calvi.

Executive producer Hewitt professes not to know *why* people watch
*60 Minutes.* "Maybe it's because they like the show," he says. "Maybe
it's because they just think they ought to watch it. I don't understand at
all." Av Westin, Hewitt's counterpart on ABC's *20/20* newsmagazine,
thinks *60 Minutes* is so successful because it airs on Sundays. "Newspapers are so fat, filled with magazine sections and reviews of the week.
And there is *Face the Nation* and other interview programs. On Sundays
you are supposed to reflect and contemplate, go to church, walk in the
park, talk. The viewer can sit back and admit he hasn't read a book all
week, hasn't kept up with the papers, but if he watches *60 Minutes* maybe
he can say he's informed." *20/20* is on Thursday nights at ten, says
Westin, so that when the program starts, the viewer can sink back and
say, "Thank God, tomorrow's Friday."

The network news divisions have always stressed journalistic responsibilities over moneymaking, and nonfiction television is tricky when
it comes to revenues. A one-hour documentary is still cheap—usually
budgeted at $240,000 in production, plus another $200,000 in administrative overhead costs—but sponsors won't plunk down the top dollars
they spend on *Dallas* and *Dynasty* and "reality programming" is losing.
NBC has reduced its ninety-minute *White Papers* to sixty minutes, ABC
is airing about twelve *Closeups* a year, carefully avoiding the sweeps
weeks when every market is "swept" by A.C. Nielsen Inc., to determine how each station is faring against competing stations, thereby establishing the rating positions and how much each station can charge for
commercials for the next several months. In the mid-1960s, *CBS Reports* averaged twenty to twenty-four hours a year. Van Gordon Sauter
cut that back to less than fifteen hours. In election years, CBS gives
itself credit for an additional five hours of election specials. News
documentaries are thrown on the air at times when they can do the least
harm to ratings—Christmas Eve, New Year's Day when few people watch
anyway—and news series are scheduled for July and August when all
ratings are depressed. In late April, May, and June, only one segment
of *60 Minutes* is new every week. In July and August, all segments are
reruns. *The Rock,* a piece Safer did on Gibraltar and Gibraltarians head-

ing determinedly into the nineteenth century, was first broadcast in December 1972. It was rerun in January 1976 and May 1980 and will no doubt get a fourth go-around.

*60 Minutes* has its own spin-off in Australia. In 1981, Sydney's channel 9 made arrangements with CBS to use the format and logo, and in less then two years the down-under newsmagazine was among the top ten shows in the country. In 1983, Hewitt ran an Aussie *60 Minutes* segment on *60 Minutes:* the story of a Taiwanese baby kidnapping and smuggling ring selling infants to childless Australian couples.

To call the show *60 Minutes* is hyperbole. When the minutes that go to commercials, network bumpers (those plugs for upcoming fare), and visual transitions to commercials are deducted, *60 Minutes* is forty-seven minutes long. Each of the three segments averages thirteen minutes. Andy Rooney is allocated three minutes but sometimes uses less, and the remaining five minutes are spent on the upfront "Those stories and more tonight" intros, updates, letters from viewers, and the end credits.

Nearly 70 percent of the mail CBS News receives about its broadcasts concerns *60 Minutes*—almost 80,000 letters a year. The spur is of course to have one's invective or praise quoted on the air. Viewers don't always get the stories they write about totally right. When Safer did a piece on Liberia and said many young Liberian men went to the United States and then returned from abroad with brides, feminists wrote in to say he had insulted all women by saying Liberian men went to the United States and then returned with broads. A Reasoner segment called *Bloody Ivory* about the slaughter of Kenyan elephants for their tusks, impelled a fifteen-year-old girl to write that she was as guilty as everyone else and had decided to change soap.

*60 Minutes* enjoys a wide age spread in its demographics. Besides the retired, the housewives, and younger kids who watch a lot of television, the program has the "news seekers"—the selective, upscale viewers who seek out programming, and are often the same people who are frequent watchers of public broadcasting. The American Federation of Teachers has no statistics on how many teachers regularly assign *60 Minutes* to students, but *60 Minutes* staffers estimate 10 percent of the audience is under seventeen. They arrive at this figure by counting the letters from students begging for transcripts of stories they have missed so they can finish their homework.

The permanent staff numbers seventy, and the show shares some camera crews with the rest of the CBS news division. There are only eight staff researchers, and the ninth-floor headquarters above a Ford showroom at 555 West 57th Street in New York City is less than opulent considering that *60 Minutes* is the biggest moneymaker of CBS News. The work areas are spacious, decorated in office tower chic. Hewitt's corner office features a sumptuous Persian rug and autographed photos of Presidents and First Ladies. On his big, wide desk is a picture of his wife. The huge simulated stopwatch on the wall in the reception area reads twenty-six minutes to the hour—any hour; there is only one hand.

*60 Minutes* and *20/20* are what keep the CBS and ABC news divisions profitable. Industry cynics like to say the newsmagazines are *designed* to make money, that their function is simply to make the news divisions break even, but that, as the example of NBC illustrates, is to put the wagon before the horse. The peacock network would dearly love to have a matching winner and since the *First Tuesday* attempt in 1968 has never stopped trying. Before the 1982 effort was named *Monitor,* waggish staffers suggested *Ninth Try, Eight Maids-a-Milking, Seventh Son,* and *Third Base.*

*20/20* has more women on its staff then *60 Minutes* and a number of stories reported by women correspondents. Corporate CBS and Hewitt are sensitive to the lack of visible femininity. Diane Sawyer, the coanchor of the *CBS Morning News,* is expected to take Reasoner's place when he retires, but there are rumors that she has her eyes on a coanchorship with Dan Rather or, failing that, that the $800,000 a year "Princess Di" may seek evening stardom on another network. Hewitt says he is no more looking for a woman than for an Eskimo or a Samoan, that when he hires, what he wants is the best broadcaster available. There are half a dozen women producers on *60 Minutes,* a fact that one of them, Suzanne St. Pierre, says isn't parity, "but it isn't tokenism either." Since there are no production meetings and memos at *60 Minutes,* a producer with a hot idea to sell to Don will follow him into the men's room. This, the in-house joke goes, puts women producers at a slight disadvantage.

If all segments are new, one Sunday's edition of *60 Minutes* costs about $385,000; reruns cost practically nothing. (One hour's worth of adventure series or sitcoms costs between $500,000 and $1 million.) Entertainment programs are also repeated, but only once a year, and because of ten-year-old FCC rulings, the networks acquire rights to only one original and one repeat airing from independent producers such as Paramount-TV, Spelling-Goldberg, Glen Larson, or Lorimar. ABC, CBS, and NBC own their newsmagazines outright. There are no fees to outside producers or studios, no sharing of the profits. What further adds to the profitability is that there is no "season" in news and public affairs. *60 Minutes and 20/20* can be on the air fifty-two weeks a year.

Over 1,300 stories have been produced and aired since 1968. To get those stories, producers average 100,000 travel miles each a year, while the four correspondents log as many as 200,000 miles each. Mike Wallace has found water to be the best antidote to jet lag. He takes Mountain Valley Spring bottles on his trips and says that when they did a story on jet lag, he discovered he flew more than some airline pilots. Ed Bradley never travels without a silver Halliburton case fitted with two miniature stereo speakers, tape recorders, earphones, cassette tapes (Willie Nelson's *On The Road Again* is Ed's theme), camera, books, and a pocket-sized television set to catch the news. There is a standard story told, with any one of the quartet as the leading character. One version has Dan Rather in an airport arrival area slipping into a phone booth to call Hewitt in New York. Don asks where he is calling from. Rather pops his head out and asks a passerby. With an odd glance, he is told, "Atlanta." When Reasoner heard about this, he is supposed to have remarked that Hewitt should have guessed that without asking. "One of us is almost always at Atlanta airport."

The four correspondents are paid handsomely for their heavy travel and hard work. As the junior team member, Bradley's annual salary is estimated at $500,000. The final year of Wallace's 1983–88 contract will pay him $1 million, about the same as Hewitt's reported annual salary. Addressing the 1981 MIFED broadcasters' convention in Milan, Don said *60 Minutes* earned $50 million a year for CBS News. Telecommunications economist Alan Pearce conservatively estimates the show's annual profits to be over $60 million, or some 60 percent of the entire CBS broadcast group's profits. The group accounts for about 55 percent of total revenues and half the pretax earnings of CBS Inc.

But at *60 Minutes'* headquarters the talk isn't about making money. The emphasis is on journalism, of getting 100 stories a year, of continuing the show's reputation for fearless, controversial, provocative journalism. By a judicious use of show business flair and journalistic candor, by presenting a variety of subjects in crisply edited stories that often leave audiences wishing for more, by getting striking pictures that dramatize and amplify the words, the newsmagazine has become a TV phenomenon and a national habit. Flaws and all, it is the most influential, most informative, and best-produced public affairs program in prime time television.

# 3

# Newsflesh
*The star correspondents*

Along Broadcast Row on Manhattan's Avenue of the Americas and at Alfredo's, the newscasters' Sardi's, the famous restaurant frequented by stage and film stars, they are top newsflesh. To corporate CBS, they are what makes the news division profitable, and to Richard Leibner, who negotiates several of their golden contracts, they are celebrities. To Van Gordon Sauter they are folk heroes and Hewitt's Angels and, to Don himself, they are his "tigers." In their own considered opinion, Mike Wallace, Morley Safer, Harry Reasoner, and Ed Bradley are pros who have paid their dues: Wallace triumphing over his lurid 1950s talk show called *Nightbeat;* Safer as second-string war correspondent; Reasoner because he worked for and survived both Fred Friendly and Roone Arledge ("that's a little like having served under both Napoleon and Custer," Harry claims); and Bradley coming up through the affirmative action double bind—the same preference that lets you in the door also makes fellow workers constantly test your mettle. ("Hey, you're the news dude," cries a black kid in Philadelphia executing a beautiful double take. "Yeah, I'm the news dude," Bradley retorts, wincing, a little jaded about the fast upturns in his professional life.)

24

"Without those four guys, there's no broadcast," says Hewitt. "The success has to be due to the four correspondents, a sensational staff of producers and film editors, but the viewership comes from the fact that each Sunday night people ask themselves, 'I wonder what Mike or Morley is going to do tonight.' "

A niche on *60 Minutes* is a plum for television newsflesh and Ed Bradley's promotion had to do with excellence and politics. The time was March 1980, and Dan Rather was plucked from Hewitt's tiger cages to accede to the evening news throne. Bradley had drawn attention to himself with his reporting from Southeast Asia. Ed's range had been Vietnam and Cambodia and, his former cameraman Norman Lloyd would remember, he had an eye for the telling detail. Like the time outside a refugee camp on the Cambodia-Thai border when Ed noticed something strange about a couple of young Cambodians. While drinking a couple of beers in a local bar, Ed found out that the kids were trying to find their parents, but that the authorities wouldn't let them into the refugee camp. After some finessing and finagling, Ed got them in and, with Norman and camera in tow, spent most of the day following them around, hoping for a miracle. When it happened and one mother and one son ran forward to a tearful embrace, Norman caught it on camera. In 1975, Ed and Norman had been aboard one of the last helicopters to leave Saigon when the United States decamped.

Born in Philadelphia in 1941, Ed was the only child of separated parents, living with his mother and spending summers with his father in Detroit. "I was raised by people who worked twenty-hour days at two jobs each. They had middle-class goals and values, but no middle-class money. I was told, 'You can be anything you want, kid.' When you hear that enough, you believe it." Bradley graduated fronf Pennsylvania's Cheyney State College, got married, taught fifth and sixth grades in Philadelphia while working nights at soul music radio station WDAS. The marriage ended after five months, and Ed went into broadcasting full time, moving to New York and joining WCBS radio in 1967. Four years later, he quit and moved to Paris. In the tradition of Richard Wright and James Baldwin, he was going to write the great American expatriate novel. Instead, he dabbled in poetry, bought a motorcycle, and stayed with musician friends. When the money ran out, he persuaded the CBS Paris bureau to hire him as a stringer. "When he first came over, he spoke not a word of French," says correspondent Peter Kalischer, who remembered Ed flying through the streets on that motorbike. "When he left, about eight months later, he spoke four words." What persuaded

Bradley to leave Paris was a one-year contract from CBS New York and assignment to Vietnam. He spent three weeks living with the Vietcong in the Central Highlands in 1973 and was wounded by enemy mortar while covering a firefight in Cambodia—a chunk was taken out of his left arm, and shrapnel was peppered across his back. In the CBS News tradition, the Southeast Asia tour was followed by assignments at home, first as *Sunday Night News* anchor, then as correspondent on the Jimmy Carter campaign. It was at the 1976 Democratic convention in New York that Bradley first met Hewitt and Mike Wallace. Working alongside Wallace, he said, "was like taking Advanced Journalism 907." When Carter was elected President, Ed did a stint at the White House. He found the third-fiddle role behind Bob Schieffer and Robert Pierpoint confining, however. "Oh sure, somebody had to be there all the time to cover the ceremonies," Ed said, "and it was me." He spent a lot of time standing on the White House south lawn, waiting for Carter to escort visiting dignitaries from the Oval Office to their cars while Schieffer had the front row seat at presidential news conferences. People in the Washington news bureau found Bradley egocentric and cantankerous. He came close to quitting.

Instead, he moved to *CBS Reports,* the prestigious news special unit, and went to China and Saudi Arabia.

In 1978, Ed reported on the Vietnamese "boat people." After weeks on the South China Sea, thousands of Vietnamese beached rickety, unsanitary fishing boats on Malaysia's coast, only to be herded into guarded camps until Canada, France, and the United States agreed to accept the refugees. Other waves of boat people followed, some being pushed back to their boats by Malaysian soldiers. In November, 2,500 refugees were kept aboard a crowded freighter riding at anchor when the government in Kuala Lumpur refused to allow them to land—a scene repeated in Hong Kong. Among those who saw the footage Ed "birded" back to New York via satellite was Hewitt. Don was so impressed by pictures of Ed carrying refugees ashore through the breaking surf that he ran part of the footage as a *60 Minutes* segment.

A homegrown triumph was *Blacks in America—With All Deliberate Speed?* The two-hour *CBS Report* opened with reactions from a white and a black student elicited by Edward R. Murrow in 1954 following the Supreme Court decision outlawing segregation in public schools, and the two 1979 segments were concerned with what had happened during the quarter century since. Ed visited Tupelo, Mississippi and his hometown to see what had changed for blacks in the South and in Philadelphia. "We have the same problems we had twenty-five years ago—race, poverty, hunger, the lack of medical attention, and all the things that go with poverty,'' said a member of a Mississippi community action group. To the credit of Bradley and his producer, Philip Burton, Jr., the program reported both failures and occasional improvements and concluded that court actions, attempted enforcement, and massive media attention hadn't brought much change.

CBS News President Richard S. Salant and Mike Wallace were early advocates for making Bradley a fourth correspondent—Hewitt and Morley Safer reportedly had reservations—and the move was smart politics. In 1980, the newsmagazine was finishing its twelfth season. Hewitt and crew were good at weighing contemporary trends, sensibilities, and perceptions, and they were aware that on camera *60 Minutes* was all male and lily white. ''I hired Ed Bradley because I don't know of a reporter who is better at finding out and better at communicating what he did find out,'' Hewitt told *People* magazine a few years later. ''He jumps off the screen at you.''

Ed had difficulty adapting to the producer-correspondent caste system. The two dozen producers of *60 Minutes* are its unsung heroes, who often spend months in the field on a story before calling out correspondent and camera crew to put the piece on film. (When David Brinkley ran *NBC Magazine,* he said reporters, not producers, were going to run the show, that reporters were going to make their own decisions, an attitude that is regarded as the main reason why *NBC Magazine* came to an early death.)

Bradley married Priscilla Coolidge—Rita Coolidge's sister and a singer in her own right—and began criss-crossing the earth, logging more than 100,000 miles during the first year with *60 Minutes*. Ed may have been chosen because he had been overheard saying he thought sleeping on the floor can be fun (he usually stays in the finest hotels and runs the biggest expense account). ''The pressure never ends,'' he says. ''There is the pressure in competing for stories, not just among the four of us, which is friendly, but with other broadcasts. It would be a lie to say I'm not concerned about ratings.'' The Bradleys' Manhattan co-op was decorated with mementos of Ed's tour of duty in Vietnam, including a pair of enormous Burmese Buddhas, photographs, drawings, and a vast collection of jazz and pop records. His nomadic life and his wife's career cut the marriage short after two years. The divorce became final in 1984.

''There have been sacrifices, but the rewards are so much greater,'' Ed maintains. ''The bottom line is, this job is fun. And when it stops being fun, then I'll stop doing it.''

Harry Reasoner is the one tiger who strayed from his cage, consorted with television's premiere tigress, Barbara Walters, but was snared back again. Reasoner and Hewitt go back to 1956 together, when Don was the boss of Douglas Edwards's *With The News* (a broadcast that a Hewitt-inspired card at the end claimed gave more people the news than any other single source in the world), and Harry was offered a summer job.

Reasoner was born in 1923 in Dakota City, Iowa, which made him just old enough to serve in World War II. Once back home, he married Kathleen Carroll, his high school sweetheart, and after newspapering on the *Minneapolis Tribune,* he became the one-man news department of the Twin Cities' KEYD-TV. His connection with far-off New York was Sig Mickelson, one of his teachers at the University of Minnesota who, for a few tumultous years in the 1950s, was the president of CBS News. Leaving Minneapolis for the CBS News presidency, Mickelson had told Harry that if he got some experience, he (Mickelson) might be able to give him a chance. Harry was thirty-three and, in addition to the experience in the Twin Cities, had behind him a stint with the United States Information Agency (USIA) in the Philippines, when he wrote to his former teacher and said he was ready. Mickelson offered him the summer job on the network assignment desk, guaranteed for eighteen weeks at $157.50. Harry thought that sum ridiculously low, but his wife told him he'd better take it, because she didn't want him to spend his forties blaming her and the children—there were to be six in all—for keeping him from his chance at the big time. Money was always to be a delicate subject in the Reasoner-CBS relationship. When he was in his fifties and making $200,000 a year anchoring the *ABC News,* Harry and Kay split up.

Hewitt was the jack-of-all-trades of the evening news, a feisty, trim bantamweight with machine-gun bursts of energy. His people swore by him. And feared him. Reasoner among them. Knowing his fate lay almost entirely in Hewitt's hands, Reasoner, like other newcomers, went to great lengths to win Don's approval. Harry's big chance came when Don assigned him to cover Nikita Khrushchev's 1959 tour of the United States. Goaded by Hewitt, Reasoner finagled his way past a tight security cordon to get a brief but exclusive interview with the Soviet leader. Later, when the State Department admonished Reasoner, pointing out he could have gotten into serious trouble for pulling a stunt like that, he said, "You don't understand. I'm more afraid of Don Hewitt than I am of the Secret Service." (Maybe he still was in 1981 when he published his once-over-lightly autobiography *Before The Colors Fade;* it was dedicated to Hewitt.)

Harry has a talent for making broadcast journalism look easy. His flat drawl and sly humor have added to his way of seeming a little lighter than many, as evidenced in his description of an anchorperson's first duty: "Do not interfere with people's understanding of what the news is about."

He has described his approach to a story as "going for the jugular with an electric razor." He can do profiles, essays, and interviews, and his versatility is valuable to Hewitt. His low-key demeanor is the opposite of the generating-electricity-from-every-pore hype that news directors go for in picking newsflesh. His diffidence, however, has given him enemies in high places. His lack of enthusiasm for boning up on election night arcana in 1970 led to the reassessment that led to his defection to ABC. It was the first time a senior news star had jumped from one network to another for a new job and better money. You weren't supposed to *want* to leave CBS for those lower rungs of television newsdom. You were supposed to be willing to throw yourself in front of a moving train if that was what it took to get ahead at CBS. That Reasoner was allowed back into the fold—a lot calmer and with a new woman in his life—was a measure of his newsflesh appeal and of an evolution not entirely to the liking of CBS News executives. Nicknamed Warren G. Harding around the shop for his Ohioan roots, his avuncular persona, and less than zealous work habits, he has been called on the carpet by Hewitt and by Robert Chandler, vice president of documentaries and operations, for not putting enough of himself into his broadcasts. Not pulling one's weight is the biggest no-no on a show with a frantic pace and onerous work loads. Although five years younger than Mike Wallace, Reasoner is expected to be the first of the original twosome to retire.

In his book, he wrote that journalism is the current events of anthropology. It should be human without being maudlin, aware of sentiments while shying from sentimentalism. It should be alive. On camera, he has reported a string of nostalgia pieces that have delighted his fans. He re-viewed *Casablanca* and set us straight on what Humphrey Bogart *did* say and Ingrid Bergman *didn't* say to Sam the piano player in the 1942 Warner Brothers classic. He has had a look at the French Foreign Legion, taken us through the urban decay of Camden, New Jersey, "the saddest place you can see," showed us creeping capitalism in Communist Hungary, coed prisons in Denmark, and has visited with the king of Morocco. *Go North Young Man* was a Reasoner arabesque, a craggy essay on another chapter of the white man's burden coming to an end, a piece of irony and melancholy on another absurd outpost of Western illusions. There he was, the collar of his anorak turned up, standing on the lip of the immense glacier that is Greenland, and slouching along a street in Nuk (formerly Godthaab), telling us that nearly three centuries of Danish rule, of Danish decency, paternalism, and determination to do the right thing may be summed up in the alcoholic Eskimo staggering home under the midnight sun. "The twentieth century," he concluded, "doesn't seem to work in Greenland." He did a story on Texas rough-necks drilling for oil off Scotland and journeyed to Ireland to explain the republic's tax shelter, which allowed British and American six-fig-ure writers like Frederick Forsyth and Richard Condon to live tax free— a status not available to homegrown authors and artists earning their liv-ing in Ireland. The piece was called *The Keepin' of the Green,* and Rea-soner's grating laugh was heard in the corridors at 555 West 57th Street as he suggested *60 Minutes* move to Ireland so they could all save a bundle. "We can qualify as writers," he joked, "by publishing our scripts."

Reasoner is the most trusted journalist on television. Fifty-six per-cent of Americans express greater confidence in his appealing mix of urbanity and Midwestern common sense than in any other newscaster. A 1982 *TV Guide* opinion poll put Mike Wallace in second place, with 49 percent, followed by *20/20*'s Hugh Downs, 47 percent.

Morley Safer is the gifted writing talent among the correspondents. He is the sardonic observer of life who says he doesn't like to walk into closets and rattle skeletons, but whose persistent prodding elicits reveal-ing, even startling, avowals from such disparate individuals as Nissan assembly-line workers in Tennessee, IRS bureaucrats, basketball players turned senators, call-in radio station hosts, and first ladies of arts and politics. It was to Safer that Katharine Hepburn, long a liberal, confided an urge to see censorship established so pornography could be stemmed, and it was to him that Betty Ford, the wife of the conservative thirty-eighth President, delivered the famous headliner that she wouldn't be surprised if daughter Susan Ford was having an affair.

Safer's finely honed essays have dealt delicately with the dangers of both canine and nuclear wastes, with Tupperware parties, fashion shows, "impaired" physicians—doctors who may be drug addicts, alcoholics, or potential suicides—welfarism in the South Seas, and men's strange urges to climb high mountains. He has explained tennis boot camps in Florida, corruption in Lagos, Nigeria, and, in *Plumbago Carpensis and All That,* what it is that drives the English to obsessive gardening. In

*The Collection,* he dwelled on the constant kissing and pecking of cheeks that accompany the unveiling of Paris fashions. In *Dutch Treat,* he explained the Netherlands' infinite social welfare as "reverse Orwellian." He prefers what he calls "the observed kind of story." He is good on exotic locations and admits he needs the variety to keep his sanity.

Safer is smaller than he seems on television, also stockier and blonder. His face, as they say in romance novels, is craggy and lived-in. He says he hates doing celebrity profiles but is perfectly aware of his own notoriety and ready to trade on it. He has a knack for slightly daffy tales about the Internal Revenue Service, about sentimental rides on the Orient Express, explaining the game of croquet, and Caribbean scams by people who call themselves latter-day Visigoths. On the wall of his office hangs a chewed-up propeller. The mangled blade is a souvenir of his attempt at piloting a test plane in a segment called *The Flying Machine.* "It didn't fly," he recalls, "and it didn't stop either. I knew I was going to die, and I really didn't want to."

The son of Austrian Jews, Morley Safer was born in Toronto. He has never given up his Canadian nationality. "I have never had a compelling reason to change my citizenship, but then I don't believe the color of your passport should matter," he said in 1979. "I believe that a reporter should be stateless. It is not a matter of loyalty, but integrity." Still, that navy-blue passport of his allowed him into China at the height of Mao Zedong's cultural revolution, and it, plus his convenient bachelorhood, has something to do with his being sent to Saigon in 1965.

Safer had joined the news staff of the Canadian Broadcasting Corporation in 1955. He had put in time as a reporter and had produced and occasionally appeared on *CBC News Magazine* when he was assigned to the network's London bureau in 1961. He covered virtually every major story in Europe, the Middle East, and Africa for CBC during the next three years, and was recruited by CBS for its London office in 1964. Together with veteran correspondent Charles Collingwood, he had covered the 1964 British elections and the death and funeral of Winston Churchill when CBS asked him to cover the guerrilla war in South Vietnam. He believed he was chosen because no one really expected the war to last very long once the United States threw its military might behind Saigon, and because the idea of sending a Canadian bachelor, newly arrived at CBS, seemed attractive—meaning he was someone expendable, with no widow to prick the network conscience should anything happen to him.

When he sent in a filmed report showing U.S. Marines methodically leveling the village of Cam Ne, and Walter Cronkite decided they just had to go with this devastating piece on the evening news, President Johnson called up CBS Chief Executive Officer Frank Stanton. "Frank, this is your President, and yesterday your boys shat on the American flag!" Lyndon Johnson began. How could CBS employ a Communist like Safer, how could they be so unpatriotic as to put on enemy film like this? When presidential aides kept insisting Safer wasn't a Communist, merely a Canadian, Johnson ordered the FBI to ask the Royal Canadian Mounted Police to check out everything about Safer and got the Joint Chiefs of Staff to investigate the officer in charge of the Cam Ne operation, to make sure the officer hadn't been bribed. By the time Safer was in Cam Ne, he had covered combat and guerrilla warfare in the Mideast and Cyprus and the Algerian revolution. He had seen French paratroopers inflict cruelty in Algiers. He had thought Americans were different. Safer's Cam Ne report marked the beginning of gnawing questions about American motives in Vietnam.

Morley married at thirty-six, after going with lots of glamorous women. His choice was Jane Fearer, an American anthropologist he met while she was studying for her doctorate at Oxford. Every summer the Safers and their daughter Sarah repair to their retreat in Spain, where they watch no television. The rest of the year, Morley relaxes at his and Jane's four-story Manhattan townhouse, reading, painting, baking pies and cakes, which he rarely eats, and watching "everything" on the tube. Jane is a scientific consultant to the American Museum of Natural History and is alleged to be responsible for Morley's affection for pieces that deal with the origins, social customs, and cultural developments of aborigines in Micronesia and elsewhere. "Breakup is not a danger in our house," he says. "That's a threat when one or the other secretly *prefers* to go. I prefer to be home. I love it. And my wife and daughter prefer it."

Safer is the intellectual. He has no high opinion of the human race and, like the Greek stoics, believes that as social creatures we must play our part in the body politic, that a man's virtues and vices are a private matter but that the good and bad in each of us have very definite effects on everyone else. Unquestionably the best writer of the foursome, he is not really comfortable doing hardball investigative journalism, but prefers stories that demand a reporter's eye, thinking, and composition. Straight interviewing often appalls him. "You interview people and they lie," he told *The Los Angeles Times* in 1980. "They know they lie, you know they lie, they know you know they lie." He likes to reassure interviewees that he is no Mike Wallace, that he won't throw any nasty curves while at the same time making people realize he is an important personage. While they were setting up the camera in the Indiana State Prison for Women to do a story on a woman who had murdered her sadistic husband after twenty-three years of marriage, Morley told everybody he had just flown in from the Mideast, where he had almost as much to do with the "peace process" going forward as President Carter. And after Indianapolis, he would be off to see a king after a rest stop at the Safer villa in Spain. On the show, Morley is admired for his elegant "bridgework." Good bridgework leads the viewer from one scene to another and, among esthetes in broadcast journalism, is regarded as more effective than the "stand-upper," in which the reporter stands stock-still while delivering his on-camera "bridge copy."

Virtually everybody who has worked with Mike Wallace agrees he is a driven man. "If Hewitt sets the pace in that office, it is Wallace who's created the aggressive style and the intense in-house sense of competition," says producer Bill Brown, who defected to NBC's *First Camera*. "Had there been no Mike Wallace, *60 Minutes* wouldn't be anything like it is." Wallace has a slightly different perception of himself and the newsmagazine. He believes his own, and the program's, success has to do with audience feelings of fairness. "I think we're perceived as fair, more daring and innovative than other broadcasts," he says. "Also, our pieces are constructed almost like morality plays."

As a character in an allegorical drama, Wallace would be cast as both Truth and Everyman. With a well-phrased accusation on his lips— and with documentation, bills, and cancelled checks in hand—he catches more people lying, or stammering in self-indictment, on camera than most attorneys ever hope to nail on witness stands in a lifetime in court. Both wrongdoers and celebrities make startlingly candid and sometimes damaging admissions. "In other words," he told a shaken director of one poverty program, "you, in effect, stole $2,974.66." Questioning an accountant about tax skimming, Mike whispered, "Look, between you and me, you do it." "Yeah, okay," the man confessed. Between you and me and forty million viewers.

For someone who is the toughest and probably the most feared interviewer on television, Wallace is exceptionally ticklish about his own projection. He has refused to be the object of a Barbara Walters profile. When interviewed, he will snap off a reporter's tape recorder if he senses the questions are getting too personal. When *Parade* magazine, a Sunday supplement for many newspapers, did a story on the broadcast in 1979, he showed up at the magazine's offices asking to see the galleys. Managing Editor Walter Anderson turned him down, telling him he was surprised that one of America's premier journalists would be worried about a magazine article. Said Anderson, "He seemed genuinely surprised and flattered to hear me describe him that way."

Like Johnny Carson on the *Tonight Show* and Phil Donahue on *Donahue,* Wallace has made himself at least as much an object of interest as those he interviews. He brings to his work a finely tuned sense of moral outrage. Like Safer, he believes most people won't tell him the truth if they think they can get away with lying. Why will people agree to submit to him then? "Because they have an idea to sell, because they like the intellectual tussle," he says. "People aren't hard to get."

Audiences love Mike Wallace. In him they not only have someone engaging to listen to, but someone to root for. His style has spawned a legion of imitators, some of whom confuse toughness with nastiness. Wallace knows the value of silence and will often let the answer hang for three or four seconds to embarrass subjects into revealing even more. And he's a great blinker, nodder, and smiler, egging on the person he's interviewing with facial expressions. "I confess to a certain amount of role playing," he admits. "The vaunted toughness is just an awareness of what to ask, of what would be on the public's mind." Behind the mastery of the confrontation interview lie years of work to develop both style and reputation. And behind each interview lies a lot of plain homework. Research, to him, means reading everything he can about an individual. As he reads, he writes down questions, between 100 and 150 questions, although he uses only 8 or 10 during the actual interview.

Wallace almost became the President's man at the receiving end of tough questions the year *60 Minutes* was born. After covering the Richard Nixon election campaign in 1968, he was offered the post as President Nixon's press secretary. He was tempted—not for partisan reasons, as he had voted both Democratic and Republican over the years—but because it was a chance to get out of broadcasting, to learn the Washington scene from the vantage point of the White House. He talked to a number of his friends and finally decided against it. "As I look back on it now, I don't suppose I would have changed the history of anything," he told *Playboy* in 1981. "But it could have changed *my* history some."

He is viewed as a tough customer, but over the years his image has become respectable. He is our ombudsman, our national district attorney, leaning in and uttering, "Are you trying to tell us . . ." before dramatically exposing the wrongdoer. Letters arrive at Manhattan's 57th Street, suggesting that if Mike, Morley, Harry, and Ed can't do a story on corruption in our town, won't you please say you're *thinking* of doing it. That would help us. "People will come out of the woodwork," Harry says, partly out of their belief that if there's something wrong in their life, Mike Wallace can fix it.''

True believers on the far left and right don't like Wallace. The counterculture magazine *Mother Jones* called him ''semi-tough'' for going after individual instances of malfeasance in society while refusing to tackle structural flaws in the American Way. And he's the bogeyman of AIM (for Accuracy in Media), the conservative watchdog newsletter, for reminding us at the height of the Teheran hostage crisis that the CIA helped train the Shah's hated secret police. Although a Jew—''a backsliding Jew,'' he has termed himself—he has angered mainstream Jewish organizations for letting Syrian Jews say they are better off under anti-Israel hardliner Hafez al-Assad than under previous regimes in Damascus, and for letting Jacobo Timerman denounce former Prime Minister Menachem Begin's messianic geopolitics. Tel Aviv is one of the few places outside North America (Canadians tune in on U.S. border stations or catch the program on ITV on Sundays), where *60 Minutes* has been shown in its entirety. An enterprising showman bought the rights to screen it in a hotel. ''Some Israelis wanted to see the program partly so they could gaze at events—civilian casualities in Lebanon, say—that their censors ban from indigenous television,'' E. J. Kahn, Jr., reported in a two-part *New Yorker* article on the program in 1982.

Myron Leon Wallace was born in Brookline, Massachusetts, in 1919, one of the four children of Frank Wallace, a wholesale grocer and insurance broker, and Zina Sharfman Wallace. The family's original surname—Wallik—was recorded as Wallace by an immigration officer when Frank arrived from Russia around the turn of the century. Following graduation from Brookline High School, Mike Wallace enrolled at the University of Michigan in Ann Arbor, paying for his education by waiting on tables, washing dishes, and working part time for the National Youth Administration. Like Ed Bradley, he wanted to become a schoolteacher. A job as an announcer at the university radio station, however, changed everything. After receiving his B.A. degree, he became a writer-announcer on a pair of Grand Rapids radio stations jointly owned by a furniture company and a laundry. In 1940, he moved to Detroit and made his network radio debut as a narrator, announcer, and actor on such adventure series as *The Lone Ranger* and *The Green Hornet*. A year later, he was in Chicago, writing and broadcasting the news at the *Chicago Sun*, and making his stage acting debut. His narration of *First Line*, a dramatic series that was part of the Navy recruiting program, prompted him to enlist in 1943. The Navy promoted him to the rank of ensign, and he spent the remaining war years as officer in charge of radio entertainment at the Great Lakes Training Station north of Chicago, and in Hawaii and Australia. He married Norma Kaplan and, returning to civilian life and radio in Chicago, became the father of Peter and Christopher. Both sons eventually showed interest in becoming journalists. Peter worked as a desk assistant for Hewitt at the 1960 political conventions and fell to his death while on a camping trip in the mountains of Greece shortly after his nineteenth birthday. Chris became a newsman at NBC.

Mike Wallace's ascent was neither irresistible nor straightforward. The marriage to Norma ended in divorce when Mike met and worked with Buff Cobb, the granddaughter of humorist Irvin S. Cobb. Mike and Buff married in 1949 and cohosted a daytime television talk show that took them from Chicago to the Big Apple. Critics noted approvingly that *Mike and Buff* lacked the usual domestic cooing and idle chatter of most husband-and-wife programs. Their disagreeing on the air as part of the show led to off-camera bickering, according to Buff, and to their divorce in 1954. He made his Broadway debut in Harry Kurnitz's mildly successful comedy, *Reclining Figure,* playing a young art dealer with what one critic called "ingratiating ease."

Mike married Lorraine Perigord, a painter, in 1955, and the next year started hosting the explosive *Night Beat* interview show that soon made him famous and earned him such endearing nicknames as the Grand Inquisitor and Mike Malice. The studio set was bare and the stark key-lighting, which one reviewer likened to a third-degree setup in a police station, silhouetted Wallace on a high stool with smoke from his cigarette curling into the eyes of his spotlighted victims. He was a feisty interviewer who had no qualms about asking celebrities embarrassing questions. "Everyone who came on my show knew the rules of the game and exactly what he or she was doing," Mike recalled. "They weren't subpoenaed after all. They came on because they wanted to." Among those who refused were General Douglas MacArthur, Charles Lindbergh, Alger Hiss, and Irene Selznick, who said, "I don't want to spend my privacy that way."

It all worked fine as a local New York program but became hypersensational when it went network on ABC, and a few of Mike's victims fired some hard shots of their own on the air. When Mike interviewed Mickey Cohen, the mobster promptly libeled the Los Angeles Police Department in general and one police officer in particular, whom he called "a sadistic degenerate" and an "alcoholic." Libel suits for $3 million followed. They were settled for much less, but ABC had to apologize on the air. The show lost its sponsor. Wallace lost his job and, over the next year, drifted between acting in commercials and all-smiles-and-gush personality parades, earning sums in the six figures endorsing Parliament and other cigarette brands.

Peter Wallace's death in Greece in 1962 had a devastating effect on Mike. He had encouraged his son's journalistic aspiration and, with the boy's mother (Norma married Bill Leonard, the future CBS News president) had helped get Peter the job at the CBS news desk at the 1960 conventions. After burying his son in the Corinthian Hills, fifty miles west of Athens, he decided that, if it wasn't too late, he would like to become the journalist his son had aspired to be. After a depressing winter in New York offering his services to the three networks, he accepted the anchor position at independent KTLA in Los Angeles. When CBS News President Richard Salant heard that part of Wallace's turning over a new leaf included buying back his own cigarette commercials, Salant called and told him to forget Los Angeles. There was a job for him at CBS.

Not everybody in the news division believed Wallace deserved the anchor position on the new *Morning News*. Epithets like "interloper" and "sleazy Madison Avenue pitchman" swirled around his debut as an anchorman, and it was only two years later, at the 1964 political conventions, that he convinced his colleagues he had the credentials to be on the team.

Lorraine and Mike Wallace live in an opulent townhouse in Manhattan. They spend summers at Martha's Vineyard and take winter vacations, when possible, in Haiti, where Lorraine has family and property. What Mike and his son, Chris, have in common with Ed Bradley and Dan Rather is that they are both clients of Richard Leibner, a balding newsflesh agent with an insatiable appetite for current events, who during heavy news weeks monitors three TV sets simultaneously. Leibner is the man who played ABC and CBS against each other for Rather's favors and, more recently, negotiated the deal that will keep Mike Wallace the first among the equals on *60 Minutes* until 1987. The deal was unprecedented. The CBS iron rule of sixty-five and out wasn't bent for Frank Stanton at the height of the Watergate crisis when the White House was getting to Chairman Paley. Keeping Stanton would have looked statesmanlike. It wasn't bent for Walter Cronkite. But it was broken for Mike Wallace.

Dan Rather's tour of duty lasted only five years. Dapper Dan, as he was affectionately nicknamed during those years, came to hate the traveling. More important, momentous things were happening to his career while he tried to concentrate on fraudulent auto insurance schemes in Los Angeles and shoddy workmanship in nuclear reactors in Bay City, Texas.

When Roone Arledge, who came from sports and was partial to open shirts and gold chains, became the ABC News boss in 1977, he was given a free hand and the megabucks it might take to pull ABC's *World News Tonight* out of perpetual third place. He spent a lot of money luring $35,000-a-year CBS News producers by offering them $85,000 a year to "come across the street" (from CBS News at 555 West 57th Street to ABC at 7 West 66th Street actually). By the time Arledge began wooing Rather during the summer of 1979, more than twenty-five CBS newspeople had defected to ABC.

The infusion of this on-air and behind-the-cameras personnel plus Arledge's knack for firing up his troops caused the *World News Tonight,* with its tricky Washington-London-Chicago "desk" concept, to climb in the ratings. And when Rather and Leibner began meeting Arledge in cabs, Chinese take-out restaurants, or at night at Roone's Park Avenue apartment, it occurred to the CBS high command that what might vault ABC News over the top and actually take away the long-standing news supremacy of CBS once Cronkite retired might possibly be their very own Dapper Dan.

The Arledge offer was calculated to bowl over. And it did. So Cronkite is earning $600,000 in his final year? Come across the street, Dan, at $2 million a year. We want you to be our chief correspondent, the principal presence at breaking events wherever they occur. If you wish, you can anchor our answer to *60 Minutes—20/20—*or the late-night newscast we're working on, specials, elections, political conventions, live events. We want you to be the logo of ABC News, if you will.

Beyond money and air time, Roone offered Dan not only a chance to be part of the decision making, to decide what stories should be covered and by whom, but to help conceptualize the whole idea of news. Heady stuff. Not even Walter sat in on CBS News planning sessions on major coverage. He had the coveted title of managing editor of the *CBS Evening News,* and he had veto power in matters that concerned him personally, but he was not consulted on hiring, firing, and day-to-day operations, nor asked to help formulate broad policy questions.

To keep Driven Dan, as some colleagues called him, CBS came up with its own stunning package. And Arledge overplayed his hand. Rather and his wife, Jean, talked over every offer and counteroffer and neither of them could quite square the ABC pitch that Dan would be both the premier network correspondent dispatched to any hot spot on the globe and the executive team player sitting in on news division decisions on 66th Street. From the beginnings at KSAM radio station in Huntsville, Texas, up through local station journalism, network reporting, overseas assignments in London and Vietnam, the tumultuous White House years from the Johnson to the Nixon presidencies, to the power and the glory on *60 Minutes,* Dan Rather skillfully managed his ascent, working excruciating hours, cultivating his image, and, at the network affiliates' conventions, pressing the flesh.

The long ordeal of Watergate and President Nixon's resignation almost killed Rather's career. He had stayed on in the White House to the bitter end because he—and CBS Chief Executive Officer Frank Stanton—couldn't let Nixon's men hound him out. When it was all over in August 1974, Rather had been summoned to New York, taken to lunch at Alfredo's, and offered the job of anchor-correspondent on *CBS Reports,* a job unfilled since the days of Edward R. Murrow. Dan should have been flattered, but as he was to write in *The Camera Never Blinks,* "What I wanted to hear, and did not, was whether I had a choice." He flew back to Washington, wondering whether the network was pushing him out of the White House correspondent's job. If that was the case, would self-esteem mean he'd have to quit CBS? He was confused. He and Jean talked into the night.

He had vacation time coming and the next morning took his fifteen-year-old son Daniel, nicknamed Danjack, fishing. The story got out that Dan Rather had "gone fishing." When he called Jean from a pay phone 100 miles from Washington, she told him to get in touch with New York. He did and, between the roar of passing semitrailers, learned that to contain the "gone fishing" damage, Salant needed his answer. Rather didn't know what to say but agreed to be in Washington two days later to meet Salant. He spent the intervening time sounding out friends, including a television writer who said it all looked suspicious, that whatever the facts, the story would play as if Rather had been pushed over the side. The meeting with Salant satisfied Dan that he indeed had the choice to stay on as White House correspondent, that no one was caving in to pressure from conservative owners and managers of affiliate stations, who thought Dan's bull's-eye questioning of the tottering Nixon had contributed to the President's downfall. Rather accepted the move to *CBS Reports* (a number of affiliate owners and managers boasted they had pulled the right strings and managed to get him).

In newsroom parlance, *CBS Reports* was the "back of the book," as opposed to front end news. *CBS Reports* was documentaries and specials, and Dan had withdrawal symptoms after the hectic pace of the evening news. After a while, however, he got to enjoy getting into in-depth subjects that left more than a two-minute imprint on viewers, and over the next year he tackled the assassinations of the Kennedys, Martin Luther King, and the attempt on George Wallace's life in four specials. He also did meaningful documentaries on I.Q. tests, environmental causes of cancer, and special interest money in politics. He was learning to write documentaries, he realized, to put together something more than declarative newswire sentences. People told him Murrow's 1950s broadcasts were the best-written television prose. Dan went through the film library and looked at every show Murrow had done. But he was also wondering about his career, about his visibility.

If there was one CBS News executive who had found Dan's tussles with Nixon "sexy," it was Hewitt. And if Wallace and Safer needed a colleague, it had to be Dan. Salant wasn't too difficult to convince; nor was Rather. When Salant and Hewitt offered him the third correspondent post on *60 Minutes,* he jumped.

A residue of anti-Rather resentment still carried over from the end-of-Nixon period. Letters from viewers complained he was too combative, too argumentative. But Hewitt assigned him to celebrity pieces and noncontroversial stories, and by the time the bidding for Rather's services on the evening news reached the stratosphere five years later, Rather was immensely popular.

Andy Rooney doesn't like the federal budget, can't decide whether he's a Republican or a Democrat, hates candy wrappers and parking meters, has a dog and four grown kids. He doesn't find time to throw things out or to get things done. He thinks that if the government can pay farmers not to grow stuff, it might also want to pay writers like him not to write too much. He hates corporate bosses who think they can make their own TV commercials. He loves Christmas, dislikes New Year's Eve, and has turned his Mr. Everyman's disquisitions into television stardom and book bestsellerdom.

Andy might still be writing caustic ruminations for others to mouth on the tube if he hadn't gotten mad at the way they treated his *Essay on War* in 1970. Maybe it wasn't the right time. The war in Vietnam wasn't going so well, and Vice President Spiro Agnew was after those nattering nabobs of negativism, so Hewitt said he'd cut by half the essay on man's inhumanity to man. Andy made an issue of it and quit. That step, strangely enough, got him where he is now, but how could he have known that quitting CBS would put him on the air at CBS?

Andy and Marguerite Howard have been married since 1942. They

live in a white frame house in Rowayton, Connecticut, in which they
raised three daughters and a son. A year younger than Wallace, Andrew
Aitken Rooney comes from Albany, New York. He arrived at writing
via campus newspapering at Colgate University in Hamilton, New York,
and, after conscription for military service in World War II, via journalism in *The Stars and Stripes*. With Bud Hutton, another staffer on
the GI newspaper, Rooney recounted the wartime experience in two books,
*Air Gunner,* a collection of crisp sketches of the B-17 gunners stationed
in England, and *The Story of the Stars and Stripes,* a breezy, anecdotal
account of the newspaper operation itself, with colorful portraits of staff
members and previously unrevealed facts about wartime events, including a frustrated Nazi plan to kill or capture high-ranking Allied officers.
Hutton and Rooney returned to Europe in 1946 to see what had happened since the end of the war. Their book, *Conqueror's Peace: A Report to the American Stockholders* was in the brisk, hardboiled vein of
*Stars and Stripes,* but the authors also described GIs doing black mar-
keteering, looting, and committing sexual offenses in France and Germany. When Metro Goldwyn Mayer bought the screen rights to *The Story
of the Stars and Stripes,* Rooney went to Hollywood. Nothing came of
the project and two years later he became a writer for Arthur Godfrey
at CBS.

Andy managed the feat of working both network news and entertainment and once likened the mutual wariness of the two divisions to two
men forced to sleep in the same bed and both scared of touching each
other for fear of giving rise to the wrong impression. In the entertainment department he served up words for people like Victor Borge, Sam
Levenson, and Garry Moore. On the news side, he scripted such programs as *The Twentieth Century* and *Adventure.* In 1961, he was assigned to *Calendar,* a rather sophisticated late-morning show cohosted
by Harry Reasoner and Mary Fickett, an actress who had played Eleanor
Roosevelt in *Sunrise at Campobello* and was to become the star of the
soap opera *All My Children.* Andy became the head writer on *Calendar*
and, with Reasoner narrating, went on to do back-of-the-book features.
Their *Essay on Women* began, "This broadcast was prepared by men,
and makes no claim to being fair. Prejudice has saved us a great deal of
time in preparation." For his part of the collaboration, Harry received a
Peabody Award. They won attention for other hour-long film essays on
such insistently uneventful things as chairs, bridges, hotels, whiskey—
all written and produced by Rooney and narrated by Reasoner. The turning point for Rooney came during Richard Salant's first tenure as CBS
News president. Andy was standing in the doorway to Salant's office,

trying to convince the boss he should be given a chance to write and *act* out some essays. What sort of stuff could he do? Salant asked. "I can do anything," said Andy, "I can do doors."

Naturally inclined toward ease if not indolence, the two of them did one-hour specials entirely from helicopters: *Birdseye View of America, Birdseye View of Scotland,* and *Birdseye View of California.* It beat slugging out along byways to set up cameras, and height could make Andy's prose soar. Coming up on the new Verrazano Narrows Bridge in the Hudson River estuary in *An Essay on Bridges,* he was moved to say, "Man has made a sewer out of the river and spanned it with a poem." Andy returned to airborne reporting in 1984. Unkindly, *The New York Times* reviewer called this series update "vanity programming."

Rooney would love to be able to do long pieces and has had his fights with Hewitt over the short form imposed on him. Ten years after the *Essay on War* disagreement, he nearly quit again. This was after the roaring success of *A Few Minutes with Andy Rooney* on the air and in print (the Atheneum hardback edition was by Andrew A. Rooney; the Warner Books paperback by Andy Rooney). He felt hemmed in by the three-minute format and talked Don into letting him do a regular twelve to fourteen-minute piece on *60 Minutes.* His segment was on Washington astrologer Jeanne Dixon and he came up with an adversary-style piece à la Mike Wallace, full of loaded questions about her track record in interpreting the influence of the heavenly bodies on Washington affairs. When Hewitt cancelled the segment just before the scheduled August 1981 airing, Andy threatened to walk. "I was sore, plenty sore," he told *The Washington Post*'s John Carmody, "until I realized I probably had the best job in the world, a real plum . . . I guess I got over it." Hewitt can be positively lyrical when it comes to praising the resident grump, calling Rooney a true latter-day H. L. Mencken.

Andy keeps his distance. His office is in the old CBS Broadcast Center at 528 West 57th Street across the street from *60 Minutes'* glass-partitioned and floor-to-ceiling curtained home base. It is to his office that a crew comes to tape his weekly three-minute contributions. The place is the amiable mess it appears to be on camera. It cannot be otherwise, he claims; creativity comes from chaos. He refuses makeup but is very particular about camera angles ("The camera can make you look bald if they hit you wrong with the light, and there's no sense looking balder than you are"). The ideas he gets are banged out on one of the two black typewriters that he identifies as Underwood 5s, "born the same year I was—1920." (He was born January 14, 1919.) He loves them and would never trade up to newer models or to a word processor. "I hate a typewriter that's smarter than I am."

Since composing three minutes worth of text on a vintage Underwood isn't quite enough to occupy a grown man for an entire week, he has taken to writing a syndicated column that appears in over 100 newspapers three times a week. How to classify him has posed a similar problem for print editors to that of some of his electronic bosses. The *Los Angeles Herald Examiner* and the *Philadelphia Inquirer* run his column on the editorial page; before it folded, the *Buffalo Courier-Express* put him on the comic pages. That these comments on bosses, repairmen, checkout cashiers, and Presidents —gathered in book form—could become runaway successes astonished both Atheneum, his publisher, and the author himself. He got a $480,000 advance for the second book and, at the age of 65, admitted to having money for the first time in his life. Too many people are bugging him about investments these days, but Marge and he managed to remodel the kitchen, spending $29,000 on the job (exactly what their Fairfield County home cost when they bought it in 1951). He would like to be taken a little more seriously to make us all realize that beyond his wry comments on cereal boxes and toothpaste advertising he is talking about a culture that is better at selling things than at making them. His sweet revenge is that he can be churlish about television's own taboo. As he said in a *60 Minutes* complaint about those irritating subscription inserts we find in all magazines, "It's a good thing television doesn't have commercials we could tear out. The living room floor would be a mess."

# 4

# Getting the Story
## *Being a "60 Minutes" producer*

By the time Bradley, Reasoner, Safer, or Wallace introduces a segment, facts and events will have been turned into a story. The facts will "say" something, the segment make a point. Ideas and issues become dynamic when they are translated into "people stories," preferably people confronting each other. The politics of busing acquired the right punch when the *60 Minutes* segment focused on the private schools where Washington's liberal politicians sent their own sons and daughters. Government invasion of privacy became meaningful when a California couple's bank and credit card statements, plus a year's cancelled checks, were turned over to a private detective who, solely on the basis of the financial records, came up with an eerily accurate portrait of the two and even deduced that the husband had been convicted of a traffic violation while driving another woman's car. Teenage drunk driving became affecting, gripping even, when we attended the funeral of two Massachusetts honor students and, in the company of parents and friends, came to realize what promising lives a few beers too many had ended.

"The story" is the fundamental principle of all the deals, hype, and celebrity glamour that make up the entertainment industries. The writer, producer, and filmmaker who, singlehandedly or in collaboration, can resolve the story and, even better, top it with a twist that takes us by surprise, can carry a project toward realization. "What's the story?" are the words that are second nature to people in Hollywood, television, and publishing.

An inordinate amount of creative juices is spent shaping the material into story form. Lines and situations are created to give exits bombshell or cliffhanger effect (in television so we will stay tuned through the commercials), action is "planted" in the opening for a payoff in the chase sequence, new "cut to" scenes are inserted to accommodate time spans, stakes are built up so as to make us root for the heroine and the good guys. The story is given "hook"—dramatic premise in the jargon of the trade. It is given "pipe" (the history of the characters) and "top-spin" (to propel us into the next scene).

The Federal Communications Commission may forbid the staging of any action for the benefit of the cameras in news programming, but dramatic structure is as important in nonfiction television as it is in teleplays for series and movies of the week. So is the need for strong plot, clear characterization, and the sharp editing that helps improve audience understanding. Making current events compelling has blurred the frontiers between fiction and nonfiction. (ABC had former cabinet members play crisis managers in a TV dramatization of a nuclear confrontation game.) To get death in the opening chapter of *The Right Stuff*, Tom Wolfe presents us with crashing test pilots and young widows who, he admits in back-of-the-book notes, are made up. Jay Cantor writes Che Guevara's biography as a novel, and NBC retells the Kennedy tragedy with actors playing Jacqueline and JFK and calls the result "the whole story."

Getting the story in television journalism means getting pictures with punch and getting not only the essential but the colorful characters. Hewitt will candidly admit he is not as much interested in issues as in their effect on people, that the governing factor is a subject's entertainment value, not its importance. A perfect strike in prime time programming is something that combines high quality with easy popularity. To be a producer on *60 Minutes* is to be spending the best part of your waking hours, if not your life, looking for just that.

Lordsburg is a dying railroad town baking under the sun in western New Mexico. Mile-long Southern Pacific freights rumble through, but Interstate 10 and the Houston to L.A. tractor trailers now bypass out between the cactus hills and the salt flats. The older motels along arrow-straight, east-west Railroad Avenue have closed, and tumbleweeds grow in parking lots and have-been gas stations. A surprisingly cheerful note is a movie theater run by a sweet old couple—she in the Art Deco box office out front, he up in the booth, with a hefty Hispanic girl taking care of the popcorn. Lordsburg is a place that makes producers, directors, and cameramen itch. The town itself is a movie set!

But you, as a hypothetical producer, don't drop into the aggressively air-conditioned sheriff's office to say that. You don't talk about photogenic tumbleweed on Main Street when you check in with the mayor's office at the other end of the municipal building. You don't tell the theater couple their Bijou looks like something out of *The Last Picture Show*. You say you're doing a documentary on the last real wide-open spaces that folks where you come from really envy. You show you know the local folklore—it was just over those hills they finally caught the Dalton gang, wasn't it?—and you listen to expressions of civic pride. The sheriff and his eight men cover Hidalgo County, which runs all the way down to the border. You note the beat before he adds that Hidalgo County is about as big as Connecticut. You know that if you're going to get the Bijou, you have to get the owners to cooperate and turn on the remnants of the outside neon striping just before dusk (your cameraman calls the shot a Hopper painting). So you try to express the right surprise and enthusiasm, maybe mention the movie house where you saw your first picture. And you never say anything is quaint or gothic.

You make sure the sheriff knows you're staying at the Best Western, and you nod to him in the squad car when you drive your El Paso airport station wagon rental down Railroad Avenue with your cameraman on the roof doing one of those *High Noon* shots. A few days later, you even con the sheriff into driving the white state trooper Chrysler into another shot. You watch your cameraman zoom in on the face, with its sunglasses, the toothpick between the lips, and that Buford T. Justice hat cocked just right. And you know you have one of those pictures worth a thousand words.

Anyone who has worked in "nonfiction" television knows this is how it goes. It's not a matter of being deceitful, but of being tactful to people. It's second nature. You establish good will, you go through the motions of listening and filming because you're getting it all for free. There are disappointments; things that just don't pan out; people who won't talk; and there are lucky breaks—that *Last Picture Show* movie theater you can turn into a clever counterpoint, or your lawyer contact phoning quickly enough so you can get an affiliate crew to the cemetery for Susan Stitzel's funeral.

But you know what you're after, what answers in interviews you will use. You're doing a story, a story you've pitched to the boss, that you got him excited about. You had to punch out a ten-page outline—embellishing a little maybe—to get the budget you're now blowing on lunches for people who're trying to sell you something. Themselves, usually.

If you're working for *60 Minutes,* the only difference is that when you're ready to shoot the interviews you've got a celebrity flying in. He's jet-lagged, of course. On the plane he finally got around to the xerox of that ten-page outline you wrote six weeks ago. But it takes one dinner and another session in his suite (yours is a room) to bring him up to date, to cue him in on developments, new leads and opportunities.

You're responsible for getting the story in the can, which means directing Mike, or Ed, or Morley, or Harry. You know the street address of the doctor who refuses to see you. You tell your correspondent to walk along the sidewalk here, that you and the crew will be right behind. "Then we'll be shooting you off the tailgate of the Avis station wagon rental," you tell him. "You walk along here, turn left, and ring the bell and face this way." Sometimes the home office pulls the correspondent right out of your hands. You remember doing a stand-upper in a chemical dump in Stockton, eighty-two miles east of San Francisco, when they called to say Ayatollah Ruhollah Khomeini had agreed to an interview. Only your producer-colleague Barry Lando could have pulled that one. While the rest of the world press cooled its heels in Qum awaiting word from the Imam on the fate of the Americans now held hostage for one week in the Teheran embassy, Barry had started haggling with Sadegh Ghotbzadeh. Barry knew Ghotbzadeh from previous stories in Iran, and the former aide and confidant of the Ayatollah was now running Iranian television.

You all tooled back to the hotel. Mike had no passport on him. They called from New York and told you to get Mike on the first polar to London, and never mind the passport. His secretary would ferry the passport to Heathrow and be waiting there for the polar flight from San Francisco. How'd she do that? you asked stupidly. By taking the next Concorde out of Kennedy. You delivered Wallace to the San Francisco airport and tooled back to Stockton, trying to figure a way to shoot the remaining stuff without him. In your hotel room the next Sunday, you tuned in and there was Mike, sitting on a prayer mat next to the Ayatollah and asking whether the hostages' release was conditioned upon the United States turning over the ailing ex-Shah to Iran. That was indeed so, Khomeini answered through an interpreter. The next time you talked to Don, he told you NBC's John Hart and PBS's Robert MacNeil had already been in Qum when Mike arrived, and ABC's Peter Jennings is winging in with his crew. Wallace was the first American reporter the Ayatollah had agreed to see since the hostage ordeal began. Later, of course, Barry told you how cleverly Ghotbzadeh and his hip media assistants had played the American networks, Eurovision, and Japanese stations against each other, splitting hairs between exclusive interviews and exclusive *program* interviews. They wanted the Ayatollah's message out and were open for bids from the news organization delivering the best audience numbers.

The title *producer* is deceptive. The motion picture producer started out as a kind of primitive studio business representative and overseer of the director, jockeyed himself into financial control in Golden Era Hollywood. He ended up as a money raiser, deal maker, and packager, often an agent or a lawyer, who knew very little about actual film making. In television, the producer is the general head honcho of a show, often a writer who has assumed administrative and some creative control over his project. Hewitt is the one who adopted the title for television news, finding the idea of producing the evening news snazzier than directing it.

On *60 Minutes,* the producer is the prime source and the work horse. He or she is a skilled journalist entrepreneur who does most of the research, collars the people for interviews, arranges schedules, directs the taping, and tries to come up with the lines that Bradley, Reasoner, Safer, and Wallace will say to make sense of it all. "The producer does the donkey work at every level, and it's his neck that's out," says former *60 Minutes* second-in-command Palmer Williams. "If his cast—and that includes his big-name correspondent—doesn't perform up to expectations, it's a blot on the producer's escutcheon." Less charitably, Safer says the producers are all mini-Hewitts.

The producers try to stay near the epicenter of social tremors. They constantly check the flow of news, afraid of missing something big. They cultivate a network of sources and find raw material through reading, tips, research, by tuning in on the idle noodlings of the very hip, by checking out rumors, and by getting people to talk. They think in terms of adrenalin, dynamics, and what they can get on camera, of what lends itself to interesting television reporting. Once they have the story in the can, they think in terms of the pace and scope of the segment, of keeping it moving. Their imagination is the spark at the beginning of complicated confections, in which are fused the interests of top-rated prime time television, fierce competition with rival producers, and Hewitt's energy and enthusiasm. Selling Don on the idea is the first step.

"Fifty percent of the time the ideas will find you," says Les Edwards, who was the youngest (twenty-nine) and only black producer when he joined in 1980 and became one of Dan Rather's favorites. If another 20 percent of the stories originate with the viewers, where do the remaining 30 percent come from?

Hewitt and Company are not above a discreet buy. The Community Informational Project in Los Angeles is one such investigative agency that works on retainer. There is some irony in the collaboration of the big CBS machine with its hundred lawyers and this collective of leftover activists who are wired into California politics, subsist on the fringes of KCET, the Los Angeles PBS station, and come with impeccable reputations for dead accurate research.

It was the Community Informational Project that delivered a major medical fraud exposé, dramatized in the person of Dr. Edward Rubin. The California attorney general's office has investigated Dr. Rubin's practices for almost as long as MediCal, the state's Medicaid program, has been in existence. At the time of the airing of *Edward Rubin, M.D.*, in 1979, he was alleged to have overcharged MediCal and the federal Medicaid program $12.9 million. Mike Wallace visited Dr. Rubin's clinic in a rundown section of downtown L.A. and got a doctor who worked eight months for Dr. Rubin and a former nurse to spill the beans on camera. Patients were always diagnosed as having acute symptoms of ailments, requiring extensive lab tests and often hospitalization at Stanton Hospital, owned by Dr. Rubin and several partners. A baby brought into the emergency room with an ear infection invariably would be admitted with acute otitis media. One woman correctly diagnosed as suffering from a tubal pregnancy ended up with severe brain damage and an out-of-court settlement. Dr. Rubin's lawyer told his client not to meet with Mike Wallace, but producer Marion Goldin and crew managed to film the doctor coming to work. They also filmed his Beverly Hills home, which he had just put on the market for $1,950,000. After stalking him for days, Wallace managed to negotiate a deal with his lawyer that allowed Goldin and crew to film the doctor coming out of the clinic. Wallace tried: "My understanding is that your attorney says that until these legal matters are over you don't want to talk, and he's advising you not to talk about it. Is that correct?" To which Dr. Rubin said, "Yes, he's— yes."

The Community Informational Project's Nancy Salter led the investigation into higher political spheres. On camera, Wallace could report that one California state senator got a $77,000 insurance contract from Dr. Rubin, that the senator and a lieutenant governor received $13,000 in campaign contributions. California Governor Jerry Brown, running for the Democratic presidential nomination, declined to explain why he twice vetoed a $125,000 appropriation for nine more MediCal investigators. Senator Edward Kennedy, another presidential hopeful in 1979, refused to explain why a report on Dr. Rubin calling a substantial portion of the doctor's income "improper" had never been made public. Senator Kennedy denounced *60 Minutes* in letters to his constituents, saying he had turned over to the Justice Department the 167-page report his investigators had prepared on Dr. Rubin. The senator never mentioned that the report had been turned over long after the statute of limitations had made the material inoperative.

A number of stories are always in the pipeline, and a percentage of them unravel en route. Sometimes a story seems to work at the outset; down the line it may not. So each producer is working on five or six projects at a time, hoping that no more than two of them fall apart. A reunion of John Lennon, Paul MCartney, George Harrison, and Ringo Starr ten years after the Beatles split up was a high-priority project in 1979. Hundreds of pages of documentation on the world's millions of refugees were assembled, but what Mike Wallace agreed may be humanity's biggest collective scandal proved too unwieldy for a fifteen-minute treatment. Stories on South Africa, on the Atlanta slayings of twenty-eight black youths, and on the Equal Rights Amendment were abandoned for various reasons. South Africa denied *60 Minutes* the necessary visas; legal nitpicking unraveled the Atlanta murders as Wayne Williams was convicted of one of the killings in 1981; while the ERA story just never came together in a satisfactory manner.

*60 Minutes* producers are harried individuals spending half their time on the road turning leads, hunches, and events into filmable segments and, in New York, racing down hallways on 57th Street, carrying thick transcripts and stacks of cassettes, slipping into screening rooms with Hewitt between endless phone calls. In the field, they work tirelessly to put together the elements before arranging for Ed, Harry, Morley, or Mike to fly out and finish the story, in which the correspondent will seem to be the author and protagonist. "You have to book these guys like opera singers," says Jeanne Solomon, a producer based in London. "Sometimes you almost have to call up a subject you've been working with and say, 'You're going to have to miss your mother's funeral Thursday, because my correspondent is going to be in town and is going back to New York Friday in order to make it to Fiji over the weekend.' "

Ed may hate to do black and minority stories, and Morley hates big-name interviews. Mike may be identified with bare-knuckled investigations, and Harry with nostalgia pieces. Hewitt nevertheless tries to avoid typecasting the foursome. Bradley has done royalty; Reasoner has done hard-hitters on nuclear power plants and prison reform; Safer Third World corruption; and Wallace a story on dispossessed blacks at Harris Neck, Georgia. The producer-correspondent relationships are made by Don and some pairings seemed to be made for life—or the length of a contract. Before she quit to become the second in command on *20/20*, Marion Goldin worked permanently with Wallace. So do Barry Lando and Steve Glauber. Monika Jensen usually has Bradley as her correspondent. Drew Phillips and William McClure are comfortable old Reasoner hands, and John Tiffin works well with Safer.

Solomon, Tiffin, and McClure work out of London; Lando lives in Paris, and two other producers live in Washington; the rest of them are based in New York. Holly and Paul Fine are the first husband-wife producer team. Suzanne St. Pierre and Goldin came out of research, Al Wasserman came from documentary film making, while Tiffin and McClure are former cameramen. Together with Howard K. Smith, McClure did the first serious reports on South African apartheid in the mid-1950s, two thirty-minute specials that became a theatrical feature in England and got CBS banned in South Africa. A more recent McClure feat was getting film out of Poland by switching his exposed film into cans marked "unexposed." Lando carried a forged Cézanne—a copy of a painting stolen from the Chicago Art Institute—from New York to Montreal to show how easy it was to spirit purloined art across borders. His encounter with Canadian customs agents was duly shadowed by a cameraman with a hidden camera and became part of *The Stolen Cézannes*. Other producers have had peripheral roles. Goldin had been seen obtaining unnecessary prescriptions for Valium for herself; Glauber has been seen dealing with unscrupulous auto repairmen and crooked used car salesmen. Paul Loewenwarter popped up in *Who Pays . . . You Do* talking to a cost contractor and a construction superintendent at an Illinois Power nuclear building site.

The show has to contend with impostors and other CBS news teams taking the *60 Minutes* name in vain. A sheriff in Texas once phoned to check the credentials of a camera crew that was on the border filming a story on illegal immigrants for, the sheriff thought he'd been told, *60 Minutes*. Hewitt had somebody look at the week's assignments. Nothing there appeared to relate to the Mexican border. The sheriff was about to slap handcuffs on the film crew when its director got on the phone and explained they were from WBBM, the CBS-owned Chicago station, and

that they had told the sheriff they were doing "a *60 Minutes–type* piece."
Don let him off with a warning.

Producers work in the shadow of a permanent Murphy's Law in-
junction: whatever can go wrong, will, and at the worst possible moment. They have all been caught short at least once, and they are full of
stories of how they outmaneuvered fate in a tight corner. Drew Phillips
once had Reasoner buy drugs in Manhattan's Bryant Park behind the
main branch of New York City's Public Library when the pusher spotted the camera and became aggressive. Phillips got Harry and the
cameraman out fast, Harry with the heroin.

In their humbler moments, both correspondents and producers will
admit they don't get the story. Either crews get it, or there is no story.
The three-man crew of camera operator and light and sound technicians
is the indispensable part of a show of *60 Minutes'* stature, where film is
preferred over videotape for its greater shadow and contrast emphasis
(news crews dispense with the lightman, and state-of-the-art equipment
can have one person record both video and audio, although the two-man
setup is still the union standard). Hewitt is partial to stunning camerawork and, more than once, has bought exceptional footage from outside
sources. Cameras, microphones, and lights often make crews hostage to
cooperation from their subjects, and one of the main tasks of the producer is to negotiate ground rules and to present the crew's best side.

The networks say they are quick to discipline news producers and
crews who stage events, but as the financial pressure blurs the border-
lines between fiction and nonfiction television, so does it tend to make
such distinctions a matter of semantics. Hewitt asks, "Which is the more
honest reporting—taking the word of people who said this happened to
them, or going out and showing it happen?" The FCC rule forbidding
the staging or replication of any action in news programming is the result of the so-called WBBM Pot Party Case, in which a producer on the
Chicago station executed an assignment to do a story on marijuana by
arranging a party, supplying the smoking material, and filming the lighting up as "typical." The WBBM Pot Party rule says that what is shown
on the air in news programs must really have happened the way it appears on the air or a narration must explain what was created for the
cameras. Television viewers, Hewitt maintains, want much more documentation than newspaper readers to be convinced.

For an elaborate *Arson for Profit* story, a *20/20* producer tried to
consummate a bribe on camera. Filming from an unmarked van, the crew
caught an exchange of money between a Chicago insurance inspector

and the *20/20* producer who had maneuvered the man into position in the hidden camera's field of vision. As finally edited, we are told in the voice-over narration that what we are about to see is an insurance inspector accepting a bribe. What in fact we saw, later investigation revealed, was an insurance inspector with no record of corruption receiving $100 when it was offered to him. Did the television crew reveal corruption or did it create it? Commenting on the 1979 *20/20* story, Columbia Graduate School of Journalism professor Fred Friendly said, "When you move investigative journalism into entrapment or anything close to entrapment, and then do that in a media, which, by itself is show business, you're dealing with a witches' brew, and you can destroy a person or an institution by what is so close to entrapment that it is entrapment."

The guiding lights of high-powered television newsmagazines don't see themselves as brewers of witches' concoctions. To newspaper reporters who profess shock at arriving at a harbor drug bust to see a TV crew asking the cops to bring up the marijuana sacks from the boat one more time because the cameraman missed it, Hewitt says the action was staged not by TV, but by police, and that print reporters were as much a part of the pseudo-event. And what about political protesters who inform the media of their intentions and then stage demonstrations in front of the assembled reporters and their cameras? A 1983 ABC *Viewpoint* on pressure groups manipulating television made the point that terrorists asking for air time in a hostage situation are of course using television, but it may be the only way they can get their message across, since the media are owned by the rich and the powerful. If the President of the United States can manipulate television, said Ted Koppel in introducing the program, why can't a two-bit convict? Presidents offering "photo opportunities" in the Rose Garden and street demonstrators who "perform" when the cameras are rolling represent only the extremes of a constant and mutual exploitation. A year earlier, retiring *60 Minutes* second-in-command Palmer Williams haggled with labor when he and Harry Reasoner were doing a story on whiskey. When Suntory of Japan sponsored a British golf tournament, Scottish distillery workers planned to picket the event to show their anger at Suntory's having bought large quantities of pure Highland malt whiskey, shipping it to Japan for blending before reexporting it to England. When Williams asked a labor leader if there really was going to be a visible protest, he was told, "We'll picket if you're there with the cameras." To which he answered, "If you'll picket, I'll be there." They did and Williams filmed.

Hewitt feels a newspaper reader is convinced when he reads interviews with people, whereas television viewers want to be convinced that
what people are telling television reporters is, in fact, true. To have a
sound man pose as a wealthy leukemia victim as *60 Minutes* did in *This
Year at Murrieta*—an undercover investigation of a California cancer
clinic—is no less honest, he says, than to have people who were victimized by the miracle cure clinic tell their story on camera. It's a matter
of documentary evidence. Av Westin, the executive producer on *20/20*,
says production devices must never be allowed to distort the viewers'
understanding of a story's real element. "TV news is show business,"
he admits, "but it uses show business techniques to convey information
rather than to distort it."

Few people targeted for *60 Minutes* investigation will actually try to
evade the spotlight. Yet it is pretty simple. If there are no visuals, if no
principals will talk, there is no show. In a number of interviews, Wallace has confessed to his own amazement at how rapidly and willingly
people go on camera. Hoping to score points by collaborating is one
reason. Overconfidence and ego, plus a fascination with television seem
to be among the others. And, Dan Rather has observed, people lead
themselves to believe an interview will be friendlier than in fact it is, a
misconception that a skilled interviewer will not try to correct.

When film maker Roman Polanski agreed to be profiled on *60 Minutes* in 1979, he was itching to have his say about the tawdry troubles
that had caused him to flee the United States and put his career in jeopardy. His alleged rape of a thirteen-year-old in the Los Angeles home
of his friend and *Chinatown* star Jack Nicholson, while the actor was
away skiing in Colorado, had led to accompanying charges of child mo-
lestation, oral copulation, sodomy, and providing drugs to a minor. After
preliminary hearings that turned into a media circus and voluntary in-
carceration for psychiatric evaluation, the Polish-born director, to his own
lawyers' bafflement, fled to his adopted country, France.

Friends prevailed upon him not to give press conferences, but as he
had managed to raise finances to film Thomas Hardy's *Tess of the D'Ur-
bervilles* with his seventeen-year-old girl friend Nastassia Kinski, the *60
Minutes* chance was too tempting. With a crew, Mike Wallace flew to
the location in Normandy (Polanski didn't dare film *Tess* in England for
fear of extradition to California) and filmed the director instructing his
green-eyed heroine on doing repeated pushups so that her arms would
tremble for a scene. When Wallace asked why he got involved with a
thirteen-year-old girl, Roman was ready:

POLANSKI: Since the girl is anonymous, and I hope for her sake that she will be, I would like to describe her to you. She is not a child, she is a young woman. She had, and she testified to it, previous sexual experiences. She wasn't unschooled in sexual matters. She was consenting and willing. Whatever I did that was wrong, I think I paid for it. I went through a year of incredible hardship, and I think I paid for it.

Friends were appalled when they saw the segment. Author Jerzy Kosinski immediately phoned Paris and heard Polanski defend himself again by arguing the girl's complicity, that she wasn't a child. Kosinski shot back that the point was that a thirteen-year-old *is* a child; even Roman himself had been a child at thirteen. "Yes, well, yes," Polanski admitted on the transatlantic connection, "but, you know, in terms of everything else." They got into an argument. In terms of everything else, that was not the point, the writer said. Had she been twenty-seven or seventy-five there would have been no case and no program. Why had Roman even talked about it? "Well," came the reply, "I had to talk about *something.*"

The chance to outwit Mike Wallace is a challenge few people can resist. Stanley Rader is a Los Angeles attorney who thinks he outfoxed Wallace when *60 Minutes* investigated him and the Worldwide Church of God. Rader cried foul on camera, but he still thinks he came out ahead on *God and Mammon,* a tale of backbiting and power struggle, of fat expense accounts and disinheritance in a church whose 100,000 members each year contributed $80 million—more money than was collected by Billy Graham and Oral Roberts combined.

Producer Norman Gorin had first heard of the power struggle in 1977 when church members had gone to California Attorney General George Deukmejian, saying Stanley Rader was ripping off the church. Gorin had called Rader saying that the "immortality" of church founder Herbert W. Armstrong had come to his attention and he planned to do an episode about it. When Rader queried Gorin about how these matters had come to the attention of *60 Minutes,* the producer's reply convinced the lawyer the information came from dissident church members. Rader told Gorin neither he nor any responsible member of the church would give him an interview. Orally, and later in writing, Rader informed Gorin that most of *60 Minutes'* information was untrue, warned that use of it in a story on the Worldwide Church of God would be construed as evidence of malice and, if aired, would result in a lawsuit.

But in 1979, Deukmejian went to court to force the Worldwide Church of God to open its books and account for tax-exempt millions pouring into its Pasadena headquarters. The attorney general's action came on the heels of the People's Temple massacre and mass suicide in Guyana, the reported brainwashing of young people by cults and of counter deprogramming efforts, and reports of huge sums collected by charismatic television preachers. Gorin's interest picked up again, but he let Wallace approach Rader this time.

During a Los Angeles stopover on his way to Thailand, Wallace called the lawyer and, over dinner, explained that *60 Minutes* was interested in exploring the constitutional issue of separation of church and state, which the California attorney general's action had raised. The press—written and electronic—was increasingly concerned about violations of the First Amendment, he said. The two of them had a mutual interest in constitutional guarantees.

Rader relented. *60 Minutes* would not be able to see the eighty-seven-year-old Armstrong, in seclusion in his home in Tucson, but Wallace and crew could film him, Rader, in his Beverly Hills home, his office, and on the church grounds in Pasadena. Mike said he would of course have to bring up the dissidents' charges, but assured Rader that the story would be balanced.

When Rader, Wallace, Gorin, and crew sat down in the lawyer's office, the session turned into a four-hour grilling that at one point featured one of Wallace's neater one-two steps, and an equally elegant parry by Rader. Wallace asked Rader about an $8,000 expense item for two first-class round-trip Amsterdam–Tokyo tickets for a Dr. Singh. Rader responded that this member of the International Court at The Hague had gone to Tokyo, with his wife, to appear on Armstrong's behalf. Wallace said he had already spoken to Dr. Singh and gotten a different answer.

WALLACE: Do you know something, Mr. Rader? Dr. Singh told us he was too busy, he couldn't make the trip to Tokyo. Never appeared.
RADER: I'm not surprised. I'm not surprised that's what he would say.
WALLACE: You mean he was there?
RADER: Yes, he was.
WALLACE: So he lied to us?
RADER: Yes.

Toward the end, Mike played parts of two surreptitiously recorded telephone conversations between Herbert Armstrong and unnamed sources. Here, the church founder was heard reading part of a letter he allegedly was about to send to Rader, asking Rader to step down from any church posts he held that might put him in line as successor to Armstrong. The tape playback produced one of those on-camera "moments" that top ratings are made of. "Mike, look, I think you'd better scrap everything, because you're on my list, okay," said Rader, visibly controlling himself. "You're ne—you're never going to live it down, Mike, I guarantee it. I'll use it as a springboard to show just what the press is, because you're contemptible. I mean this; not for the camera. I'd like you to get out of here, immediately. I hope you got it, and I hope you have the guts to use it."

For reasons that had nothing to do with *God and Mammon,* Stanley Rader would be eased from power a year and a half after the *60 Minutes* broadcast. His separation from the Worldwide Church of God came at financially advantageous terms to him, and he would tell anyone who cared to listen that he had bested Mike Wallace. How? By being disarmingly candid. Was he living in a million-dollar home? Wallace had asked. He had just turned down a $1.2 million offer for the home, Rader had answered. Was he paid $200,000 a year? Closer to $300,000, Mike. Did Herbert Armstrong in effect have the right to do with the church what he wanted? You bet, because Armstrong was responsible and accountable to God alone. Was there a constitutional issue here, as far as Rader was concerned? No. People had a constitutional right to be stupid if they wanted to. They had a constitutional right to be generous, to give money to Herbert Armstrong to light cigars with if that was what they wanted.

Morley Safer was told to get out of the offices of Ashley Books for obtaining an interview under false pretenses, but producer Suzanne St. Pierre and crew kept the camera rolling while the publishing president covered her face and insisted the camera be turned off. The occasion was an investigative report on vanity, or subsidy books—the publishing of writers whose work is so bad, or so uncommercial, that they must pay to see themselves in print. The segment, which aired in January 1979, focused primarily on Vantage Press, the largest subsidy publishers in New York City, but also included an interview with Billie Young, the president of Ashley Books, a Port Washington, New York company. On camera Safer produced a letter that Ashley Books had allegedly sent to potential vanity authors.

BILLIE YOUNG: Well, why don't you talk to me about my established authors?

SAFER: Well, for the moment because the point of this story . . .

YOUNG: Because the point of this story is that you didn't level with me, that's the whole point of the story.

SAFER: No, we leveled with you. We're talking about new authors.

YOUNG: No way. Let me tell you something, Morley.

SAFER: . . . and . . .

YOUNG: I'm a former reporter. I worked for Cowles. I've had your job. I know what it is. But there's a way of doing it honestly, and I think you're doing it dishonestly.

SAFER: How are we doing it dishonestly?

YOUNG: By sitting there with that letter.


A moment later, Young covered her face with her hands. At the time, her lawyer claimed Safer and St. Pierre were offered interviews with several of Ashley Books' established writers and a literary agent, but that the *60 Minutes* crew wasn't interested in them. Five years later, Young refused to talk to this author about the incident.

Getting the people in the story to show their emotions is what makes for powerful television, and *60 Minutes* producers and crews are smart enough to keep the cameras rolling when a Billie Young tells Safer to get out of her office or a Stanley Rader says he hopes Wallace will have the guts to use what they just filmed. Getting the anger, the joy, the sorrow is getting the emotions that reach out and touch us. Bradley brought Lena Horne to tears, prodding and coaxing her to bare her soul, and producer Jeanne Solomon intercut shots of the entertainer's one-woman show on Broadway with Horne and Bradley walking through New York's Central Park absorbed in talk. (Impulsively, Horne took Bradley's hand.)

There are moments of truth that no one could have foreseen. When Barry Lando and Wallace set up *60 Minutes'* most elaborate sting in a Chicago storefront, there were no guarantees that anything would come out. The idea behind *The Clinic on Morse Avenue* was to catch owners of medical testing labs paying kickbacks to clinics catering to Medicaid patients, but Lando and crew behind the one-way mirrors and hidden microphones had no idea who would come through the door. The ravages of deindustrialization were in the faces that Paul Loewenwarter and crew caught in Midland, Pennsylvania in *Bye, Bye Benefits* as much as in Bradley's sober reporting. A clip of a Beirut nightclub singer belting out *I Will Survive* became the theme song of Safer's essay on the destruction of the Lebanese capital.

What makes nonfiction television so riveting is that the emotions are not scripted, that special moments are indeed the real thing. What constitutes reality programming, however, is being redefined. "Hybrids"— fictionalized biographies, docudramas—attract big audiences, and entertainment producers are increasingly finding "gut instinct" stories in newspapers and magazines. Programs based on news or at least on real-life scenes are the hottest trend.

In a first for a network news division, ABC News' *Nightline* in 1983 produced and broadcast for four nights running a make-believe U.S.-Soviet confrontation sliding toward the brink. For *The Crisis Game,* ABC News hired *The New York Times'* national security correspondent Leslie Gelb to help shape a program that would try to penetrate the minds of American and Soviet leaders as they reeled toward a nuclear faceoff. Gelb in turn recruited seven experts, called the controllers, who wrote a hundred-page briefing book and picked the players. Former Secretary of State Edmund Muskie was cast as president, and his advisers included two former defense secretaries: James Schlesinger, who had that title again, and Clark Clifford, who played secretary of state. Former Army Chief of Staff General Edward Meyer, who reluctantly wore his uniform for the taping, acted as chairman of the Joint Chiefs of Staff. For eighteen hours one weekend in Washington, the cameras rolled as "President Muskie" and his advisers deliberated the deepening crisis in a post-Khomeini Iran. The make-believe cabinet members didn't recite scripted dialogue, but, within the parameters of the briefing book, argued the twists and turns of the escalating confrontation while Gelb and his controllers, watching on TV monitors, played the rest of the world—Moscow, NATO, Congress, the news media.

Six months earlier, NBC Entertainment broadcast, over the objections of NBC News President Reuven Frank, a simulated newscast reporting the instance of nuclear blackmail by terrorists. Many viewers called in to complain that the show was too real and that it might inspire real terrorists. On CBS, a docudrama told the story of the real-life disappearance and death of six-year-old Adam Walsh. The movie showed pictures at the end of missing children, and within two days, a three-year-old boy was reunited with his mother in Louisville, Kentucky, and a fifteen-year-old girl, abducted when she was twelve, called her grandparents in Arkansas.

This new way of presenting issues that hover just below the news account consciousness has affected the conceptualization and the ethics of newsmagazine programming. A *60 Minutes* segment is still hard-core reality programming, but the means of getting the story, and producing it, have been broadened. Unlike a Hollywood film maker or entertainment-side TV producer, a *60 Minutes* producer-correspondent team cannot invent what isn't there. They must work inventively with the facts, convince on the strength of their documentation. Since *60 Minutes* is a news program, producer and correspondent are under FCC obligation to present a filmed reality, but once that responsibility has been met, the ethical question facing them is how much the facts can be reworked and the result remain news programming.

"What is drama, after all, but life with the dull bits cut out," Alfred Hitchcock once said. A *60 Minutes* producer must strive to dramatize by cutting out the dull bits. And with the limits of what constitutes factual material being tested in hybrid programming, the primary concern of *60 Minutes* teams is no longer the ethics of getting the story, nor is it the use and abuse of the power and attention that the program's enormous success bestows on those working for it. The First Law is to come up with facts rearranged in such a way as to grab the viewer by the throat and prevent him from thinking about what else might be going on.

# 5

# Hewitt

## *Executive producer Don Hewitt*

When Don Hewitt went to work in the newsroom at the Graybar Building on Lexington Avenue and 42nd Street in 1948, CBS was already a formidable news organization. And not only in the person of Edward R. Murrow. From the beginning, William S. Paley had let himself be enlightened by newspeople with a sense of standards. In 1928, when Samuel Paley gave his son $400,000 of his Chicago–Philadelphia cigar manufacturing fortune to buy into a shoestring radio network, the money was accompanied by sound advice: hire smart people and be smart enough to listen to them. The network was grandly called United Independent Broadcasters, a name chosen more as a protest against the Radio Corporation of America hegemony than anything else. UIB was soon in desperate straits and for one year became the very junior partner of the well-heeled Columbia Phonograph Company. When the partners split, the record press company allowed UIB to keep the Columbia name. Within a year Columbia Broadcasting System was shortened to CBS.

Television news began on CBS in 1946 with one regular weekly Saturday night broadcast with Douglas Edwards. The program was seen only in New York as there was no television network. CBS News was radio. Murrow had his daily news program, carried coast to coast, and he had his far-flung correspondents, picked and trained personally: William Shirer, Charles Collingwood, Dorothy Thompson, Winston Burdett. Murrow didn't want breathless wire service "rip-and-read" news bulletins but original, thoughtful reporting. He wanted a sense of the issues at play and a sense of the mood and feelings of the country covered. And he had leverage. He had become a friend of Paley during the war and he was the one man the chairman exempted from his policy of separating friends from business associates (Janet and Ed Murrow had been invited to the small wedding of Bill Paley and Barbara Cushing Mortimer, the ultimate social marriage of 1947; CBS President Frank Stanton had not).

Murrow had no doubt the little screen was the future, but he viewed the coming of television journalism with misgivings. Television forced a reporter to rely on camera crews. Unless the camera was rolling, the lights were on and the sound was recording, there *was* no story. Murrow's reservations about TV news were matched, albeit for a reason, by Paley and the upper reaches of CBS management. News didn't make money. Paley had never been a poor young man and moving from his father's cigar business to broadcasting had turned out to be a singularly shrewd move. Yet nothing in radio prepared him and his lieutenants for the wealth and influence television would bring. A year after the fifteen-minute Douglas Edwards newscast began, there were a million television sets in the United States; ten years later, there were fifty million and CBS was the single biggest advertising medium in the world. But it was not until the mid-1970s that networks and their affiliated stations discovered there was money to be made in news. During the formative years of television, news was a drain on corporate profits, a stepchild lumped together with documentaries and classical concerts as the public service justification for making money on the rest of the programming.

Murrow was leery of trying any kind of hard news formula, but his bosses were just as eager to have CBS News' brightest star make the leap to television. It was decided that what he needed was a producer, someone with technical skills. Their choice was Fred Friendly, with whom Murrow had worked in radio. Friendly was a driving, insecure, born salesman with superb technical skills, matching ambitions, and enormous energy, who was to become one of the founding fathers of the Public Broadcasting System (PBS). He was a big bear of a man with large hands and a powerful presence, who relished challenges and difficult ideas.

Friendly began his own conversion to television by going to the Museum of Modern Art and studying everything in the film library, from Pathé newsreels to the classical British documentary school of John Grierson. His idea for Murrow was to do a *Life* Magazine of the Air, a televised version of Murrow's *Hear It Now* program. Together, Murrow and Friendly had collaborated on a talking history of World War II, a series of record albums, or radio documentaries, they called "I Can Hear It Now." The records were a hit. Why not do a *See It Now?*

Murrow and Friendly contracted with Hearst-MGM News (Twentieth Century Fox-Movietone was already delivering newsreel footage to the nascent NBC-TV News) for camerawork on a cost-plus basis and for library footage as needed. They also acquired Palmer Williams, a former Borscht Belt actor who had spent the war working for the Army-Navy Screen Magazine. The year was 1951. Twenty years later, Williams was to become the second in command on *60 Minutes.*

Hewitt was a born and bred New Yorker, a breezy cocksure young man who looked a lot younger than his twenty-five years when he went to work at the CBS newsroom in 1948. The son of Ely S. Hewitt, an advertising salesman for the Hearst newspapers, and of Frieda Pike Hewitt, Don loved the news business. His boyhood idol was the Hildy Johnson character in Ben Hecht and Charles MacArthur's *The Front Page,* the hard-boiled, wisecracking reporter played by Cary Grant in the movie version. At nineteen, Hewitt didn't make it to sophomore at New York University, but went to work as a copyboy at the *Herald Tribune.* New York had eight daily newspapers in 1942, all itching for scoops and banner headlines and, in the Hildy Johnson tradition, reporters were supposed to run after hot leads and to get the story, never mind how. Don loved it. He spent World War II as a frontline correspondent in Europe for the War Shipping Administration. Since his demobilization, he had gone through a number of journalistic jobs. He had spent a year as night editor at the Associated Press in Memphis and, coming back to New York in 1947, found a position on the suburban *Pelham Sun.* His latest job was as night telephoto editor for Acme News Pictures. He found the idea of telling stories with pictures fascinating. When he gave notice saying he had been hired by Edmund Chester, the guy in charge of the embryonic CBS television news, his boss said he was crazy. Television was a fad. It would never last. Maybe, Don agreed, but he was curious about the new fad. If it didn't work out, he could always come back to newspapering. He was used to moving around.

Don went to work in the control room on the Douglas Edwards news show. The thirty-one-year-old Edwards was no Ed Murrow, but he was

well established in the second echelon of radio newscasters. He had started
his career at fifteen in Troy, Alabama and three years later moved to
WSB Atlanta, first as an announcer then as a newscaster on what was
to become Ted Turner's superstation. In 1938, he had moved to WXYZ
in Detroit. Newscasts were named after their sponsors, and Douglas became a Cunningham News Ace. Another News Ace he worked with was
a young man from Brookline, Massachusetts, named Mike Wallace. Since
WXYZ also put on several popular radio shows, Edwards and Wallace
were also radio actors, announcing the thundering hoofbeats of Silver,
the Lone Ranger's great horse.

Edwards' fifteen-minute television news show (sponsored by Olds-
mobile) was seen in Boston, Philadelphia, and Washington, as well as
in New York. As more and more stations were hooked into the CBS-
TV network, Edwards opened the show by welcoming them to the
broadcast. For Paley and Stanton, this announcement of the expanding
network was any night's most important story. When the West Coast
was tied into the coaxial cable at the end of 1951, Edwards opened with
the words, "Good evening, everyone from coast to coast."

There were no videotapes, no graphics, and no filmed reports.
Whatever film clips were used came from movie newsreel companies—
sports attractions, beauty contests, dog shows, or similar events planned
in advance or staged especially for pictorial coverage. Ninety percent of
the time, Edwards simply read the news.

Hewitt was one of the guys in the control room who tried to tinker
with the system, asking himself and everybody else how they could improve the nightly broadcast. The man in charge in the booth was called
the director ("we invented titles as we went along, too," Hewitt remembered). By midsummer, Don was one of several guys who took turns
directing the fifteen-minute newscast. One day in the fall, Edwards went
to Ed Chester and said he thought his show would have more stability
and continuity if there were one permanent director. Chester wasn't against
the idea and asked which one of the young men Edwards wanted.
"Hewitt," Edwards said. "You got him," Chester replied.

Like Friendly, for whom he was to direct a couple of *See It Now*
broadcasts, Hewitt had unfettered enthusiasm for finding out why everything worked.

Was television news merely radio with pictures? What do you take
pictures *of*? What do you say about the pictures? Where do you put your
reporter—on camera reporting into the lens, or off, explaining the pictures? To have the reporter tell the story of an apartment fire on camera,
with flames and firemen in the background, was not only a way of il-

lustrating the story, it was a way of making the reporter responsible for his report. And if you couldn't have film, why couldn't you use still photos? Or maps, while Edwards was reading the story. In the early days, these graphics could only be shown full frame, and Hewitt worked obsessively to figure out a way of showing the charts or maps behind his newscaster. At home one sleepless night, Don covered parts of his TV set with brown paper to decide how large Edwards' head and shoulders should be in relation to the graphics. In the office the next morning he knew the proportions he needed.

Then there was the double projector system. If you shot film and sound separately, you could have the cameraman concentrate on silent footage of a story and, once back in the editing room, lay the reporter's narration over quick cuts of the action. To make it work better, Hewitt ordered correspondents on the scene to remain in close touch with the camera crew, but not to narrate the pictures while they were being taken. The correspondent would then stand up in front of the camera and record an on-camera opening and closing to the story. Finally the reporter would write and record a narration on film, again standing up so he could be seen at the scene of the action.

Edwards read the news as he was accustomed to doing it on radio, by glancing down on his script. Don wanted his newscaster to look up and, as a first step toward the teleprompter, had someone copy the text in big black letters, which were held up in front of Edwards. The eye level was seldom right, and in a flash of inspiration Hewitt suggested Edwards learn Braille. All Doug would have to do then was to stare into the camera and read the news with his fingers. Edwards refused.

A lasting invention was the lineup, issued early in the day and holding the scrambling and confusion to a controllable level. A lineup tells the staff what stories are scheduled for broadcast; where stories will originate; what priorities should be set for processing film; what graphics need to be prepared; what scripts must be written and by whom; in what order the items appear; and for how long each is expected to run. Drawn up by the executive producer some six hours before air time, the lineup allows the entire effort to be coordinated. Since the amount of air time is rigidly fixed and an executive producer can't add five minutes on heavy news days, stories expand and contract at the expense of each other. Leftover seconds are rounded up to the nearest five and are negotiated with anchor and correspondents practically up to news time. The executive producer lives by his stopwatch—something Hewitt remembered when it was time to invent the *60 Minutes* motif.

During the 1950s ABC was so pathetically weak as not to count (it had been split off from NBC by government decree in 1941), and the opposition Hewitt and Company were watching was John Cameron Swayze. Camel cigarettes was the sole sponsor of the fifteen-minute NBC television news, and the program was called *Camel News Caravan.* On camera, Swayze sported a carnation in his lapel. He had a brisk, lively delivery and a breezy style that was the forerunner of the 1970s "happy news" affectation. Toward the end of each broadcast, the boutonniered Swayze bubbled with enthusiasm and said, "Now let's go hopscotching the world for headlines."

More important than Swayze on camera was NBC's commitment to its own film crews and a larger staff dedicated solely to TV news. At CBS, television was a stepchild; radio—and Murrow—still reigned supreme. Grudgingly, they allowed Hewitt to expand. Av Westin and Andy Rooney were a pair of future news magazine luminaries who passed through Hewitt's shop. Westin, who started out as a desk assistant while still a student at New York University, would eventually become Don's chief rival—executive producer of ABC's *20/20.* Rooney was a writer on his way to script dialogue for Arthur Godfrey.

Godfrey had two hit evening presentations on television, in addition to a popular morning radio show. By the early 1950s, he reached over eighty million viewers and at one point accounted for 13 percent of the network's revenues.

Shortly after *See It Now* made its debut in November 1951, they all got a new boss. Sig Mickelson was a former journalism teacher from the University of Minnesota, who had worked as news director at WCCO, the CBS affiliate in Minneapolis. A few months after joining the network in New York, Stanton asked Mickelson to take on the job of building up the news operation.

Mickelson had none of Friendly's mercurial enthusiams or Hewitt's energetic gall. He was aloof and professional in manner and, unlike Murrow, had little corporate clout. As a result he tried to build up television very much against the grain of Murrow and his "boys"—the elegant Collingwood, the cerebral Sevareid, the premier correspondent Howard K. Smith—whom Murrow had encouraged to think independently and to analyze news. Mickelson deferred to Murrow and his crowd when they recommended new people. Ernie Leiser was a former foreign correspondent with years in Europe, who was taken on as a writer at Collingwood's recommendation. Mickelson's own expertise was his shrewd eye for spotting journalistic talent. Walter Cronkite was his catch and when he was finally given the budget to hire reporters exclusively for television, his first recruits included Harry Reasoner and Charles Kuralt.

As plans for covering the political conventions, both to be held in Chicago, were being made, it became clear to Mickelson that Edwards—like Swayze at NBC—was something of a lightweight. Hewitt would direct, but Mickelson wanted someone who could give a sense of the whole, someone acutely aware of complexities and nuances, but who could at the same time convey a sense of being on top of events. Mickelson wanted someone at a central station who would introduce and focus the long broadcast, sum up and tie together the coverage coming from a number of reporters and camera crews moving around freely with delegates and on the convention floor. Hewitt was all for it, but who?

Radio was still bigger than television, and when Mickelson asked for either Murrow, Sevareid, or Collingwood to become his "anchorman," he was told to get lost. From the second-stringers, Mickelson and Hewitt picked Walter Cronkite.

This former United Press reporter had been hired when the Korean War broke out on the strength of his war correspondent work in Europe. There was a manpower shortage in the CBS News bureau in Washington, however, and he was asked to delay his departure and spend his first few weeks at WTOP, the CBS station there. There was little war footage to put on the air, so Cronkite took Hewitt's advice and for his stand-uppers for the evening news began using maps and a blackboard to tell the day's action in Korea. He worked hard, developed his own sources at the Pentagon, mastered the subject and, while everyone else explained the confusing war in complicated geopolitical terms, he tried to simplify the story. When he inquired about the Korean assignment, he was told the CBS brass felt he was doing such a good job "explaining" the war from Washington, there was no reason to send him to Seoul.

At the conventions that made General Eisenhower the presidential candidate for the Republican Party and, a week later, Adlai Stevenson, the Democrats' choice, Cronkite, and Hewitt in his control booth, were superb. "We were learning how to serve it up," Hewitt told Theodore H. White, "how to make it more dramatic, more exciting. We were dealing with something called the attention span. My job was to capture and hold the attention of the American public by putting on the best show, like putting a frame around a picture. Only it wasn't a picture of the convention, it was a picture of Cronkite."

Cronkite saw himself as Walter Burns, the mythical managing editor who sent Hildy Johnson on those hot assignments in *The Front Page*.

His job was to arrange the episodes of the convention as a managing editor would. And he came prepared: he knew the weight of each delegation and during the long hours in the Conrad Hilton ballroom, showed his professionalism, stamina, and gift for ad-libbing. On the second day, Murrow and some of his people began drifting around to let Mickelson and Hewitt know they were available.

Don's opposite number at NBC was the *Camel News Caravan* editor Reuven Frank. NBC fielded Bill Henry, a respected newscaster, as its main commentator, but compared to Hewitt's cleverly structured focus on Cronkite, Frank's coverage was diffuse and sprawling. Ever expedient, Hewitt created that great staple of television news—the super. His problem was to identify important delegates on the floor without breaking Cronkite's commentary. Inspiration came over breakfast with a colleague one morning when Don noticed the coffee shop's sign with movable letters advertising ham and eggs. The sign and accompanying box of letters were his for $20, and supers—lettering superimposed on the screen—were born. Don also managed to steal one superb moment from the opposition. When Richard Nixon was nominated as Eisenhower's running mate and hordes of reporters—2,000 were accredited to the convention—gathered around the young California senator to get his reaction, Hewitt in the control booth suddenly told his floor reporter to take his headset off and give it to Nixon so Murrow and Cronkite could interview him.

NBC's *Camel News Caravan,* with Swayze happily hopscotching datelines, was gaining on *Douglas Edwards with the News*—now also sponsored by a cigarette manufacturer, Pall Mall—but Edwards came across as personable in a low-key and thoroughly businesslike manner, and there was no question of replacing him. To keep Cronkite visible, Walter was given a Sunday showcase, a hokey but popular piece of pseudojournalism called *You Are There.* "The place: the plains of Ilium outside the great walled city of Troy; the date: 1184 B.C. and you are there," Walter began his intro to a dramatization of Homer's telling of the sacking of Troy. Playing a sort of immortal reporter on a time warp, Walter one week was in Rome for the murder of Julius Caesar; the next in Philadelphia for the signing of the Declaration of Independence; then, a few weeks after that, in Moscow for one of Stalin's 1930s purge trials.

Cronkite was not alone in stooping to visibility. Murrow did his own "Lower Murrow," as New York critic John Lardner would call his *Person to Person* show. Showbizzy and fatuous, the interview show took Murrow into the homes of celebrities. Joseph Wershba, who was to become a *60 Minutes* producer, remembered his own embarrassment at seeing Murrow do silly patter with instant, often empty-headed stars.

Murrow was himself embarrassed, but he was also aware he could do only so many controversial shows. And *See It Now* was heading toward confrontation with Senator Joseph McCarthy, the ogre of the Cold War, whom not even President Eisenhower was ready to take on. McCarthyism was already coming to be known as the practice of making accusations of disloyalty, in many instances unsupported by fact or based on hearsay or questionable and irrelevant evidence. The demagogue from Wisconsin made his charges and then went on to his next accusations, smearing with an ever bigger brush. The media didn't investigate his charges, and an astonishing number of people were cowed, including Bill Paley.

Murrow, Friendly, and their team spent endless nights poring over footage of McCarthy. They told Stanton and Mickelson they planned a March 1954 broadcast. Paley was not about to tell Murrow *not* to do a McCarthy show, but he was not very eager to be associated with it, and as much corporate distance as possible was put between the program and CBS. Asked at the last minute whether he wanted to see a screening of the segment, the chairman said no, but suggested Murrow offer McCarthy equal time. Mickelson also refused to see it and, as David Halberstam would write in *The Powers That Be*, "the most potent and sensitive television show of a decade was thus broadcast without any prior screening from CBS superiors; such a thing would be inconceivable a decade later."

The program used an alarmingly simple technique that Hewitt, Palmer Williams, and Wershba would use decades later on *60 Minutes:* it let McCarthy hang himself. The senator's inconsistencies had always been hard to nail down. As put together for *See It Now*, McCarthy was heard to offer exact numbers of Communists working for the federal government, but his numbers kept changing. He waved papers providing "documentation," but the papers' contents were never revealed. The *See It Now* producers had no exclusive material on the senator. They merely edited three hours of clips to make the inconsistencies stand out, showing McCarthy for what he was, not for what he said he was.

Paley felt Murrow was becoming a potential liability, that his broadcast had too much autonomy. Alcoa dropped *See It Now* for a different show in 1955, and Paley suggested that instead of a weekly *See It Now* show, it might be an idea to do it now and then as a sixty-minute or, even occasionally, a ninety-minute program. Wasn't thirty minutes awfully confining? The idea of longer, fewer programs flattered Murrow and Friendly. They fell for it, and their weekly time slot was sold to Liggett & Myers Tobacco for a quiz show.

By the 1956 national conventions—boring, drawn-out affairs that renominated Eisenhower and Stevenson—Reuven Frank fielded *two* anchormen. Chet Huntley's unflappable and objective reasonableness combined with David Brinkley's wry observations created a unique chemistry. Backing them was a team of smart floor reporters and for the first time NBC challenged the CBS supremacy. NBC was not about to let Huntley and Brinkley slide out of the limelight after the convention, and a few months later the Swayze broadcast was replaced by *The Huntley-Brinkley Report.*

Hewitt made history of a sort that year flying over the sinking Italian luxury liner *Andrea Doria* with Edwards and a cameraman. On the morning after the ship collided with the *Stockholm,* a Swedish cruise ship, off the coast of Nantucket, a Navy commander at the rescue station at the Quonset Naval Station in Rhode Island recognized Edwards from the evening news. That allowed Edwards, Hewitt, and cameraman to get aboard a seaplane, which reached the scene just as the ocean liner began to sink, with a loss of fifty-two lives. With camera whirring and Edwards doing an eyewitness report, the plane circled until the *Andrea Doria* disappeared beneath the waves. The scoop beat the pants off the opposition—the only thing Hewitt cared about—but it also showed how effective television could be in covering a certain kind of event. Six years later, when an American Airlines plane crashed into New York's Jamaica Bay, Don pulled another "Hildy Johnson." Because of a tugboat strike, it was impossible to get to the site, but Hewitt made a few inquiries, located the owner of one tugboat at his home in Connecticut, and offered twice the going rate. The owner found the offer irresistible and, within an hour, Hewitt and his people left rival network crews on the dock to chug out to the site of the wreckage.

More important, he explored the techniques of film making to find new ways of dramatizing and magnifying news events. Legends grew up. While on a trip to Berlin during the pre-Berlin Wall days when the East Germans harassed Allied, and especially American, cars trying to travel to West Germany on the autobahn, Hewitt supposedly tagged along with CBS correspondent Daniel Schorr and his crew to Checkpoint Bravo to do the story. Schorr and crew decided he would stand a hundred meters from the East Germans and, when the camera rolled, point to the checkpoint. Hewitt couldn't help asking a few question. What would happen if Schorr went up to the East German border guards? Would they stop him, refuse to let him through? Schorr nodded and Hewitt asked if the crew had a radio microphone. Yes, it was part of the standard equipment. Within minutes, Don had persuaded Schorr to hide the wireless mike in the folds of his necktie and, with cameraman and sound engineer following in a car, walk up to the East Germans and ask, "Why can't I go through? I'm an American. I want to go!" As Schorr would remember, it was immensely successful. "It made the story much more concrete. All the menace of East German troops and their guns and all the rest. Being stopped personally . . . I represented the whole United States. And that was the kind of eye Hewitt brings to these things." Years later, Hewitt would tell this author, "Nice story, except it never happened."

Don cultivated a bouncy, hip guy style and sported a nonconformist Hollywood look: open collar, sports coat, and a racy crewcut. He called male acquaintances "pal," and the scores of young women who passed through CBS News were "honey." He had pazzazz. On early afternoons, he and his cronies played sizzling games of poker. The perverse dare was to get to the lineup as late as possible.

Relentlessly, however, the Huntley-Brinkley team closed in. Don called the two-man anchor team Mutt and Jeff, but Reuven Frank worked the kinks out of having Huntley in New York and Brinkley in Washington. The two hated their scripted end-of-broadcast "goodnights," but by sometimes having them deal with divided aspects of the same story, Frank gave the broadcast a new pace. The lineup copy was tightly written, and the news half hour often seemed to be in more places where things were happening than the Doug Edwards broadcast. By 1960, NBC News was number one in the ratings, to Paley's mortification and Hewitt's peril.

The entertainment side of CBS was so extraordinarily successful that the chairman couldn't tolerate having his news division slide into second place. At the Democratic convention in Los Angeles, which chose John F. Kennedy as the presidential candidate, Hewitt panicked and persuaded Mickelson to meet the Huntley-Brinkley threat with Cronkite and Murrow. Instead of playing off each other, however, the two big guns of CBS News played the same avuncular role. Besides, Murrow was no good at ad-libbing. The result was a disaster and, years later, Hewitt would admit the Cronkite-Murrow team-up was the worst idea of his life. In a postconvention purge, Mickelson was fired and, ominously, replaced by a lawyer. The news operation had always been run by people with journalistic backgrounds, but Richard Salant was an attorney. He had come aboard in 1952 on the condition his duties not be confined to legal work. "Next to a disbarred lawyer," he told Stanton, "there's nothing worse than a house lawyer, a *kept* lawyer." The news division soon realized this slight barrister, with a boyish appearance, enjoyed a special relationship with the network president—that he was Stanton's number one troubleshooter.

Stanton made Ernie Leiser the assistant general manager. With his granite face and his horn-rimmed glasses, Leiser's camera presence had been all negative. He had realized it himself and for a year had plotted to get behind the camera. He quickly became the strong man on Salant's team. He was one of those who pushed the hardest to have Cronkite replace Doug Edwards and was the force behind the expansion of regional news bureaus and the push toward a half hour evening newscast. When CBS went to the thirty-minute format in 1963, Leiser moved imperceptibly in on Hewitt's turf, suspecting Don was too wedded to the fifteen-minute tabloid form to see that the half hour newscast required a different approach.

RCA Chairman David Sarnoff, NBC's ultimate boss, thought of himself as the elder statesman of broadcasting, someone above being identified with either Democratic or GOP politics, and ABC's Leonard Goldenson also found it expedient to steer clear of being personally identified with partisan politics. Paley, however, was openly a Republican, which didn't help Hewitt when Don became Nixon's fall guy for the disastrous Great Debates of 1960. Howard K. Smith was the agreed-on moderator and Hewitt the agreed-on director of the first debate. In September, the candidates and their retinues assembled in Chicago, at WBBM, the CBS owned and operated station. Edward A. Rogers, principal television adviser to Nixon, immediately objected to the studio background. It was too pale for his candidate's light-colored suit. The backdrop was hurriedly repainted—it was still sticky at debate time—and Rogers was still fussing over lighting and camera positions.

Hewitt was setting things up when Nixon entered from one side, Kennedy from the other. "I assume you two gentlemen know each other," Don said, smiling to break the ice. A minute later, Don asked Kennedy if he wanted makeup. JFK had been campaigning in California and looked tanned and vigorous. He declined makeup, but let an aide run to the nearest drugstore to buy Max Factor Creme Puff. When Hewitt turned to Nixon, the Republican candidate first refused, but relented and let someone apply a bit of Lazy-Shave, a product recommended for "five o'clock shadow."

Hewitt had his own bosses, including Stanton, up in his control booth.

Once he got behind the controls, Don was appalled at the way Nixon looked. Nixon had had a brief illness and had lost a few pounds. His collar looked loose around the neck. Hewitt told Salant to take a look on a monitor. Salant made Rogers come up and have a look. Was Rogers *sure* Nixon looked all right? Salant asked. Rogers said yes.

What television audiences noticed that night was not so much the ritualized questions and answers, but the air of confidence, the alert patrician, slightly disdainful mien of the young JFK in contrast to the sweaty, drawn Nixon. Don cut to occasional reaction shots of each candidate listening to the other. Rogers furiously objected to the reaction shots. Perspiration was streaking the Lazy-Shave on Nixon's haggard face. The control booth turned into a madhouse. Kennedy's man pointed to his cue sheet, shouting to Don, "You owe us two more of Nixon, you've had sixteen of Kennedy and only fourteen of Nixon," and Rogers shouting, "No, No." Hewitt told everybody to shut up.

Nixon lost the presidency to Kennedy almost as narrowly as he won it eight years later, emerging in 1968 as a much smoother, more mature politician, with one of the most expensive and professional campaigns ever mounted. As President, he once asked Hewitt about makeup and listened carefully while Don explained the best makeup was a good natural tan.

The nightly *Huntley-Brinkley Report*'s lead over the *CBS Evening News* was becoming so commanding, and so personally embarrassing to Paley, that Doug Edwards' days were numbered. Hewitt, whose drive and personality dominated the broadcast, tried to prod Edwards to take a more active role in the newscast, telling him that if viewers didn't like the show, they wouldn't blame the guy in charge in the control room. They would blame Edwards. The ax fell in April 1962. The "pioneer" of the evening news was out and Cronkite in. Despite Ernie Leiser's reservations, Hewitt was made executive producer of the *Evening News with Walter Cronkite*.

All three networks went to thirty-minute evening newscasts in 1963. CBS cancelled a late-morning news and chat show hosted by Harry Reasoner and Broadway actress Mary Fickett and replaced it with *The CBS Morning News*. The anchor was a newcomer to the network, a newsman and former talk-show host named Mike Wallace. The executive producer was Av Westin, a young man from the Hewitt stable who had impressed Salant after a tour of duty as field producer in Bonn and London. Deeply interested in the mechanics of TV news, Westin had become convinced the BBC was way ahead in delivering news about the duller subjects in life: the minutiae of international relations, economics, trade balances. The trick was to *anticipate*, to film "backgrounders" and analyses in advance and to "bank" these reports until the appropriate news peg came around. Knowing in advance that a congressional committee was about to investigate hospital costs, for example, would permit a crew to shoot a short feature on hospital routines. Anticipating the regularly issued FBI reports on crime meant you could do a carefully researched piece on a police precinct in a high crime area in advance. Newspeople should be able to apply experience and judgment to unfolding trends. The mixture of hard news and such background material would bring a different texture to newscasts.

Viewer response, however, was as favorable to Wallace as it was to Cronkite and, like Hewitt on the evening show, Westin worked furiously to whip the morning show into top form. Westin was flexible and inventive and Mike could handle unforeseen on-the-air situations with confidence. The person who booked the guests for the show was Barbara Walters. The future "queen of television news" also worked on a short-lived show, which starred Cronkite and Dick Van Dyke—Walter doing the news and Dick songs and chatter—and moved up to be the one female writer on various news and pubaffairs programs, all of which went off the air. She got to meet Hewitt, who kindly told her she wouldn't make it on camera in television. *The Morning News* benefitted enormously from its 10 A.M. time slot where it was safely beyond the reach of the already eleven-year-old *Today*. Because there was more money in airing *I Love Lucy* at ten, Wallace and Westin were moved to a 7 A.M. slot in August 1965. *The Morning News* promptly lost everything it had carefully cultivated over two years: identity, morale, Westin, and Wallace.

The switch to the half hour evening news—twenty-two minutes once commercial time out was deducted—cost Salant the presidency of CBS News and lit the fuse under Hewitt's executive producer chair. Since taking over from Mickelson, Salant had made vast improvements but, by making a big deal of the longer evening format, he escalated the Cronkite vs. Brinkley-Huntley battle to the point where *Newsweek* made it a cover story and Paley demanded results. By the end of 1963, when it became clear the thirty-minute Cronkite show wasn't going to knock Huntley and Brinkley off the air, Salant was kicked upstairs. His replacement was Fred Friendly, the "brilliant monster," as the domineering, energetic head of the documentary division was nicknamed.

Hewitt and Leiser were in the newsroom and, as chief of a newly opened southern news bureau, Dan Rather was in Dallas that November afternoon in 1963 when President Kennedy was shot. Although unconfirmed, CBS radio quickly reported the President was dead, but Hewitt waited an agonizing seventeen minutes before he had Cronkite announce the tragedy on the tube. Television was different from radio; it gave a different weight, a different intensity to news. But it was the distant war in Vietnam that President Johnson tried to win, which showed how television coverage of events had a way of sweeping past politicians and their calculations. With guile and appeals to patriotism, LBJ might be able to control the flow of news about the war in Washington, while in Saigon, General William Westmoreland could appeal to the press corps not to forget the "big picture." Neither could control the TV crews in the field, however.

Morley Safer was a correspondent who suddenly brought a new dimension of candor to the television coverage of the war. Instead of relying on the State Department and Army briefings—nicknamed the "five-o'clock follies" by the press—in Saigon, Safer and Ha Thuc Can, his cameraman who doubled as interpreter, regularly went "jungle bashing" with the troops. While touring a Marine staging area near Danang, Safer and crew were invited to accompany a unit that had orders to "waste" the nearby village of Cam Ne, which, according to the local province chief, was a Vietcong sanctuary. There, they watched in horror and filmed as the Marines methodically leveled the village. At one point, the cameraman saw a group of Marines about to fire a flamethrower down a deep hole from which came voices of women and children. Can started arguing with the Marines, screaming at them while he began to talk the people out of the hole, eventually saving perhaps a dozen lives. Safer watched in shock. An hour later, standing in front of the smoldering huts, he concluded his stand-upper, "This is what the war in Vietnam is all about. The Vietcong were gone . . . The action wounded three women, killed one baby, wounded one Marine, and netted four old men as prisoners. Today's operation is the frustration of Vietnam in miniature. There is little doubt that American fire power can win a military victory here. But to a Vietnamese peasant whose home means a lifetime of backbreaking labor, it will take more than presidential promises to convince him that we are on his side."

Hewitt's downfall came in the wake of the 1964 political conventions that chose Barry Goldwater and Lyndon Johnson as the Republican and Democratic hopefuls.

At the Republican convention in San Francisco, Chairman Paley was committed to William Scranton, a middle-of-the-road candidate favored by Eisenhower. This open endorsement angered Senator Goldwater and made the party conservatives suspicious of CBS. What hadn't helped was that Daniel Schorr, the network's correspondent in Bonn, had linked Goldwater with certain right wing military men in West Germany, whom the senator was to visit immediately after his expected nomination. In his report, Schorr noted that the meeting with the Germans was to take place at Berchtesgaden, Hitler's former hideout in the Bavarian Alps, without mentioning that since the war Berchtesgaden had been a U.S. Army recreation center. The Hitler angle was a cheap shot and, for a time, CBS was barred from Goldwater's convention headquarters. Paley was furious and demanded that Schorr be fired. Friendly, who had just taken over from Salant, consulted Hewitt and his staff and all agreed that to sack Schorr would be an unseemly cave-in to naked pressure. As Schorr remained unfired, Paley became convinced he had too little control over his own news department.

Hewitt fielded a younger team than NBC's Reuven Frank did, including newcomer Roger Mudd, but didn't miss many stories. The difference was all showbiz image, "casting" of Huntley-Brinkley vs. Cronkite, concept, and tone. It was a particularly galling moment for Paley to have the news division clobbered in the ratings. On the entertainment side, CBS was at the height of its power and glory. CBS Inc. was buying into publishing with the purchase of Holt, Rinehart & Winston and acquiring a stake in sports with the New York Yankees baseball team. The corporate headquarters moved into a brand-new skyscraper, quickly named Black Rock after its ebony granite facade, on 52nd Street and the Avenue of the Americas. The news division didn't rate space at Black Rock, but left its crammed quarters in the Graybar Building for a block-long former milking plant fronting 57th Street on Manhattan's far West Side.

Back from San Francisco, Chairman Paley asked Friendly what he planned to do about the coverage of the upcoming Democratic convention in Atlantic City. Nothing, basically, Friendly answered after much soul-searching. NBC would no doubt dominate again. The best thing was to grin and bear it and plan for the future. This was not what Paley wanted to hear and he told Friendly to come back with the names of possible replacements for Cronkite. Friendly tried to stand fast but, at the next meeting, Paley called Roger Mudd a born anchorman. How about combining Mudd with Bob Trout? Paley wondered. Mudd was young and terrific, Trout the seasoned pro.

The Mudd-Trout duo failed to impress at the Atlantic City convention, which was less a representative party assembly than a coronation of LBJ. NBC's Sander Vanocur scored a marvelous exclusive with the President the night Johnson accepted the nomination, the only scoop at a scoopless convention. CBS bounced back with a superb election coverage that November, and Cronkite was rehabilitated. Paley was heard wondering why he had let Friendly argue him into using Mudd and Trout at all.

But there was to be another fallout. Friendly was among those who felt the evening news needed a new executive producer. Hewitt was great, but maybe he wasn't current. Hewitt's forte, his flair for visuals, his innovations with double projectors and graphics had been absorbed into everyday newscasting. Leiser's passion, on the other hand, was the news itself, the angle, meaning, and impact of a story. Leiser considered himself superior in intellect and news acumen to Hewitt. Editorially, he *was* stronger. And he was Cronkite's man. Together they were beginning to grope with the big questions: What *is* news? What is the emotional reality of a piece of information? How can you show a *feeling?* Is there a better way? The same questions would preoccupy Van Gordon Sauter nearly twenty years later when Dan Rather took over from Cronkite.

Friendly didn't exactly rush to Don's defense when Ernie suggested he take over. The definition of news was being broadened to include more and varied information. Friendly and Cronkite regarded the authoritative Ernie Leiser as a more serious producer than Hewitt, as someone who would give the evening news both a larger scope and a stronger tone. A month after the election, Don sensed something was afoot and went to Friendly only to be told he was secure in his job, that he had nothing to worry about. A few hours later, he was summoned back to Friendly's office and told Ernie was replacing him.

"Best decision I ever made," Friendly said twenty years later. "Don has lots of dazzle, lots of pace—that's what he's good at. But the daily news had to have a steady administrator, had to have coolness, and Don's a hot person. He always wanted to change things day by day, even hour by hour. Under him, the program had great cosmetic value but no content. If I had wanted to do one Cronkite show—just one—Don would be the man. But 250? No."

Hewitt was both angry and demoralized. With Cronkite he had made the *CBS Evening News* the model of its kind, and this was Friendly's reward. Don was forced to think a lot of things over. He had been with CBS for sixteen years; maybe it was enough. He came close to quitting, but accepted the offer to produce and direct in "soft news," as the documentary operation was called.

The following April, they all attended Ed Murrow's funeral. A year later, Friendly himself was out.

# 6

# The Back of the Book

## *From idea to demo reel*

Don Hewitt called his years in documentaries his Siberian limbo. "Documentary" had no magic and the word made him, and nearly everyone else in television, cringe. As far back as the 1930s, people working in documentaries had tried to come up with a more exciting name for it. John Grierson, the British theoretician and father of a remarkable documentarist school, tried "realist" and "factual" cinema. At CBS News, they called documentaries news specials, reality programming, or news features.

Television abandoned early on the immediacy of live broadcasting for canned entertainment, the punch of reality for the safety of rehearsed make-believe. Time and again, the awesome forces of televised events—tragedy in Dallas, the reach for space at Cape Kennedy—kept the nation riveted to the tube and turned the world into that new cliché, the global village, but sponsors and audiences preferred the *Beverly Hillbillies, Andy Griffith Show, Red Skelton Hour, Candid Camera, Lucy Show, Dick Van Dyke Show*, and *Gunsmoke*, with which CBS dominated the 1963–64 ratings. *CBS Reports* might document the plight of migrant workers in *Harvest of Shame*, incur the wrath of the American Medical Association

78

with *The Business of Health,* and take on the gun lobby with *Murder and the Right to Bear Arms.* The program might confect such specials as *Trujillo—Portrait of a Dictator, Our Election Day Illusions,* and *Thunder From the Right;* at Black Rock it was a pain in the ass. And always had been. Coming out of the 1954 Army-McCarthy hearings, Murrow and Friendly had realized they would have to go easy on controversy and, to be able to continue making hard-hitting documentaries—or "fact films," as they called them to escape the stigma—they had invented the *Person to Person* pap. Still, Frank Stanton killed *See It Now* because of lack of sponsor enthusiasm.

In 1959, however, the quiz scandal had made it necessary to do more in public affairs programming. President Eisenhower was shocked at revelations that contestants had been lying about their appearances on *The $64,000 Question,* that program personnel had admitted winnings were rigged. Amid congressional agitation for cleaning up network practices, Stanton promised the Federal Communications Commission (FCC) that everything on CBS would henceforth be "what it purports to be." Canned laughter and applause would be banned and, starting immediately, CBS would make regular one-hour documentaries in prime time on important issues. NBC also set up a "creative projects" unit in its news division. *CBS Reports,* as the new program was hastily called, would be broadcast once a month, Stanton asserted, perhaps every fortnight or even once a week, "if the networks are permitted to retain their present structure" (meaning that self-regulation, not legislation, was the American way). The radical idea of doing away with laugh tracks was soon abandoned, but *CBS Reports* became, for a while, a monthly staple.

The last *CBS Reports* story Murrow narrated was a harbinger of a reporting style to come—investigative journalism. Chiefly the work of Jay McMullen, a reporter Friendly was so impressed with he let him go "underground" for months on a story: *Biography of a Bookie Joint* was an exposé of gambling and police corruption in Boston. McMullen began filming the entrance of a bookie parlor, disguised as a key shop, from across the street and, with the help of Palmer Williams, the newsreel jack-of-all-trades Murrow and Friendly had hired when they were babes in the wood in TV, developed an 8mm camera concealed in a lunch box. With his "lunch box," McMullen shot entire sequences of gambling operators, customers, and the protective machinery inside the bookie joint. *Biography of a Bookie Joint* led to the resignation of the city police commissioner.

The man Hewitt went to work for as a back-of-the-book producer was a former radio personality named Bill Leonard. For eleven years, Leonard had been the roving reporter on *This Is New York,* a popular six days a week radio program on WCBS, first as an early morning show featuring Leonard with offbeat stories he had collected during the night on the prowl, later as an expanded daytime information magazine. A massive heart attack had forced Leonard to alter his lifestyle at forty. Many considered him too New Yorkish for the network, but Friendly moved him to *CBS Reports* after Leonard proved himself with *Trujillo—Portrait of a Dictator.* Leonard had a few contacts in the Dominican Republic and spent the better part of 1960 there, digging into the life and times of Rafael Trujillo and even persuading him to appear for CBS cameras on a white horse. *Our Election Day Illusion* and *Thunder From The Right* had followed, and in 1962 Leonard had been chosen to run the network's long-range planning for election coverage.

Leonard, who had none of Friendly's mercurial temperament, was an early computer enthusiast. He realized such machines could be used to project election returns. Together with political pollster Louis Harris and IBM computer programmers, he devised a system on statistical probabilities whereby a small sample of voters would represent the entire electorate. A "model" of each state was programmed and constantly refined with ethnic, economic, and other demographic input. His baptism of fire was the 1964 political conventions, where he became Friendly's indispensable deputy (once shouldering a TV camera himself to muscle in on an NBC exclusive with President Johnson), and the presidential elections, where the 172,500 precincts in the country were reduced to 2,000 key models in the CBS computers. He had been in on the Dump Cronkite postmortem and found top corporate politics too savage for his taste. When Friendly offered him the vice presidency of public affairs, Leonard accepted.

Friendly's presidency of CBS News was tumultuous, invigorating, controversial, and short-lived. From the beginning he was under tremendous pressure to make the news division match the glitter of the entertainment side. The tone was set three weeks after he took over when an earthquake in Alaska became "my Bay of Pigs," as he told Hewitt. While the *Huntley-Brinkley Report* had camera teams on the scene and broadcast updated film reports, *CBS Evening News* was reduced to rewriting wire service accounts. With threats of mass firings, Friendly drove the news division to the limit. His enthusiasm, ass chewing, and violent tantrums were both inspiring and intimidating.

Leiser was interested in performance and drove himself as hard as anyone. He was impatient, often brutally critical, but was considered to be fair. He had none of Hewitt's showbiz jive and fire storms, and he soon began purging the more enthusiastic Hewitt apprentice sorcerers. One was Bill Crawford, a sharp-featured intellectual who had worked up from writer on the old Doug Edwards show to middle management. The son of the distinguished journalist Kenneth Crawford, who had written the "TRB" column in *The New Republic* in the 1940s, Bill called Hewitt "the maestro" and refused to cower to Leiser's new rules. Crawford was shipped off to Washington, where he was to stay and groom a number of younger reporters working for him. Roger Mudd and Dan Rather were to be members of the Bill Crawford fan club.

Back at the fishbowl, Leiser's high standards inspired a kind of surly awe and affection. His quest was for excellence, for scope and redefinition. He quickly adopted the anticipatory news formula that Av Westin was using with great effect on the *Morning News,* and, on his own, made other breaks with the Hewitt tabloid practices. Whenever possible, he balanced the lineup and had front-of-the-book news on politics, government, war and disaster followed by what, in wire service jargon, was called "enterprisers," in-depth, back-of-the-book pieces. Headline items were usually filmed reports running a minute or a minute and a half. Enterprisers, of which were always a number in the "bank" for slow news days, could run as long as six or seven minutes, Leiser decreed. He considered this an important advance in broadcast journalism, a way of giving a broadcast a more assertive tone and more breadth. Field producers from the Mekong to Minneapolis were told to come up with more enterprisers.

Friendly had agreed to take over the management of the news division on the condition he be given direct access to Paley and Stanton. The chairman and CEO had acceded to this demand, but soon tired of Friendly's constant complaints and requests for meetings. They had their own meetings to attend as they isolated themselves in corporate reorganization. CBS was becoming a giant—profits for 1965 reached $50 million—and in the Wall Street fashion of the day, the company was split into the Broadcast Group, embracing news, TV and radio networks, plus the five owned and operated stations in New York, Philadelphia, Chicago, St. Louis, and Los Angeles, and the Columbia Group, encompassing the flourishing record, music, and publishing subsidiaries, the toy and guitar manufacturing, and the baseball club. John A. (Jack) Schneider, a fast-rising thirty-nine-year-old executive who had started his television career as a time salesman in Chicago, was named president of the Broadcast Group. Henceforth, Friendly was told, Schneider was the man to contact in dealings with top management.

In August 1964, President Johnson told a hushed nation that North Vietnamese patrol boats had attacked U.S. destroyers in the Gulf of Tonkin. The incident was a provocation, and the President's response—bombing of North Vietnamese harbors—was wrapped in solemnity and the flag. The media fell into step with the country, trusting the President, who, after all, had all the information. Johnson used the incident to get an all-purpose resolution through Congress. A few senators wondered why the rush, but Senator William Fulbright, head of the Foreign Relations Committee and Johnson's old friend, said the President needs the resolution *now;* otherwise the Communists would know Americans were divided.

Among the few who were made uneasy by this rush to give the President war powers was the dying Ed Murrow. The night the Tonkin Resolution passed, he called Friendly and criticized his former protégé. Why had *CBS Evening News* handled the story the way it did? What did they all know about what had happened in the South China Sea? *Why* had it happened? And why couldn't Rather and the boys do some sort of special analysis? Friendly was both shocked by Murrow's interference and felt a little guilty. Earlier in the day, Rather had told him on the phone from the White House that it all smelled a bit tricky.

In January 1966, Senator Fulbright challenged the President in what was to be the only congressional hearing on Vietnam in ten years of war. Fulbright had felt used by LBJ in the Tonkin Resolution and now wanted both supporters and critics of the administration's war to testify before his Foreign Relations Committee. A constitutional confrontation was shaping up.

Secretary of State Dean Rusk was the first witness, and it soon became apparent his testimony and the Senate committee's questions were no gentlemen's exchange of lofty views. Fulbright lost his temper and made no attempt to hide it. The Cronkite show that evening carried three minutes of this constitutional drama. Friendly wanted more. On the phone, he learned from Bill Small, the bureau chief, that they had twice as much excellent footage of this first real foreign policy clash between the executive and legislative branches since World War II. Would the Senate committee have permitted live coverage? Friendly asked. "Certainly they would have," Small snapped back. "But you could never have gotten the air time and you know it!"

Six days later, when David Bell, the head of the AID program and a proxy for both President Johnson and Rusk, testified, Friendly got permission to go live for thirty minutes. The half hour passed and the hearing continued. Goaded by his people, Friendly kept the Bell testimony on the air. On and on into the morning. The Bell testimony became richer and more fascinating by the hour. Pushed by CBS, NBC also stayed live, but NBC had a weaker daytime schedule and was losing less money. Into the afternoon, the testimony continued. The next day, both NBC and CBS were back live, but on the third day, when former ambassador George Kennan, considered one of the most effective critics of the Vietnam policy, began testifying, only NBC was covering. Paley and Stanton had had enough. CBS broadcast a fifth rerun of *I Love Lucy,* followed by the eighth rerun of a *Real McCoy* episode. At a crucial moment, Friendly couldn't get past Schneider to Paley and Stanton, who alone could authorize preemption of air time.

Stung by criticism, CBS quickly resumed coverage (Schneider lamely defended his decision by saying housewives weren't interested in public debate on Vietnam). Five days later, Friendly quit. "I am resigning," he wrote in a letter released to the press, "because CBS News did not carry the Senate Foreign Relations hearings last Thursday . . . I am resigning because the decision not to carry the hearings makes a mockery of the Paley-Stanton Columbia News division crusade of many years that demands broadcast access to congressional debate . . . We cannot, in our public utterances, demand such access and then, in one of the crucial debates of our time, abdicate that responsibility." Press accounts called the resignation the real end to the Murrow era at CBS and praised the mercurial Friendly for sacrificing his career for the public's right to hear and see the Vietnam hearings (while Schneider stepped deeper into it, saying leading opinion makers weren't watching TV during the day). The farewell on 57th Street was subversive and dramatic. Friendly was cheered as he told everybody to keep up the fight to safeguard the honor and tradition of broadcast journalism. A few weeks later, he began a new career in the nascent public television. His influence was to be so strong that, during its formative years, PBS was dubbed "Friendlyvision" along Broadcast Row.

As Paley saw it, the news department was not only losing money while every other division was profitable, but it was also more threatening to the company. With his socialite wife, the chairman moved in the increasingly isolated and conservative circles of the very rich.

It became Stanton's job to put the tumultuous era behind him. Schneider suggested the new CBS News president be either Bill Leonard or Friendly's news side vice president Gordon Manning. On reflection, however, it was decided that both Leonard and Manning had been too close to the deposed Friendly. Cronkite and Sevareid invited themselves in on the deliberations and recommended that Dick Salant be given his old job back. The idea of rehabilitating Salant, now a special assistant to Stanton, appealed to everybody except Salant. A lot of the people who had helped kick him upstairs two years earlier were still around. He had no intention of having this happen to him a second time. A fig leaf was found: he was appointed *acting* president.

The networks had enough controversy on the evening news. Television magnified the Vietnam War, brought it into the living room, emphasized the awesome American fire power and the fact that it was hard to distinguish between civilian and combatant in this war. In October 1967, the Pentagon announced that American casualties—killed and wounded—since 1961 had climbed past 100,000, but insisted steady progress was being made. Morley Safer, Dan Rather, and the other young correspondents in the field were beginning to doubt, but Cronkite and many of the older men at 57th Street couldn't admit the United States might be wrong. During a 1965 visit to Saigon, Cronkite hadn't liked the way the younger correspondents tore into officers at military briefings. As a stateside VIP, he was himself briefed by the brass. Safer tried to put Cronkite in touch with young officers who knew the day-to-day reality, but Air Force generals put on air shows for Cronkite, showed off their newest weapons, and told him it was a small war, a quick war. One thing bothered Walter. If it was going to be over so soon, why were they constantly enlarging the huge Camranh Bay base?

The war overshadowed all other areas of foreign policy in 1967, and in June the Middle East exploded into the Six Day War. At home, cities in all sections of the country experienced racial violence on an unprecedented scale. Antiwar demonstrating increased sharply. On 57th Street, they went through more color-coded lineup revisions than there were hues in the rainbow. During the long hot summer, Leiser drove himself harder than anyone else. In September, he could no longer take the hectic pace. Pleading total exhaustion, he had to ask Salant to take him off the evening news.

With Salant, Leiser picked his own successor and it was not Hewitt. It was Leiser's old Paris pal Les Midgley, currently executive producer of a Special Reports unit and just finishing a four-hour inquiry into the Warren Commission's report on the Kennedy assassination. Midgley was marrying Betty Furness, the Johnson administration's special assistant for consumer affairs, and was looking forward to a relaxing honeymoon when he was told to take over as executive producer.

Leiser remained Cronkite's field producer and was with Cronkite four months later when the Tet offensive sent Walter back to Vietnam. Again, General William Westmoreland was unwavering. The Vietcong's Tet assault was actually a great and dramatic victory for the American side, he explained, adding that the battle for Hue, for example, was already over. The next day, when Cronkite and Leiser choppered to Hue, they found Marines engaged in a fierce battle to recapture the city. On the last night in Saigon, Walter had dinner with a group of correspondents. How could it have happened? The whole sorry mess had been a mistake from the start, he was told. Deceit had been employed at every step. On the way back to New York, Leiser sensed Walter knew he had been had.

To show they hadn't totally lost the touch for hard-hitting stuff, *CBS Reports* came up with a seven-part series, *Of Black America,* and the most controversial documentary in ten years, *Hunger in America.* Directed by Martin Carr, *Hunger* aroused such indignation—and claims of Communist propaganda—that the FBI investigated Carr. Still, Hewitt only had to look around him to see discouragement. Carr, McMullen, and Gene DePoris were the three best investigative reporter-producers in the house. Carr, however, left to join NBC shortly after *Hunger in America* (with Chet Huntley he was to do another documentary on the migrant farm worker dilemma ten years later in *Migrant*). After *Biography of a Bookie Joint,* McMullen proposed he either do a special on patent medicine or corruption in Saigon. Both had been ordered cancelled. DePoris had started a special on the military-industrial complex and *that* had been scuttled.

The problem was of course that nobody watched documentaries. Most documentaries, no matter how laudable, managed a rating of only four, while it took at least a rating of twenty to interest an advertiser. To be perfectly cynical about it, documentaries just weren't good business for the networks. CBS, NBC, and ABC were spending $250 million for production of nighttime entertainment for the 1967–68 season—$20 million more than in 1966–67. Sponsors stood in line to buy time on the *Smothers Brothers* and *The Man from UNCLE,* not on *CBS Reports* specials, which, as a result, were aired in weak and irregular time slots. Hour-long documentaries were not cheap, although cheaper, usually, than *Gunsmoke* episodes, but they were troublesome to advertisers and to special interests. The latter often meant an added cost of legal defense when feathers were ruffled. But most of all, courageous journalism didn't come easily to a company that not only had to answer to stockholders, advertisers, and affiliated stations, but to the source of its license—the government—before it answered to the public.

Although Martin Carr had left to go to NBC, things weren't any better at the other networks or even on the new public television. Documentaries were getting "blander and blander," as ABC producer Stephen Fleischman said. Conditions had become rigid and frozen since the crusading days of *See It Now* and, short of a fundamental change, there was little chance that experimentation in ideas and techniques would be more than a memory of the *belle époque*. Steven H. Scheuer, of New York City's noncommercial WNYC station, felt the depressing blandness of commercial TV documentaries was already descending on National Educational Television because here, too, documentaries recited lists of social ills instead of coming to grips with the people and institutions responsible for social abuses.

Hewitt looked at the dilemma differently. It was a question of marketing, he felt. Nobody read a document, so why should anybody want to watch a documentary. He hated the word. To work on television, reality had to be packaged right. Also, few stories warranted the full-hour treatment. To fly, a subject had to have a rich menu of components, and it had to have national importance. Public affairs programming, the networks' *pro bono publico* duty, was the networks' chastity belt when profits were too hefty or when a quiz scandal hit, but pub affairs could be all sorts of things. Why should it be "talking heads" press conference programming on Sunday afternoons? (When Sunday football became a gold mine, *Face the Nation* and other "cultural ghetto" programs were unceremoniously shuffled to late morning scheduling.) Stanton and Leonard tried *Who, What, When, Where, Why* with Harry Reasoner and touted this as the first CBS News prime time pub affairs program since Murrow to have a regular host. When *Who, What, When, Where, Why* died of anemic ratings in 1967, Hewitt was ready.

He tried out his idea on Harry first. How about a prime time show, with Harry Reasoner as its star, that was more like a newsmagazine, mixing hard-hitters and soft features, a program that took potshots at chosen targets but also showed trendy people? Harry was flattered, but after *Who, What, When, Where, Why,* he didn't place much hope in Don's magazine idea.

Hewitt went to Bill Leonard. How about a sixty-minute show that combined both hard and soft features with an occasional investigative piece? It could be cheap, initially, and include back-of-the-book stories that couldn't be developed for the Cronkite show yet didn't justify the full-hour treatment, material in the "bank," enterprisers on programs, and personalities. Why couldn't you go for journalism that also works as drama? The format? The gimmick was not to have a host behind a desk, but a correspondent out doing the story, to get the reporter *involved*. Show him driving a racing car; patrolling Falls Road in Belfast with British soldiers; confronting someone suspected of having something to hide. Let people in on the story.

They got into a discussion on where you would draw the line. The traditional view was that journalists should be detached from the events they are covering. But that, too, was becoming a cliché. What's wrong with becoming involved as long as it doesn't *distort* the story? Leonard wasn't the most difficult person to convince.

The newsmagazine format was popular on Canadian television, and in France *Cinq Colonnes à la Une* (literally Five Columns on Page One) added up to such inventive television journalism that the program had become a veritable institution. Hewitt was to claim he got the idea from the news weeklies with their clever mix of cover stories and pieces on newsmakers. *Life* magazine, which concentrated its rich photojournalism on people, had especially great television potential because people were the point. Hewitt kept stressing it. People weren't interested in issues.

Leonard was receptive if it didn't cost too much to come up with a sample pilot they could take to Salant. The start-up cost was one evening's studio time, plus $13.45 for sandwiches and coffee for a couple of editors, Don, and Harry. They put together a demo reel by recutting segments from shows that had already been on the air, including a piece Charles Kuralt had done on Henry Ford. Reasoner told Hewitt he owed him a wasted evening, but he also said it was a hopeless project because it involved singling out one correspondent and making him the star. Remembering having been prisoners of Murrow and already becoming involuntary prisoners of Cronkite, management would never stand for that.

Salant wasn't impressed. The demo reel Leonard and Hewitt ran for him was neither here nor there. It was entertainment trying to pass itself off as news. Precisely, argued Don when they were back in Salant's office where three built-in TV monitors glowed silently at him all day. Too much showbiz! Salant retorted. Besides, such a broadcast would encroach on the hard news side and lead to all kinds of squabbling over territory and privilege.

Only Salant would have thought of that. His rule—the "acting" had been dropped from his executive title when it became clear things would work out—had none of Friendly's volatile leadership. Salant was a corporate man who thought of himself more as a publisher than an editor. Not for him to descend into the fishbowl and sweat it out with the boys over lineup revisions between the affiliate "feed" at 6:30 and the 7 o'clock edition. Salant had no background in news and knew it. As a lawyer he was good at gauging the implication of news, what items meant legally and politically, a quality that would stand CBS News in good stead in the unraveling Watergate affairs. As a corporate figure, he was good at delegating authority, and he maintained a special relationship with Chief Executive Officer Frank Stanton. Cronkite and Eric Sevareid liked Salant's hands-off style. As CBS News pulled ahead of NBC once again to become the dominant voice in broadcast journalism, even Chairman Paley smiled beneficently down on Salant.

CBS News now had over eight hundred full-time employees, as many as on the editorial staff of *The New York Times,* and power struggles were a fact of life. There were Cronkite's people, whom Walter defended with possessive authority. There was the strong Washington bureau that had Walter commuting with increasing regularity for evening newscasts originating in the capital. There were the *Morning News* crew and the *CBS Reports* people. There were field producers and correspondents, all clawing, pleading, negotiating, for air time. As Reasoner had hinted to Hewitt the night they put together the sample show, Cronkite emanated such stature and authority that he had an intimidating, even oppressive effect on his coworkers. He had "magic time," as producers called the total amount of minutes and seconds he appeared on camera each night telling stories or introducing reports from the field.

Hewitt kept after Salant. The boss didn't quite give in, but had one suggestion. Maybe such a newsmagazine would work if Don had *two* correspondents. The multisubject format would benefit from a dual, on-camera presence, especially if the second guy was cast right, if he had a style different from Reasoner's. Over the next couple of weeks, Leonard and Hewitt tried to cast a second pilot they could show Salant. If Reasoner had a warm conversation style and a knack for wry humor, Wallace came with the reputation of the tough interviewer who wouldn't let his subjects off the hook, no matter how important they were. Like Hewitt, he saw news items as drama built around a value conflict. Unfortunately, Mike wasn't around. He was covering the Richard Nixon election campaign, but he would be in Chicago for the Democratic convention in August. And, Don discovered, so would he.

It promised to be a zinger. As the Democrats met, Chicago resembled a city under siege, and the main question seemed to be whether the convention would go on at all, given disabling telephone, taxi, and bus strikes. Security had been no problem for the Republicans, who had chosen Nixon amid the orderly opulence of Miami Beach, but the Democrats were beset by organized plans to disrupt the proceedings within the hall and throughout Chicago. A Coalition for an Open Convention had brought 1,200 dissenting Democrats to the Windy City two months in advance to plan challenges of delegate credentials and a platform repudiating the Democratic Johnson administration. Peace groups planned massive demonstrations and leaders had trained "parade marshals" in the harassment and penetration of police lines. These marshals were ready to lead the expected scores of thousands of youthful demonstrators into confrontation with Mayor Richard Daley's 11,900-man police force. Supporters of Eugene McCarthy still hoped that massive demonstrations would stop Hubert Humphrey and turn the tide toward their candidate— or perhaps Ted Kennedy—and help to disavow the Vietnam War.

CBS News sent a hundred people, with several tons of equipment. The arrangements made by the city virtually confined live coverage to the hall itself. There was an elaborate credential system, gates that people could exit through but not enter, all designed to maintain control. "No one fully understood the security system and they didn't mean for you to understand," Dan Rather remembered.

The most notorious scene came on August 28, when protest organizers assembled their followers where the TV cameras were, outside the convention headquarters hotel. The networks filmed most of the eighteen-minutes of brickbats, bottles, and bags thrown at police and officers, reinforced by National Guard units, resolved to stop the marchers with nightsticks, tear gas, and mace. In the CBS control room, Hewitt threw the incoming videotape on the air as fast as he could, giving viewers a dizzying montage of nominating speech, shouting crowds, more speech, blue-helmeted riot police, wounded people, paddy wagons, balloting, ambulances, more speeches.

Some delegates wanted to recess, but protests and questions were ruled out of order. When Senator Abraham Ribicoff criticized Daley for the repressive atmosphere around the hall, the mayor stood and gave the "cut" sign to turn off Ribicoff's microphone. Mike Wallace was removed from the floor by uniformed Chicago policemen; Dan Rather was knocked down when he pursued a man wearing a delegate's badge being literally carried out by tough-looking characters in plain clothes. In the control room, they had switched the camera onto Rather just as he was slugged. Up in his aerie, Cronkite went on the air. "It looks like we've got a bunch of thugs in here," he said, adding that if this continued, "it makes us, in our anger, want to just turn off our cameras and pack up our microphones and our typewriters and get the devil out of this town and leave the Democrats to their agony.'' In the control room, Hewitt stop-framed the tape of the scuffle and put it on the air. In his acceptance speech two nights later, Humphrey promised to bring back the politics of joy. A little more than two months later, Nixon won the narrowest presidential election in modern history.

Back from the fray, Hewitt managed to get Reasoner and Wallace together for a second pilot. Mike quickly got the drift of the ''casting'' problem. ''There was the 'white hat/black hat' business at the beginning between Harry and me,'' he remembered. ''I think Leonard and Hewitt decided it probably needed a little more 'grit'; otherwise it might turn out to be a trifle gentle or bland. So they looked to me as a contrast.''

Reasoner found his own white hat role most congenial, and Salant found the second pilot sufficiently promising to take it to his corporate superiors. Programming was dubious but agreed to give it a shot. On Tuesdays at ten every other week. In this time slot, the broadcast could do no harm. In fact, it was something of a sacrificial lamb here, going against NBC's popular *Tuesday Night Movie* and ABC's *That's Life,* a weekly musicomedy series starring Robert Morse.

# 7

# Developing Muscle

## *The first years*

❧ "This is *60 Minutes*," Harry Reasoner declared on the debut show. "It's a kind of a magazine for television, which means it has the flexibility and diversity of a magazine adapted to broadcast journalism." Within sixteen months, the new program would be at the receiving end of the first rash of Justice Department subpoenas for notes, films, out-takes, and work material. Before the end of its third season, it would air a story resulting in a libel suit that would cost CBS millions to defend, result in a landmark Supreme Court decision, and remain unresolved for more than a decade. In between, *60 Minutes* set out the parameters of a new kind of broadcast journalism that would bring it fame and fortune, scads of awards, and turn it into the most imitated show on television.

The first edition that Tuesday night, September 24, 1968, contained few indications of the future notoriety.

Reviews were few. In Hollywood, *Variety* called the Humphrey-Nixon piece old hat and the attorney general's views on police-youth clashes a restatement of the obvious, reserving its only praise for the three Europeans' comments on American politics and the Saul Bass excerpts. The broadcast, it said, wasn't much different from other network news shows, which included features such as *The Frank McGee News* on NBC. "Don Hewitt is exec producer and director and seven individuals are producers; perhaps that's too many, and too little imagination," *Variety* concluded. *The New York Times* was kinder, calling CBS's "new alternate week newsmagazine something television has long needed."

The ratings were terrible. *60 Minutes* never captured more than 18 percent of the Tuesday night audience. Hewitt felt insecure about his show's status at Black Rock, while Dick Salant and Bill Leonard lobbied on the executive level, not only to keep the magazine alive but to give Don and his people the budget they needed to pursue and develop stories.

And they all gave it their best shot.

Instinct told Hewitt that Reasoner and Wallace had to be backed up by strong, talented people, and he immediately got Leonard to assign to *60 Minutes* the best and the brightest in the shop. Palmer Williams and Joe Wershba were old hands, dating back to the Murrow and Friendly days, and Phil Scheffler came over from the evening news. Hewitt and Williams were a pair of opposites: Don the natty Midtowner who had lunch in fashionable restaurants with Art Buchwald and members of the bicoastal showbiz set; Palmer the inveterate Greenwich Village person who hardly ever wore a necktie and was unknown to maitres d's north of 14th Street. Don, still described as "boyish" in middle age, mercurial, quick-tempered, loud; Palmer the laid-back Bohemian, scholarly and with manners suggesting a professor of political science; Don the fount of ideas, Palmer the funnel of assignments and logistics.

Williams, who was eight years older than Hewitt, had taught Murrow about film. He worshipped Murrow and was proud to have his *60 Minutes* office furnished with his hero's desk, bookshelves, pen-and-pencil holder, and ashtray. Hewitt never spent much time in his office and tended to hold conferences—confrontations, others said—in hallways. "If we had meetings, the show would look like a meeting," is an oft-quoted Hewittism. "If we wrote memos, the show would look like a memo. We don't have meetings, and we don't write memos." The white-haired, scholarly Williams knew all the cameramen and film editors. He knew airline schedules and became a combination managing editor, father confessor, and one-man storehouse of information. He handled the logistics of where producers and correspondents were or should be at any given time. "Hewitt is the guy who gets us started," Wallace remembered of the early days, "but Williams was the steady hand that kept us going."

Hewitt instilled intense competition in the shop. Reasoner remembered how they all had to make details both clear and interesting to Hewitt, Williams, and Scheffler if they wanted to see their projects "make air"; how they all knew their pieces had to have dramatic elements, story flow, and some surprise. Wallace reflected the general thrust of Hewitt and Company when he said he saw a story as a drama "built around a value conflict." But on the nitty-gritty level, a story had to be developed, be made different, exciting, controversial, revealing. It had to be budgeted, checked, and double-checked. Money spent on research was "the cheapest money," because you could decide whether a story worked before you blew the wad filming it. More interviews were always done off camera than were ever filmed.

What Hewitt was looking for was emotional response. Gut journalism, he called it. The impact of television wasn't so much on the mind as on the spleen. "It's not what your eyes and your ears digest that counts, it's the impact on your gut," he would say. "I have a kind of sixth sense for seeing a piece of film and knowing what's wrong and what's right about it. I don't articulate well, but I can take a producer and an editor into a screening room and show them what's wrong." He screened every story upon completion, often suggesting last-minute repairs and insisting on up-front punch to the piece. He personally selected the weekly mix from the "bank" that at any one time might include as many as a dozen completed segments.

"Value conflict" made him take a leaf from the early days when two correspondents had covered different sides of the same story—Murrow in Israel, Howard K. Smith in Egypt. Soon producers Reasoner and Wallace were dispatched to Northern Ireland, Mike and his crew reporting the Protestant side and Reasoner and his team the Catholic side of "the troubles." Next they were in Nigeria, Reasoner with the secessionist Biafrans in the bush; Mike with the federal troops in Lagos; and in the Middle East, Harry in Lebanon and Jordan, Mike in Israel. "Mike and I were scheduled to meet up at the Allenby Bridge," Reasoner remembered, "coming from opposite directions, at 10 o'clock one Friday morning, the year Joe Namath and the New York Jets won the Superbowl. The Israelis wouldn't let you photograph anything on their side of the bridge, but my producer and I had been told you could shoot across it. Our idea was that my crew would shoot Mike, and his crew me. But Mike and his gang had heard you couldn't do that, and they never turned up. They were probably playing tennis in Tel Aviv. I'd have felt much worse about the whole thing if I hadn't won a bet from Mike on the football game."

Hewitt let just enough of the rivalry between Wallace and Reasoner show through to give the broadcast an appealing edge. In September 1969, when Reasoner did a story indicating that inflation was even hurting panhandlers, Wallace was seen at the end coming up and saying, "Pardon me, sir. I—I wonder if you could let me have a hundred dollars for lunch at '21.' " To which Harry retorted, "Why don't you get a decent job, like me?"

Eldridge Cleaver became *60 Minutes'* first controversy. Faced with revocation of his parole from the California prison system, Cleaver had fled the country late in 1968. For nearly a year, the movements of the Black Panther Party's information minister and author of *Soul on Ice* were a mystery. He surfaced in Cuba, but seemed to get a cool reception from Fidel Castro. Later, he appeared in Algiers and in Moscow, where he argued that the Soviet regime should support revolutionary movements elsewhere. He could travel freely in Communist countries, using his California driver's license and an FBI "wanted" poster instead of a passport. He was in touch with affairs in the United States and intended to continue "functioning in the struggle against the oppressive system." Wallace and crew caught up with him in Algiers and taped a half-hour interview, of which five minutes were aired in the January 6, 1970 broadcast.

Cleaver urged America's blacks to make common cause with oppressed people everywhere, but he was in North Africa. The Black Panthers' West Coast leader, David Hilliard, who also appeared on *60 Minutes,* had been arrested a month earlier for threatening the life of President Nixon during a Moratorium Day speech in San Francisco's Golden Gate Park. Now, the Secret Service and the Justice Department wanted *all* the film with Cleaver and Hilliard. Paul Sternbach, the network's general counsel, felt CBS had to cooperate in a criminal case involving people accused of threatening the life of the President. The Secret Service served subpoenas demanding the complete record of all correspondence, memoranda, notes, and telephones calls made in connection with the broadcast, including the outtakes of Wallace's interviews with Cleaver and Hilliard. Sternbach doubted if any reporter kept records of all memos and phone calls eighteen months back and managed to negotiate a narrowing of the government's scope of inquiry.

The Chicago Newspaper Publishers Association decried "dragnet subpoenas issued for reckless fishing expeditions" after four Chicago newspapers and TV stations were asked to hand over notes, film, tapes, and personal testimony of the Weathermen faction of the Students for a Democratic Society. *Time, Life,* and *Newsweek* were also told to reveal their reporters' dealings with student radicals, and a *Times* reporter was subpoenaed to tell about his meetings and interviews with black militants. Attorney General John Mitchell claimed full personal power under the Constitution to use wiretapping and eavesdropping in internal security cases and to demand the notes and working material of newsmen who had interviewed militant suspects. In the face of fierce media resistance and a legal setback when a federal court of appeals in San Francisco quashed the subpoena against the *New York Times* reporter, Mitchell announced guidelines that recognized the possible limiting effect on First Amendment rights of the subpoena, and promised "all reasonable attempts" to obtain information elsewhere.

The January 6, 1970 airing of the interviews with Cleaver and Hilliard set the standards for *60 Minutes* and, a month later, emboldened Salant to say the government didn't have the right to probe the inner workings of a news organization. But there were other outspoken interviews in the early editions of the show. Captain Ernest Medina and Private Paul Meadlo, two members of the U.S. Army platoon that had taken part in the mass killings of South Vietnamese civilians at My Lai, appeared on the program, as did Daniel (Danny the Red) Cohn-Bendit, the young radical who had led the 1968 student uprising in Paris.

Two new trends became apparent in the 1970 programming: ecology and concern for minorities. *60 Minutes* was in on both, but the shakeup of the year was the departure of Reasoner and Rooney.

Reasoner was earning a little more than $100,000 a year, but his contract was up, and at negotiation time old vexations were brought up. Bill Leonard had never forgiven Reasoner for not boning up on more tidbits about each candidate on election nights and, over on the news side, Gordon Manning was energetically promoting the career of Roger Mudd, at Harry's expense. Still, Reasoner was a fourteen-year veteran and, in the star system, which was becoming an integral part of TV journalism, his star was of a magnitude and brilliance just slightly less than that of Walter Cronkite. He was Walter's regular substitute on the *Evenings News* and was costar on *60 Minutes* and, since the contract being negotiated on his behalf by Ralph Mann of International Creative Management (ICM) would cover the unusually long period of seven years, he believed he was entitled to a substantial raise.

As the summer dragged into fall and the management of CBS News refused to up its initial offer of a modest raise, Mann proposed they make overtures to ABC. As Mann understood it, ABC might be willing to offer Reasoner the one job not available at CBS—the anchor seat on the *Evening News*. Elmer Lower, the president of ABC News, was convinced that what his shop most urgently needed to pull out of its perpetual third place was a coanchor with proven box office value. A private survey revealed that Cronkite was, by far, America's favorite dinnertime companion but, to Lower's surprise, the runnerup was neither NBC's David Brinkley-John Chancellor twosome, nor ABC's own Howard K. Smith, but Harry Reasoner.

Unaware of this audience survey, Mann was agreeably surprised by the enthusiastic response his feelers elicited. ABC wanted Reasoner. And ABC wanted him to coanchor the evening news with Smith. Negotiations moved swiftly. In October, Harry signed on a dotted line that gave him $200,000 a year in a five-year contract.

Principle and ego, not money, made Rooney follow his friend to ABC, after a brief interlude at National Educational Television (NET). With Reasoner, he had put together another of the eclectic essays. This time on war.

The Nixon administration was trying to neutralize the conflict in Vietnam by withdrawing additional troops and encouraging the Saigon regime to assume a greater share of the fighting, but a major American offensive into Cambodia sparked new domestic upheaval. Despite—or because of—Attorney General Mitchell's backdown on the subpoenas of newsmen and their notes, tapes, and work material, the administration turned the full force of its anger and hostility toward the media. Beginning with a speech in Des Moines, Vice President Agnew said the network newsrooms were full of arrogant, small but far too influential elitists, unrepresentative, unelected and, above all, overpaid people. His speeches, which found a favorable echo in a middle America appalled by a decade of tumultuous social change, were more than tongue lashings. They carried threats as Agnew reminded audiences that television was "licensed" by government. The White House got to the network's soft underbelly, the affiliate stations. Salant had to fend off affiliate owners who suggested that he go to Saigon and whip up the level of Americanism in the news bureau.

It was a delicate time to air Rooney's *Essay on War*. Hewitt, Leonard, Salant—all the way up they told him they'd have to cut it. Andy got mad and quit over the issue. Taking a sizable pay cut, he went to work for NET. CBS grudgingly sold him the *Essay on War* for use on NET's *The Great American Dream Machine* show on condition that defector Reasoner's famous sandpaper voice wasn't used. Andy did the next best thing and recorded the narration himself. In Reasoner's autobiography, *Before the Colors Fade,* Harry told of this momentous step. "Once he found out he didn't need me, he became impossible," Harry wrote. "Andy Rooney is my best friend. We just don't talk to each other." The *Essay on War* brought Andy a Writers Guild of America award; it also elicited a call from an advertising agency asking if he would be interested in doing a headache commercial. "Told me a lot about my voice," he later commented.

Rooney did fifteen more pieces for *The Great American Dream Machine,* a composite of often sardonic and even iconoclastic short items, which were inventive and occasionally brilliant. The program became a target of the Nixon-Agnew offensive. Several congressmen called it dangerously subversive and kept inserting parts of it into the *Congressional Record.* After the *Dream Machine* folded in 1972, he went to ABC to continue his collaboration with Reasoner, writing news and news specials.

Hewitt was interviewing replacements. To take Reasoner's place, Don admitted he was looking for another Reasoner. "We're looking for Reasoner's wit and style, his craggy good looks," he told *The New York Times* in November 1970. "He looks good without being pretty, and it reinforces his style." Who was good-looking without being pretty in the CBS correspondents' stable? John Hart, Dan Rather, Hughes Rudd, Charles Kuralt, and Charles Collingwood were mentioned, with Hart the front-runner. To replace Rooney, Don was testing William F. Buckley. The publisher of *National Review* would be one of several guest columnists who might become part of *60 Minutes.*

Hewitt shuffled his lineup for the November 17, 1970 edition to make room for a look at Charles de Gaulle, who had just died. It would be Reasoner's next-to-last time on the air for *60 Minutes,* but an interview he had done with Senator George McGovern would be dropped in favor of an appreciation of the late French president, to be hosted by Harry and Eric Sevareid. It would follow a rerun of an interview with Jean-Jacques Servant-Schreiber, in which the publisher of *L'Express* spoke of his understanding of de Gaulle. *60 Minutes* would close with a Wallace report on marijuana harvesting in Kansas.

Morley Safer covered the death of the last of the great World War II statesmen in a way that made Hewitt sit up and listen. As bureau chief in London, Safer flew to Paris November 10, the day after de Gaulle's death, and for the following day's *Evening News with Walter Cronkite* did something very simple. November 11 was Armistice Day. The Champs Elysées was closed to traffic for the commemoration of the end of World War I and the mourning of the chief of state. With a camera in front of him, Safer merely strolled down the Champs Elysées, with

the Arc de Triomphe behind him, reading aloud from de Gaulle's memoirs. The next day, Leonard called Safer and offered him the job as co-
star with Mike Wallace on *60 Minutes*.

Safer demurred. He had married the former Jane Fearer. They both
loved Europe and had plans to buy a place in Spain. Besides, Morley
wasn't convinced that he, or anyone else, had reason to believe that there
was much of a future in *60 Minutes*.

ABC was moving in on CBS, topping the seventy-city Nielsens for
the first time in November 1971. For the second season in a row, *All in
the Family* and *Marcus Welby* were in a constant seesaw battle for first
place in the ratings. To keep Bill Leonard, Hewitt, and the rest of soft
news moderately happy, Salant extracted a network programming promise that the *Thursday Night Movie* could be replaced by a two-hour news
offering once a month.

"I'm glad to get away from *Marcus Welby*," Hewitt said. The Sunday evening slot wasn't without sacrifices for him. The 6 P.M. air time
meant the *CBS Evening News* was dropped and the *60 Minutes* format
was changed to consist of two segments—the first a digest of the day's
news, and the second the regular newsmagazine features.

The stylishly crafted pieces Safer turned in worked well with the hard-
hitting stories Wallace reported, but they generated few headlines and,
for a while, the two star correspondents were barely speaking.

Without much enthusiasm at first, Morley began doing his share of
tough, investigative pieces. Among his early efforts were a look at My
Lai three years after the killing of the South Vietnamese civilians. Other
offerings included a tour of the White House with Tricia Nixon, visits
to the Virgin Islands, Lourdes, a report on draft dodgers in Canada, and
a probe of organized crime on the waterfront. For fun, Safer went to
Europe, and, with his one-time cameraman—now London resident producer—John Tiffin, immortalized the manufacture of Rolls-Royce motor
cars. *The Rock* was another Safer-Tiffin gem. The two of them got it
just right, down to the droll absurdity and puzzling outlandishness of the
20,000 Gibraltarians, "descended from Spanish, Portuguese, Genoese,
Moors, and dallying British seamen who fought with Nelson at Trafal-
gar." Morley talked to the keeper of the Barbary apes, and to one ape
called Barbara; mentioned the roast beef, Yorkshire pudding, and warm
beer these Latinized Englishmen or Anglicized Spaniards downed before
going for Sunday drives around the Rock, again and again, over two
and a half miles of roadway. He showed the pathos of them dancing the
latest craze—jitterbugging—and he showed the border that Spain had

closed in a pique over stalled negotiations to make Gibraltar Spanish. Spanish and British border patrols outdoing each other in their respective flag-lowering ceremonies in the evening allowed him to finish with a salute to this speck of land "where the sun does not quite set on the British Empire, and where the people dash happily headlong backwards into the nineteenth century."

In tune with the abrasive mood of the times (the war in Indochina remained the nation's most nagging foreign policy in 1972), the general tenor at CBS News and, in particular, Wallace's more muscular style, *60 Minutes* changed. The soft people in the news pieces that Hewitt felt were such an important part of the "mix" were still there, but the number of sharp journalistic investigations increased. And viewers loved it. An increasing number of viewers saw Wallace as something of a maverick, but fair in his relentless interviewing.

A month after President Nixon ordered the bombing of North Vietnamese ports and the bombing of land and sea routes in an attempt to choke off delivery of war supplies to Hanoi, *60 Minutes* aired *CBU,* a fifteen-minute probe of cluster bomb units. For the story, Hewitt employed the network's premiere documentarian, Peter Davis, fresh from his award-winning *The Selling of the Pentagon.* Safer was the correspondent and, before getting to Honeywell Corporation executives, he described the CBUs as munitions dropped in canisters that, before hitting the ground, scattered bomblets several hundred yards in every direction. "When the bomblets themselves explode, they produce a shower of tiny steel pellets," Morley went on. "The Vietnamese claim CBU pellets ricochet from one internal organ to another, producing severe wounds that are difficult to treat."

Davis and Safer got James Binger, the Honeywell chairman of the board, to explain that antipersonnel weapons, whether grenades, bombs, or bullets, have the same purpose, unfortunately: to kill people. Morley submitted the Honeywell chairman to some hard questions, wondering whether industry didn't have a duty at some point, even with an elected government, to say it would no longer make such weapons, wondering how guilty Binger would consider German industrialists had been during World War II. Binger said it was not for him to undertake or set out American foreign policy, but Safer led the Honeywell boss into invoking the sort of defense German industrialists made at Nuremberg: a corporation is not responsible for how the government uses the weapons it builds. It was powerful television. "Dozens of other American companies with household names produce weapons and other products that contribute to the war effort," Safer summed up. "If the shareholders of these companies—and that includes millions of us—told them to get out of the war business, presumably they would have to do that. So far, enough shareholders believe in the profitability and the morality of the CBU to ensure its survival.'' Aired June 11, 1972, *CBU* generated the heaviest mail to date for *60 Minutes*. A year later, *The New Republic* blamed Hewitt and Safer—Davis had left CBS a month after the broadcast—for not mentioning that the company under contract to the Pentagon to transmit photos assessing bomb damage was CBS Laboratories, a CBS Inc., division.

Barry Lando was a new producer, a crossover from the hard news side and a former *Time* reporter, who was to become the chief collaborator on some of the biggest and most famous Mike Wallace coups. While on the news side, Lando had done a story for the *CBS Weekend News* on Lieutenant Colonel Anthony B. Herbert, a former altar boy from Pennsylvania's coal country and a ramrod-straight crew-cut veteran of Korea and Vietnam. He had emerged from the Korean War as the most highly decorated enlisted man, with over twenty-five medals. At one of many ceremonies in his honor, a bayonet that had been run through his side was polished up and ritually presented to him by actress Jennifer Jones. Then Eleanor Roosevelt drew him aside, told him to leave the Army and go to college. Obediently, he got a degree from the University of Pittsburgh; then reenlisted and spent twelve years in training camps, survival courses, cold war duty, and spy work. When he was sent to Vietnam for a regular tour in 1968, he was an inspiration to his men. While most commanders watched the action from helicopters, Colonel Herbert led his troops on the ground, right down into enemy bunkers. Fellow officers often relied on artillery strikes to do the killing and the grunts to do the body counts. Partly as a result, civilian dead were regularly recorded as killed Vietcong and North Vietnamese soldiers. Herbert trained his men to ''close in and kill—just like it says in the manual''—constantly telling them he wanted results with enemy soldiers, not women, old men, and children. The results were spectacular, and Colonel Herbert was a tailor-made media hero for the Army.

Suddenly, however, the colonel was stripped of his field command, packed off to a stateside desk job, and harassed and humiliated until he was forced to retire in February 1972. Exactly why was something of a mystery, but in *Soldier,* a book he later wrote with James T. Wooten, he argued it was because he had alleged that atrocities occurred, and that they occurred regularly, mainly because of commanders' unwillingness to enforce the military codes of conduct. Specifically, he had told Brigadier General John W. Barnes and Colonel J. Ross Franklin about the slaughter of defenseless Vietcong suspects in Cu Loi village on February 14, 1969 and had asked them to prosecute the American lieutenant who had stood by and done nothing to stop the killing. This whistle blowing and finger pointing became more than Barnes and Franklin, among others, could bear. At first they were incredulous; then they called him "soft"; finally they got rid of him. When Colonel Herbert went public, the Army answered his charges by impugning his motives and his stability and by showing documentation that placed Franklin on rest and recreation in Honolulu the day Herbert made his report on the Cu Loi incident. Still, the Knight newspaper chain accused the Army of "making a scapegoat" of Herbert, *The New York Times* urged him to keep up his "battle that involved . . . the integrity and effectiveness of the U.S. Army," while *The New Republic* maintained the Army's treatment of Herbert was "a disgrace to the Army and a tragedy for the nation."

Lando thought the way Herbert had been cashiered would make an excellent *60 Minutes* story. Hewitt wasn't so sure. The country had been through the trial of Second Lieutenant William Calley for the murder of defenseless men, women, and children in My Lai. Accusations of American atrocities were becoming routine. Lando was anxious to prove himself to Hewitt and on his own continued to look into the Herbert story. In the spring of 1972, he told Hewitt and Wallace he had talked to officers who maintained Franklin had been back in Vietnam, not in Hawaii, the day the Cu Loi incident was reported; that the incident was common knowledge throughout the unit; that Franklin himself was relieved of command a little more than a year after he had sacked Herbert; and that the reason involved something called "a body bombing"— throwing a prisoner unwilling to talk out of a helicopter to his death. President Nixon was making his historical visit to China and the war in Vietnam made a daily appearance in headlines. Hewitt and Wallace weren't interested. Mike told Lando, however, that if they could shed new light on the Herbert-Army confrontation or investigate the role of the press in the affair, there might be a story. Don told Mike that as long as it didn't interfere with a piece Lando and Wallace were doing on a Georgia company town, Barry could continue looking into the Herbert case.

Three months later, Lando submitted a dramatic new outline. There was reason to believe everybody in the media had it all wrong. It might be possible to demonstrate that when Colonel Herbert's superiors had failed to act on his report of the Cu Loi incident, he had called them liars, that, in fact, this was not the story of an officer whose career had been broken because he denounced the killing of a half dozen Vietcong suspects; it was the story of an officer who, by casting himself as the martyr of a military establishment anxious to cover up war crimes, had gained national prominence. This time, Hewitt and Wallace sat up and listened.

So did the Pentagon. When Lando visited Major General Winant Sidle, the Army's chief information officer, and told him of his suspicions, Barnes and Franklin suddenly became available for interviews with *60 Minutes*. In January 1973, Wallace, Lando, and a crew went to the Pentagon to interview Franklin (they managed to forget to ask about the circumstances of Franklin's removal from command) and Captain James Grimshaw, a company commander whom Herbert had recommended for a Silver Star. Three weeks later, Herbert was taped in New York with, unbeknownst to him, Grimshaw in the audience. *The Selling of Colonel Herbert*, as the segment was ironically called, aired February 4, 1973. The broadcast challenged Herbert's account of how he lost his command in Vietnam and relied heavily on interviews with soldiers who had served under him. The climax came when Grimshaw was brought forward to confront the unwary colonel. The *60 Minutes* broadcast dissolved Herbert's celebrity. Negotiations to sell the movie rights to *Soldier* were terminated, and invitations to speak on college campuses and elsewhere for substantial fees dropped off, then vanished. Late that year, Herbert sued Lando, Wallace, CBS, and the *Atlantic Monthly*—which had published an article by Lando—for $45 million.

To prove libel under the 1964 Supreme Court ruling in the landmark case of *The New York Times v. Sullivan*, a "public" person—one who has voluntarily come into the public's collective vision—must prove not only that a news organization published or broadcast a falsehood, but that it acted maliciously in doing so. The decision said the need for vigorous public debate of controversial issues meant that stories about public officials could be wrong but not liable to a lawsuit, as long as reporters and editors did not know in advance that the accounts they were printing were false or had not recklessly failed to try to verify the stories. Malice was present, the high court ruled, if reporters and editors either knew a story to be false or recklessly overlooked its truthfulness or falsehood. A "private" person, on the other hand, need only prove that a story is false and that its incorrectness somehow injures him or her. That is a much easier legal standard to meet.

The libel suit went to the Supreme Court in 1976 for a ruling on whether CBS employees would have to answer questions about the thought processes that went into the preparation of the broadcast. Thousands of pages of sworn, pretrial depositions were taken. Lando's testimony alone filled 2,903 pages and contained all the decisions he, Hewitt, and Wallace had made, including the crucial switch from regarding Herbert as a victim of military efforts to cover up abuses during some of the most intense fighting of the war to seeing him as a soldier who called his superiors liars. Just before the Supreme Court was to hear the case, Hewitt had another of his Hildy Johnson brainstorms. Why not invite Chief Justice Warren E. Burger to appear on *60 Minutes?* Turning down the invitation, the Chief Justice showed he was not without a sense of humor. "The 'charge'," he wrote in a letter to CBS dated December 28, "would be that a) you were trying to influence me; b) you were trying to intimidate me; or c) I was trying to cultivate you. It would be what moderns call 'no-win'." When the case was heard, Jonathan Lubell, Herbert's chief counsel, maintained that in order to prove defamation as a public figure, Herbert should be able to question Lando's state of mind. Lando's CBS attorneys argued that such questioning would chill the free exchange of ideas in a newsroom. The following April, the Supreme Court ruled, 6 to 3, that a libel plaintiff obliged to prove malice because he is a public figure has the right to inquire into the reporter's state of mind. The First Amendment notwithstanding, the court said, a journalist's thoughts and decisions in preparing material involved in a libel suit are not protected from disclosure.

The time spent on pretrial motions, responses to such motions, availability of court dates, conflicting schedules of principals and lawyers made Herbert a bitter man. He was spending every penny he had on the case, along with money borrowed from friends. He told interviewers that the legal system played into the hands of big corporate attorneys, who dragged out proceedings in the hope that the witness would die before a case could go to trail. When asked about the case in 1982, Wallace estimated CBS had spent between $3 and $4 million defending this one suit, figures that network lawyers would neither confirm nor deny. Eleven years after the suit was brought, *Herbert v. Lando* was still in litigation.

# 8

## Getting
## the Politicos
### *Gaining clout*

Sweeping school desegregation plans were ordered for Richmond, Virginia and San Francisco in 1971. In August, President Nixon disavowed a federal plan of busing to achieve school integration in Austin, Texas, but a month later a federal court judge found Detroit's extensive school segregation to have been deliberate and called for remedial plans using a metropolitan approach. The year's most important school opinion was handed down by the Supreme Court in a case involving the schools of Charlotte-Mecklenburg County, North Carolina. Nixon supported the court, though he did "not believe that busing to achieve racial balance is in the interest of better education." Busing became a burning issue. In February 1972, after a stormy session, the Senate passed a combined higher education and desegregation bill with a relatively mild antibusing provision.

At a dinner party, someone asked Don Hewitt what he thought of busing. He really had no opinion, he answered, since he sent his kids, Jeffrey, Steven, Jill, and Lisa, to private schools. Ducking the question made him think, however, and the same night he was on the phone to Mike Wallace. "Hey, let's go to those members of Congress most vocal in their support of busing and find out where *their* kids go to school!''

Barry Lando was told to give it a try. Nailing the big-name liberals in Washington, D.C., who were personally ducking integration proved to be almost embarrassingly easy, and on November 21, 1971, Lando and Wallace made air with *Not To My Kid, You Don't*. Busing is not much of a local issue in the capital, Wallace began. ''There just aren't enough white children in the district to bus. The Washington public school system is 95 percent black. Still, Washington's liberals—its congressmen and journalists and jurists—have been busy advising communities elsewhere that busing is a necessary tool to achieve integration, even if it means busing your child away from your neighborhood school.''

After a visit to W. Bruce Evans Junior High, where only six of the twenty-eight seventh-graders could read at the seventh-grade level, Wallace took himself to the private Georgetown Day School, where the children of Senator Philip Hart; Frank Mankiewicz, the top strategist of Senator George McGovern; *Washington Post* editor Benjamin Bradlee; and Supreme Court Justice Thurgood Marshall went to school. He asked the wife of Democratic congressman Donald Fraser whether she saw any hypocrisy in lawmakers, journalists, and jurists talking busing while making sure their own kids went to private schools. ''Well no, I guess I really don't,'' answered Arvonne Fraser, ''because you've got to say— your kids only get educated once, and they're your kids and you want a good education. And sometimes you get a choice, you know, and—and the kids, that particular kid's education may come first.'' Mike insisted that the legislators, journalists, and judges preached integration and elicited from Arvonne Fraser that, yes, it was hypocritical since the rich had freedom of choice.

From Georgetown Day School, Wallace and crew visited St. Albans School for Boys, run by the Episcopal Church, where senators Ted Kennedy and Birch Bayh, *The New York Times*' Tom Wicker, and *The Washington Post*'s Phil Geyelin had sons. ''We asked Senator Kennedy to talk to us, but he declined,'' said Mike on camera. ''Where he sends his son to school, he said, is a private matter.'' Senator Edmund Muskie's daughter attended the School of the Holy Child, a private Catholic institution, while two other Muskie children went to another Catholic school. Said Wallace, ''We wanted to talk to the senator about this issue, but his office told us he had no time on his schedule, that he was all booked up until mid-December.''

Before *60 Minutes* and the country got to Watergate, Mike's acquaintance with International Telephone and Telegraph lobbyist Dita D. Beard led to a hot exclusive. Beard was the woman who wrote, or did not write, a memorandum that linked ITT's offer of $400,000 to under-write the Republican Party's 1972 convention with the settlement of three antitrust cases in a manner favorable to the company. Wallace knew her from having covered Republican governors' conferences and on the telephone got her to agree to an exclusive interview.

When the heat was on in Congress in April 1972, Beard had disappeared, only to surface at the Rocky Mountain Osteopathic Hospital in Denver for treatment of a heart ailment. A Senate judiciary subcommittee flew to her bedside but she collapsed while testifying. Reporters were laying siege to the hospital, but when Wallace phoned and reminded her of a promise of an exclusive interview, she told him to come on out. Her lawyer agreed, and Wallace, Hewitt, and a crew got on a plane to Denver. When they drove up in their airport rental van and Don saw the lurking press, he dropped Mike off at the entrance and told him to meet them at the emergency entrance in the back. Don waited and waited and was just about to give up when he saw Mike wheel Beard toward him in a wheelchair. The doctor wouldn't allow any TV crew inside. They packed Beard in the van, went to an apartment that had been rented for her use during her convalescence, and in thirty minutes wrapped the interview, in which she said she had not written the famous memo and that when she had approached former Attorney General John Mitchell at a party at the Kentucky Derby, he had told her "in effect, to shove off." They drove her back to the hospital, where she was readmitted, and the following Sunday led off with the Beard exclusive. Mrs. Beard Defies Her Doctors to Give an Interview to CBS, *The New York Times* headline said the next day.

Evidence suggested that the quid pro quo of settling the antitrust suit against ITT and its $400,000 "commitment to help defray costs for the Republican convention" had been arranged by Deputy Attorney General Richard Kleindienst. The Senate exonerated the Arizona conservative who also appeared on *60 Minutes* and in an extraordinary interview said, "I'm no penny-ante, two-bit little crook. I came to Washington with my honor and a little money. I still have my honor and less money." There were other singular interviews with Spiro Agnew, Nguyen Cao Ky, and Doug Van ("Big") Minh, with the antiwar activitist brothers Daniel and Philip Berrigan, but to Don's distress his newsmagazine finished the 1971–72 season in 101st place in the prime time ratings. It was doubly embarrassing because CBS was so overwhelmingly successful. It had 27,842 employees; its net income reached $82.9 million. *All in the Family* topped the Nielsens, and new hits included *Maude, The Waltons, M\*A\*S\*H*, and *The Bob Newhart Show. CBS Sports* added NBA basketball to its NFL football coverage. The bungled burglary of the Democratic Party head-quarters in Washington's chic Watergate complex, however, suddenly put the entire news division on a collision course with Chairman Paley and the upper CBS management.

Paley had made an exception for himself, and Stanton imagined that he, too, would be able to stay on after sixty-five. It was not to be and, in October 1973, he left, a restless, frustrated millionaire. Arthur Taylor was hired to "deStantonize" the company. He came from International Paper Company and was touted as the best of the new generation of corporate managers. He once told Morley Safer that when he grew up he wanted to be a CBS foreign correspondent. Safer sensed condescension in the joke. The Taylor rule was short as was the reign of his successor, John Backe. The chairman dismissed both after they moved a little too aggressively to take over from him.

For Hewitt and his people on the eighth floor, the mid-1970s were frustrating years of preemptions. Palmer Williams was becoming the Sunday quarterback, trying to guess when the National Football League game would end. Stopwatch and phone at his elbow, the *60 Minutes* managing editor sat in his Greenwich Village apartment on 12th Street, his TV set tuned to the game, while up on 57th Street, Merri Lieberthal, the unit producer originally hired as a secretary to Mike Wallace, had ready segments truncated to various lengths. As soon as *CBS Sports* called Williams and gave him a two-minute warning, he was on the phone to Lieberthal so she could throw the right length of *60 Minutes* for Eastern time broadcast. For Central, Mountain, and Pacific air time, the full forty-seven minutes were usually restored.

Hewitt talked to Salant about getting programming to allow *60 Minutes* to "bump the network"—to let the whole Sunday evening prime time slide by, however many minutes football ran over. The idea was turned down. What was especially galling was that *60 Minutes* was climbing in the ratings. On certain Sundays, it reached nearly a third of the audience share.

The mid-1970s were also the years of the Watergate affair. Investigative reporting was becoming a growth industry. Newspapers and local TV stations formed "task force" units to root out malfeasance and malpractice in government and society at large. The style was to ask questions in a tough, belligerent manner to convey the impression that the reporter wasn't letting anyone get away with anything. In Des Moines station WHO-TV filmed decoys illegally exchanging food stamps in a four-part series that resulted in federal scrutiny of food stamp abuses. WABC's Geraldo Rivera became famous in New York for an elaborate exposé of a state school for the mentally retarded called Willowbrook, causing a public outcry and official redress. The country, said *The New York Times* ace investigator Seymour M. Hersh in acceping the Drew Pearson Foundation award for uncovering CIA meddling in Chile, "is in the age of the great exaltation of the investigative reporter."

It wasn't easy. An important television exposé might take months of research and undercover legwork. It might fail to produce a "smoking gun" and be junked as too risky or too inconclusive. Too often, it meant talking on the phone to people who didn't want to be seen or quoted. And television needed pictures. As *The Selling of the Pentagon* producer Peter Davis put it, "If Woodward and Bernstein had shown up at their rendezvous with Deep Throat lugging a camera, lights, and sound equipment, the whole Watergate exposé might never have happened." You could do "talking heads" in a studio roundtable, but the result was usually experts spouting hard-to-follow facts in front of a few graphs and charts.

And there was the FCC Fairness Doctrine, which decreed that broadcasters must spend a reasonable amount of time discussing controversial issues of public importance, and do so in a way that fairly reflects opposing points of view. As the Watergate drama unfolded with ever widening implications, the Fairness Doctrine itself became a controversy. CBS and NBC argued that broadcasters should have the same unfettered First Amendment rights as the print media. CBS President Arthur Taylor told Congress the nation's broadcasting outlets now outnumbered daily newspapers by more than four to one and that the doctrine was "a potential tool of determined and unscrupulous public officials to destroy what is, in effect, the only national daily press that this diverse nation has." NBC Chairman Julian Goodman said the doctrine was fine in setting professional standards for responsible journalists, but something else when it gave "the government authority to second guess news judgments and threatens to make it a supereditor for broadcasting." On *60 Minutes,* Wallace said he had no problems with the Fairness Doctrine.

Dick Salant created CBS's own "SWAT team" in the spring of 1973 when White House press secretary Ronald Ziegler said all previous statements denying White House involvement in Watergate were now "inoperative." Salant made Stanhope Gould the head of the new investigative unit. Together with Linda Mason, another associate producer on the Cronkite show, Gould had won an Emmy for a searing report on the Nixon administration's 1972 Soviet grain deal. Eager to score again, Gould and Mason got the news division's go-ahead to have a look at CBS Records and a lingering drug payola scandal.

Clive Davis, the hip and talented boss of the record division, had just been fired. In a civil complaint CBS brought against him, the company charged him with padding expense accounts to the tune of $94,000. Davis had moved on to the presidency of Artista Records, Columbia Pictures' record subsidiary, but federal narcotics agents disclosed they had come up with evidence linking Davis's deputy to the drug scene. This in turn had touched off a grand jury probe of charges that employees of CBS Records and other record companies used drugs as a form of payola to push rock stars and labels.

Executives at the purged CBS Records were furious when Gould and Mason began snooping around, but the new investigative team apparently had the blessings of the chairman himself. Watergate was careening relentlessly towards it denouement, and the smart thinking had it that Paley saw the news division's probe as a very classy way of showing his conservative friends that *CBS News* reported *all* the bad news, including CBS's own. When Gould came up with a script in early 1974, however, the grand jury investigation of the record business had petered out, apparently for lack of evidence. Gould wanted to have his investigative report turned into a two-parter narrated on the evening news by Cronkite. Instead, Salant decided the material should be broadcast as a one-hour special. Narrated by David Culhane, *The Trouble with Rock* finally aired one hour before *60 Minutes* on August 11, 1974. Coming two days after Richard Nixon's resignation, not many viewers that summer Sunday evening were interested in a nearly two-year-old story of graft in the record business. A few weeks later, Gould quit CBS.

ABC launched a major offensive to catch up with CBS. For twenty years, CBS had dominated the overall prime time ratings but, by the fall of 1975, less than one point separated the three commercial networks. The highest rated programs were *All in the Family* (CBS), *Sanford and Son* (NBC), and *Chico and the Man* (NBC), followed by ABC's *The Six Million Dollar Man*. All stops were pulled, and Black Rock ordered the news division to throw *60 Minutes* into the counteroffensive. "I've waited twenty years for this," exulted Salant. "I always knew that if I survived in this job long enough, the day would come when those characters would turn to me to help them with a ratings problem."

"Those characters" in programming had made the astonishing discovery that *60 Minutes* had become as popular as football and, on December 7, the newsmagazine was moved back—against the advice of any number of network experts—one hour to the 7 to 8 time slot. Hewitt was ecstatic and, in his gambler's metaphor, told his people they finally had the dice in their hot little hands.

Well, almost. Programming wouldn't relent on the football overruns and allow *60 Minutes* to bump the network. Don wasn't worried about the opposition. ABC was offering *Swiss Family Robinson* and NBC *The Wonderful World of Disney,* but football meant truncated editions for Eastern time zone viewers during the NFL season.

To be the Sunday lead-in and to experience climbing ratings made everything possible. Hewitt now had seventeen full-time producers, ranging from veterans like Williams, Wershba, and Paul Scheffler, to young hands like Barry Lando (nicknamed the leading agent of the Wallace Bureau of Investigation), Harry Moses, Norm Gorin, Suzanne St. Pierre (Mrs. Eric Sevareid off-duty), Steve Glauber, Marion Goldin, and Grace Diekhaus. Before Hewitt could roll the dice one full season, Black Rock and Salant came with a second heady decision. *60 Minutes* would run year-round, fifty-two weeks a year. Don got out his pocket calculator. Even counting summer reruns, that meant they'd have to do a hundred stories a year!

Tall order. Each producer might devote two or three months to a single story before calling out Wallace or Safer plus a camera crew. Now, their problems were to manage to corral one of the two stars for enough time to get a segment in the can. "You have to book these guys like opera singers," London-based Jeanne Solomon would tell E. J. Kahn, Jr. For Mike and Morley the pace was grueling. They were now spending nine months a year on the road, sometimes regarding it as a feat merely to get to their destination.

Wallace was trim and athletic, with a mean tennis elbow, but he was fifty-seven—Morley was thirteen years his junior—and he felt a need to keep topping himself, a need, that at candid moments, he admitted was deplorable. Lorraine and he had bought property in Haiti, where she had family, but he often interrupted the infrequent vacation they took to phone New York and pitch stories to Hewitt. His two stepchildren, Anthony and Pauline, were finishing college, and Chris Wallace was getting into broadcasting. "I hate to sound sickeningly happy, but I confess that I am," he told the *Christian Science Monitor* in 1974. "My kids are healthy. I'm devoted to my wife. I like the work I do, my health is fairly good. I feel a little bit guilty about all of that, but it didn't come about easily." In the fall of 1975, he was candid enough to go to Hewitt and tell him that he, and possibly Morley as well, were stretching themselves too thin.

As indicated earlier, Dan Rather was getting worried about his visibility on *CBS Reports,* even if he managed to grin when a friend suggested he might soon qualify as a candidate for those don't-leave-home-without-it American Express commercials featuring vaguely remembered "names" (Do you remember me? I used to cover the White House for *CBS News*).

So the offer to become the third correspondent on *60 Minutes* came at just the right moment.

The first assignment Hewitt sent Dan on was a story on Robert Redford. The decision was vintage Hewitt-Dapper Dan meets the Sundance Kid. Rather was of the mind that his debut should start on a weightier note. Bill Crawford, a Washington bureau producer who had been through the Watergate wars with Dan, got the scene through the grapevine: "I can hear Hewitt's answer: 'Screw journalism, Dan, just find out what he wears to bed at night.' "

They were stars. Mike and Morley had their own retinue of producers, researchers, and secretaries, and each had a star-sized ego. When Dan joined, new spacious offices were set up to accommodate all three. Hewitt had tape measures brought in to make sure the size and shape of each "tiger cage" were the same. Everybody was on first name basis, and the air was thick with affectionate insults and open-office-door spunk. It was a charmed circle, as Kathleen Fury would write in *TV Guide* years later, "of sophisticated, rough and tough locker room male bonding." Hewitt's feisty energy, the joshing rivalry and corridor confrontations instead of preplanned meetings, the sense of being a winning team riding a popular wave paid off in enterprising fearlessness and high-powered television. The tenor of the times and the impulse of its journalism were to explore and confront, and on *60 Minutes* they confected elaborate scenarios to reveal and inform. Wallace could be seen emerging from behind a door in a Chicago health clinic to confront medical lab technicians offering kickbacks. Rather could be seen catching a government inspector mislabeling meat in a packing house. Perhaps the most famous of the undercover genre showed how easy it was to become another person by creating a new identity.

Early in *Fake ID,* Mike was seen interviewing the head of the birth records office in Washington, D.C., and asking the official whether a young woman standing next to him might not be an impostor, one of those people creating a dilemma of vast proportions for law enforcement by establishing whole new identities and lives for themselves. The official conceded the possibility but didn't take Wallace too seriously. When he handed the woman the certificate, he asked, "You're not going to use that for fraudulent purposes, are you?'' She insisted she wasn't.

The young woman was a decoy. She was CBS News researcher Lucy Spiegel, and applying for the birth certificate of someone her own age but long since dead was only the beginning. *Fake ID* showed her obtaining a phony driver's license, a false Social Security card, opening a bank account and, for final cachet, a U.S. passport. Using her new identity, she applied for food stamps and used bad checks to buy an expensive camera and a plane ticket—both dutifully honored by *60 Minutes* later. Mike tagged along and provided the ironic high point when he asked the airline ticket agent how he knew this young lady wasn't handing him a check that would bounce. "I'm quite satisfied that she is okay," the agent said, and smiled. "After all, I have been in the business for twenty-eight years."

Mocking the civics book pretensions of American life and appealing to the proverbial touch of larceny that is in every heart, Mike, Morley, and Dan exposed titillating frauds and, with a wink to viewers guiltily delighting in vice, showed the following "how to":

—How to arrange a divorce of convenience and thereby pay lower income taxes.

—How to smuggle cigarettes from North Carolina and dodge excise taxes in such high tax states as New York.

—How to write off Sugar Bowl tickets and country club dues as a business expense.

—How to become a minister of a nonexistent church and claim tax benefits for a bogus congregation.

—How to get kickbacks on Medicaid prescriptions.

—How to "double dip"—draw both government pay and a government pension.

—How to steal a Mercedes Benz from an airport parking lot in three easy steps: 1) note license plate number and dealer's decal or sticker; 2) phone the state department of motor vehicles and get owners' name from public records; and 3) phone the dealer, explain you are a police officer needing to confirm that Mr. Smith—who says he is locked out of his car—did in fact buy the silver 450 SL, and ask him to provide the serial number so a new key can be made.

*60 Minutes* has always had more trouble with the political right than the liberal left. The newsmagazine is on the perpetual hit list of Accuracy in Media (AIM), a conservative watchdog newsletter published in Washington, D.C. "Why did Mike Wallace pull in his claws when he interviewed Jacobo Timerman on *60 Minutes* on December 5?" AIM asked in 1982. Wallace was in Tel Aviv talking to the former Argentine newspaper editor about his charges that his new homeland, Israel, was a militarist state and that its invasion of Lebanon was politically stupid, morally wrong, and that Prime Minister Menachem Begin misused the memory of the Holocaust by drawing unwarranted comparisons between Palestine Liberation Organization leader Yassir Arafat and Adolf Hitler. Why didn't Wallace question Timerman about his role in laundering money that leftist Argentine terrorists obtained from kidnapping and theft? AIM asked, echoing the Buenos Aires generals' claim that Timerman wasn't jailed and tortured because he was a Jew but because he secretly supported the Montenero terrorists.

Pressure groups and special interests inevitably react to stories investigating their turf. The gun lobby went after *60 Minutes* in 1982 for a segment, reported by Reasoner, on Teflon-coated bullets that can pierce the bulletproof vests worn by police. The American Rifle Association didn't like the way its supporters came across on camera at a township meeting in Suffolk County, New York, shouting epithets during an open hearing on a proposal to ban such bullets.

The Defense Department has a standing order of noncooperation. The Pentagon may have furnished personnel for the revisionism of Colonel Anthony Herbert's story, but the standard practice is not to speak to anyone connected with the newsmagazine. *60 Minutes* was barely a year old when a story on the Navy staging World War II sea battles off San Diego for Twentieth Century Fox's movie *Tora! Tora! Tora!* provoked Defense Department wrath. In 1979, *60 Minutes* caused new pain to the military with the story of a black enlisted Army man who eighteen years earlier had been accused by counterintelligence officers of stealing classified documents while being stationed in Orleans, France. Produced by Harry Moses, the tale of James Thornwell was the stuff top ratings are made of.

Thornwell had denied stealing any documents in 1961, but Army investigators were not satisfied and had started a brainwashing scheme that went on for weeks in an old mill near Orleans and culminated in their secretly administering the hallucinogenic drug LSD. He was eventually allowed to leave the service with the matter of the missing documents still unresolved. He began to experience periods of depression, suffering from nightmares and headaches, was unable to keep a job, and became a drifter. Two marriages ended in divorce.

A 1977 congressional investigation into Army experiments with hallucinogenic drugs resulted in Thornwell receiving a vaguely worded letter from Washington advising him he had been one of the Army's guinea pigs. Using the Freedom of Information Act, a California lawyer, who had represented Thornwell in a car accident case, obtained Army documents that detailed not only the administering of LSD but systematic efforts to break him down with a variety of methods, including threats by investigators that they would make him insane.

With Dan Rather as the narrator, Thornwell's story aired on March 25, 1979. It featured a harrowing sequence showing Thornwell returning to the old mill and seemingly breaking down as he recounted his ordeal eighteen years earlier. A year later, Congress voted to give Thornwell $625,000 as compensation, reportedly the largest sum it had ever awarded an individual claimant against the government. Thornwell's lawyers said the *60 Minutes* segment was largely responsible for the congressional action.

Moses got feelers from Hollywood, asking if he was interested in working on a dramatization of the Thornwell story. Grant Tinker, president of MTM Productions, was the most enthusiastic, and a deal was made for a $2.1 million movie for television that Moses directed. To establish the accuracy of the story in still more detail, Moses and his screenwriter, Michael de Guzman, tracked down many of the people to be portrayed in the film, including one of Thornwell's ex-wives and the officer who was in charge of the Army counterintelligence unit that subjected the soldier to prolonged interrogation, lie detector tests, sodium pentothal "truth serum," and finally LSD. The former officer, now a physician in the Midwest, was a bundle of guilt when the past was brought up and seemed to want Moses and de Guzman to beat him up.

Starring Glynn Turman, who had appeared in the screen versions of *The River Niger* and in *Cooley High, Thornwell* aired as a two-hour movie on CBS in early 1981. Vincent Gardenia played the head of the Army team administering the LSD. The reviews were not too hot: Turman was considered adequate as the young soldier, Gardenia miscast, and the scene where the hallucinogenic drug is administered less than climactic.

In February 1980, Moses and Dan Rather presented *The Death of Edward Nevin*, a bizarre case of secret Army biological warfare experiments thirty years earlier. With the help of recently declassified Defense Department documents, Moses and Rather reconstituted the September 26 and 27, 1950 release into the atmosphere of San Francisco Bay of the bacteria called serratia marcescens "to study the offensive possibilities of attacking a seaport city with a biological warfare aerosol generated from a ship located some distance offshore." Serratia marcescens was chosen because of its supposedly benign characteristics. Unknowingly, almost 800,000 San Franciscans breathed particles of serratia. Eleven people reported illness as a result—all hospital patients then undergoing treatment that made them particularly susceptible to the infection. One of them, Edward Nevin, died.

The spraying of San Francisco remained a secret until 1976 when an investigative reporter on the *San Francisco Chronicle* found out about it, and Edwin Nevin III read about his grandfather's death while riding to work one morning on the subway. "I was stunned," the young trial lawyer told Rather. "I was angry. I was hurt. The government made a decision with extremely limited thought and preparation and investigation, made a decision to expose 800,000 San Francisco citizens to bacterium, live bacterium, did not investigate the potential for that bacterium causing disease to an adequate degree, and proceeded, nevertheless, to, in effect, reverse the whole process of the purpose of our military and our defense system—that is, to protect the people of the United States of America. And instead, that very branch of our government attacked the people of the United States of America." The Pentagon refused to talk to Moses and Rather.

More recently, *60 Minutes* has caused grief to the military with a report on the Maverick antitank missile and the lack of realistic tests of the weapon, and *Uncle Sam Doesn't Want You* about homosexuals' fight to stay in the armed forces. The complaint at the Defense Department is that any spokesman it might supply *60 Minutes* will be up against more than he can handle and, in any case, whatever he says will probably be savaged in the cutting room. Colonel Robert O'Brien, chief of the Directorate for Defense Information in Washington, told *TV Guide* in 1983 that one reason why the newsmagazine has problems getting military personnel to go on camera is: "General X tells me, 'I sit in front of that TV set and watch those guys take people like me apart; I'm sure as hell not going to be interviewed by them!' "

Government agencies and departments taken to task, if not apart, by *60 Minutes* include the Federal Drug Administration, the Internal Revenue Service, and the Environmental Protection Agency. *The Riddle of DMSO,* produced by Marion Goldin and reported by Wallace, was such an indictment of the FDA's ban on dimethyl sulfoxide that Representative Claude Pepper, the chairman of the House Select Committee on Aging, sent a letter of congratulations to Wallace for looking into the controversial pain-killer and the committee counsel hailed the broadcast as a "tremendous service." The Arthritis Foundation did an about-face and endorsed the use of DMSO as a local analgesic, while at the FDA the segment so politicized the agency's testing methods of the drug that research doctors were forbidden to publicly discuss their data on DMSO in the treatment of bladder disorders. Three years later, Esther Kartiganer and Reasoner did *To Your Health,* a report on what the FDA was not doing to outlaw sulphites in processed food that could kill asthma sufferers.

The Internal Revenue Service was so ridiculed in *Penny Wise,* a 1983 sendup of its handling of a small Yonkers, New York trucking firm that it reversed its administrative decision. Produced by Norman Gorin and narrated by Safer, *Penny Wise* told of how by keeping back Feuer Transportation's operating license, the government not only shut down the company and put its dozen workers on unemployment compensation, but effectively prevented Feuer from ever earning any money to catch up with its tax arrears. Safer explained the chronicle of events with gusto, but the images that stayed in the mind were pictures of the out-of-work Feuer drivers and warehousemen—beefy, solid working-class men, sitting behind their black accountant, nodding and shaking their heads as he explained the government's Catch 22. The segment provoked the IRS into returning the truck operating license to Feuer, allowing Safer to cheerfully report in an update two weeks later that all Feuer now needed was to raise $200,000 to get started again.

The Environmental Protection Agency, the State of New Jersey, and the county of Middlesex were shamed into cleaning up one man's drinking water in *David and Goliath,* an excerpt from a 1982 documentary nominated for an Academy Award. Frank Kaler of Brunswick, New Jersey fought county, state, and federal governments for six years before a neighboring chemical waste dump was closed. The Kaler family got dizzy taking showers, vegetables turned black during cooking, and one EPA expert declared "you could almost bottle the water and call it cleaning fluid." As Reasoner reported, Kaler came away bitter, saying he was teaching his kids you could buy your share of American justice if you had enough money.

But it was a report on the continued cleanup efforts in the Marshall Islands since the 1947 atomic bomb tests that lifted a *60 Minutes* story beyond exposure of government insensitivity, official inadequacy, and bureaucratic bungling to uncommon heights of humanity and left its viewers with the goose pimples that come with realizing that what we have wrought will be here for tens of thousands of years.

Producced by John Tiffin and reported by Safer, *Remember Eniwetok!* told what had happened since that island in the chain of Pacific islands was ground zero of forty-three separate nuclear bomb tests. It began with the Eniwetokians, who thirty years later wanted their island back, and with their old chief, who was bewildered by the distant government that on the one hand took his land away and now sent him a

lawyer to help get it back. Ted Mitchell was the lawyer, who remembered the first time he took the chief to the United States. For the old
man, it was inconceivable that there could be so much land available to
one people and that, having so much land, they would go so far away
to his island and destroy part of it to test their weapons. The story had
its pokes at government doublespeak. There was a visit to the Runit waste
disposal island in the company of Army people, all wearing surgical masks
and yellow boots to protect them from contamination from a place they
said was perfectly safe. There was a Defense Nuclear Agency manager
who couldn't answer straight when asked why islanders were told to grow
coconuts on Bikini but told not to eat the coconuts. But it was not a
story of government irresponsibility. Congress had continued to appropriate funds for a vigorous cleanup program amounting to over a quarter
million dollars per islander. Soil contaminated by plutonium, strontium,
and cesium was detected by gamma radiation, removed in large loads,
and deposited in a crater on Runit and sealed. The island will remain
off limit for the next 24,000 years.

"There's something more here than a simple 'made to order for television' conflict between the friendly but determined natives and the
friendly but devious big power and the random unknowns of science and
nature," Safer said in the March 1980 broadcast. After a shot of an atomic
bomb exploding, he said, "It's easy now to say we shouldn't have done
it or we shouldn't have to do so much of it or should have done it more
carefully. But it's been done and there's been nothing in history like the
effort that's been made to put things right. That, too, may be wrong,
but at least we tried. So, the dome at Runit stands, perhaps as a symbol
and a warning to future tinkerers with nature." An archeologist visiting
in a thousand years might wonder at the sealed crater but, Safer added,
he should wear a surgical mask and rubber boots and should definitely
not hang around too long.

# 9

# Scams and Hustles
*Going after crime*

🌿 *60 Minutes* became America's TV habit at a time when crime topped the headlines, obsessively. Terrorist violence reached new dimensions of savagery and scope, threatening the stability of governments in a number of countries in 1978, the year *60 Minutes* first reached the top of the ratings. Crime—especially violent crime—was the subject of extensive debate as convicted murderer Gary Gilmore was shot to death by firing squad in Utah, the first prisoner to be legally executed in the United States in almost a decade. Months later, San Francisco Mayor George Moscone and City Supervisor Harvey Milk were assassinated in their offices; and David Berkowitz, the "Son of Sam" killer who terrorized New York City, was declared mentally fit to stand trial, and pleaded guilty to six murders and seven attempted murders. In Washington, the House of Representatives Select Committee on Assassination held highly publicized hearings on past assassinations, while serious reported crime in the country increased, and the use of deadly force by and against police came under scrutiny. Calls for more severe punishment of criminals were part of every political campaign.

In February 1977, *60 Minutes* had come up with the provocative proposition that criminals cause crime, not society. Three years later, a segment that featured a murderer's repeat confession to Mike Wallace posed the question: was society trying to punish itself?

*The Criminal Mind* examined the findings of Dr. Stan Samenov of St. Elizabeth's Hospital in Washington, D.C. (where four years later, President Reagan's would-be assassin, John W. Hinckley, Jr., would be incarcerated), that hard-core criminals are learning to con their way out of long-term prison sentences by manipulating Freudian theories. Muggers and murderers, with their faces dramatically hidden, told Morley Safer on camera how their lawyers had taught them how to play insane, how to tell court-appointed psychiatrists what they wanted to hear ("Crime excites me, to see fear in people's faces, to make the getaway"). "It's a nice story to feed the public," commented Samenov on one man's story that he had to steal to sustain his drug habit, when in fact the man had avoided responsible living all his life and had never developed responsible thinking. Society's basic mistake, said Samenov, is to believe criminals think like everybody else, a mistake that twists the judicial system around and makes it work for the criminals and their lawyers to the detriment of society.

Produced by Jim Jackson, *The Criminal Mind* showed defendants being coached by their lawyers and, once convicted, telling prison psychiatrists whatever it took to shorten the prison term, from revealing the right underlying personality structure in Rorschach tests to conforming to the right thinking patterns.

Were the laws made for the criminals? The 1974 murder in Miami of nine-year-old Arnold Zeleznik by Vernal Walford, who had been released from a Massachusetts mental hospital days earlier although doctors knew Walford was dangerously psychotic, became an Emmy Award winning *60 Minutes* segment, and the subject of John Katzenbach's 1984 best seller *First Born*. It was a tale of legal injustice, madness, and a seven-year battle up to the Supreme Court for the victim's family but, as we shall see in a later chapter, *60 Minutes* would show the even more gruesome *Looking Out for Mrs. Berwid*. This segment would play back a police recording of the actual murder. In 1980, Steve Glauber and Dan Rather went to California to look into public outcries against the judicial constraints put on police. "Do you want to have the guilty go free because a policeman made a minor error?" asked Los Angeles District Attorney John Van de Kamp in the opening minutes of *Handcuffing the Police*. A minute later, we were with Cheryl Cole, who, with her husband Steve, had been accosted as they drove home by three men who tied up the husband and brutally raped her. The trio were caught, tried, and convicted, but because of an arguably irrelevant error the convictions were overturned. "Twelve citizens said, yes, they are guilty," Cheryl said on camera. "But no, the court system says, we'd better let them go because somebody made a mistake." A lawyer called exclusionary rules the price we pay for living in a free society, but a Pasadena, California police officer said each time he stopped a car or a person on the street, he'd have to run through his mind all the court decisions of the last year or last week that might be relevant. He'd have to make his decision in a minute, while courts could sit for hours and deliberate.

Glauber and Rather filmed a real CHiPs episode, in which a California Highway Patrol officer stopped a car running a red light. The officer informed the couple in the car he would run a warrant check on the driver. But a female voice over the police radio told the officer the computers were down, meaning that to detain the driver any longer than it would take under normal circumstances would make the warrant check illegal. Lawyers weren't sure if someone else's identification in the driver's wallet could be considered stolen property. A checkbook could be examined only if the officer didn't try to bend it first, thereby indicating it might conceal a weapon. Should the officer look into the trunk and find a woman's purse, a briefcase, and a card box, he'd better be extra careful, Rather explained, because there are different legal interpretations for each object. The segment ended with the case of Barry Braeseke, who confessed to the murder of his mother, father, and grandmother in their Oakland home in 1976 but whose conviction was overturned because the detective who booked him didn't repeat the entire Miranda rule that Braeseke had the right to remain silent before the detective, with Braeseke's permission, turned on a tape recorder and Braeseke made his confession. While in custody, Braeseke made a second confession on camera to Mike Wallace, who was reporting on PCP, a drug the Oakland man claimed had led to his murderous acts.

Despite the confessions to police and to *60 Minutes*, the California State Supreme Court ruled, 4 to 3, to reverse Braeseke's conviction. The majority of the justices felt there was not proof beyond a reasonable doubt that Braeseke had waived his right to remain silent. To Rather, the prosecutor wondered why the community had to be the victim of judicial reform.

Beyond such reflections on society's gropings for new definitions of crime, punishment, and justice, *60 Minutes* has proved to be a unique forum for exposure of suspicious dealings by politicians, doctors, lawyers, businessmen, bureaucrats, and all manner of rip-off artists preying on the poor, the helpless, the gullible, and the taxpaying. Facetiously,

*60 Minutes* pieces on corrupt supersalesmen, county judges, media quacks, religious humbugs, medical shysters, and bungling civil servants are called the "scam of the week" segments around CBS News, but it is the gusto with which Don Hewitt and his angels go after such stories that is responsible for making *60 Minutes* one of the three longest running evening series in CBS history. "This is one show where you don't know for sure how things will turn out," Morley Safer told *Rolling Stone* in 1978, "whether the crook will get away with it or get his comeuppance."

The occasion for the *Rolling Stone* interview was *60 Minutes'* tenth anniversary, an event celebrated on the ninth floor of 555 West 57th Street with a cake in the form of a stopwatch, with dark chocolate face and meringue minutes. Chairman William Paley cut the first piece as Don, his "tigers," wives, staffers, and freeloaders from the news side swilled champagne. Paley paid tribute to Hewitt and said the newsmagazine was the first documentary series in history to rise to the magic circle of the ten most popular programs on television.

In the industry, *60 Minutes* inspired awe *and* envy. It was not only the classiest network show on the air, but it had advertisers flocking to buy time. ABC launched its own newsmagazine, *20/20,* and at the 1978 NBC affiliates' meeting, station operators asked the network to give them a similar program. Nobody had ever dreamed that anything coming out of the news department could become a money machine. The six commercials sold by the network commanded nearly $175,000 each, meaning that *60 Minutes* "grossed," as they say in the movie business, over $1 million a week. Around CBS, the Hewitt show was now called the Candy Factory for the assortment of "bonbons" it served up each Sunday. Paley called *60 Minutes* the crowning achievement of the back-of-the-book unit. Dick Salant admitted, "This isn't the way things are supposed to happen in television—quality and numbers." Hewitt had his own crack, "Both Dick and I have one true claim to fame. Mine is that I told Barbara Walters she'd never make it in broadcasting. His is that he said *60 Minutes* would never be successful." As always, Don graciously passed the praise to his correspondents while neatly underscoring those ratings once more. "Who would have thought a program like ours could've gotten as high as, what, 30 percent of the audience? So how come we've gotten as high as 53 percent? Because this is a show about the adventures of four reporters, that's why!" The fourth man was Harry Reasoner, who, as the chairman put it, had come "home."

Reasoner's years with ABC had not been a happy time, and when Roone Arledge had been appointed president of ABC's news division,

Harry managed to get out of the last two years of his seven-year contract. Hewitt wanted him back. Salant had Ed Bradley in mind as *60 Minutes'* fourth correspondent but gave in to Don's wishes.

The tenth anniversary was its own news event. *Newsweek* said the fact that *60 Minutes* was still around represented "a rare testament to a network's patient commitment to a program of excellence. More important, the series' success offers gratifying evidence that America's TV appetite is far broader than prime time programmers have traditionally believed." *Good Housekeeping* led off with a Mike Wallace profile, saying the tiger was, in private, a pussycat—courteous, friendly, disarming. The magazine revealed that Mike and Lorraine had refused to have the tables turned and be profiled by Barbara Walters. *The New York Times* commissioned freelance author Harry Stein to do a Sunday Magazine piece that revealed how much pressure Black Rock put on Salant to clone *60 Minutes* for still more glory and profits. "Whatever its shortcomings," Stein wrote, "no other regularly scheduled network program aspires to nearly as much as *60 Minutes*—or achieves it quite as often."

And the candy factory kept the confections—and occasional sourballs—coming. The eleventh season opened with a Dan Rather-Steve Glauber scams-and-hustles piece that was so popular it was repeated three times during the next eighteen months.

*Highway Robbery* featured *60 Minutes'* own elaborate stingmobile. To investigate gas station ripoffs of out-of-state drivers, Glauber, together with Carol Graves of the Georgia Consumer Agency and her son Matthew, posed as tourists on their way to Florida. They were driving a specially inspected car that was followed by Rather and a crew in a van equipped with two-way mirror side windows for unobstructive filming. The first time out they struck home. Steve, Carol, and Matthew pulled into a Shell station off Interstate 75, asked the attendant to fill 'er up and check the oil while they went to the bathroom. The van slid to a stop nearby. Inside, Rather explained the scene as the attendant took a bottle of oil from his pocket and, while hiding it in his rag, bent down and squirted oil onto the front shock absorbers. When Glauber returned from washing up, he got the bad news.

Once the car was up on the rack, Glauber was told one of the shocks was busted and that he would have to have the front pair replaced. After paying $50.15 for two new shock absorbers, they drove on. At a Texaco station, the attendant punctured the front tire while Glauber and the Graves were in the washrooms. They bought two new radials for $154.12. At a fourth stop—a Gulf station—they were told one of the tires was splitting on the side and coming apart, a gash the attendant apparently had made with a knife or a razor. The tires weren't the only problem. The attendant said one of the shock absorbers was bad and recommended replacing all four. They paid $271.98. "Four stations, three hits, a lot of CBS money out of our pockets," Rather editorialized. "The grand total, $476.26.

From the Georgia Office of Consumer Affairs, Rather learned that the people preying on tourists weren't just local guys trying to make an extra buck, but "fifty percenters"—professionals who, after watching a station's traffic, approached the manager and offered to pump gas in a way that could make them both three, four hundred dollars richer every day. The fifty percenter went to work for the station, concentrating on elderly travelers and families with children concerned with safety. The crooks worked the Northeast-to-Florida corridor in the winter and the Southwest during the summer months.

The highlight of *Highway Robbery* came when Rather and crew revisited the three gas stations and confronted the personnel. The Gulf station attendant said he hadn't held a gun to Glauber, hadn't scared him into buying. "I didn't tell him nothing but, you know, what I thought he needed. I mean, he didn't have to buy. He could have said no." At the Texaco station, where the manager had sold them tires, Rather was repeatedly asked, "Can you prove it?" When Dan introduced cameraman Billy Wagner to the Shell attendant, the manager told them to get the hell out of there. Dan persisted and asked the attendant who put him up to it. The sheepish answer was that nobody did.

RATHER: Guy went to the restroom. You go down underneath the car, make the shock absorbers drip grease, and then you tell him "you got shock absorber trouble." We had the shock absorber marked, had a master mechanic tell us the shock absorber's fine. Now there's no question it happened.

ATTENDANT: It's his opinion, I guess.

RATHER: No, it's not a matter of opinion. It's a question of who put you up to it, how did it happen?

ATTENDANT: Ain't got any comment.

RATHER: You don't deny it happened?

ATTENDANT: I—maybe it did, maybe it didn't, I don't know.

RATHER: Well, I'm—you know exactly what he's talking about. You make a commission on it?

ATTENDANT: No, just work here. Part of my job, I guess.

RATHER: Is it part of your job?

ATTENDANT: Whatever you're talking about. All I do is just do my job.

In his wrapup of the 1980 rerun, Rather could report that the Texaco and Gulf stations had been closed and that the Shell station no longer did repairs. When Mike Wallace read the following week's mail, he quoted a letter from a lady in Colorado, who said Rather and Glauber had left out the old fan belt trick, where the attendant gives the fan belt a twist and then discovers the belt is separating. "Never let an attendant open the hood unless you're standing beside him, and break his arm if he reaches for the fan belt," she advised.

Three years earlier, *60 Minutes* itself got hustled.

Teamster union president James F. Hoffa disappeared from a restaurant outside Detroit in July 1975. Officials were inclinded to believe he had been killed, but his body was never found. Except that a North Carolina redneck, who had spent the better part of his forty-nine years in prison, and his thirty-three-year-old writer sidekick were going to lead Joe Wershba and a camera crew to a cement case on the ocean floor off Florida where they'd find the body. "I knew the guy was unsavory," said Hewitt when it was all over, "but I also knew that only an unsavory character could lead us to Hoffa. And I wanted that story so bad I could taste it."

Clarence "Chuck" Newton Medlin was a mean hulk of a man with a tall yarn to tell. Living at a Greensboro halfway house on what federal prison authorities called prerelease status, Medlin called up a lot of North Carolina newspapers in the fall of 1975. He began with a talk with Bill Hodges, editor of the *Sanford Herald* in his hometown fifty-five miles south of Greensboro, where his mother and stepfather lived. He said he had met and become a friend of Hoffa while at the Lewisburg penitentiary in Pennsylvania, and he knew who had killed the Teamster boss and where the body had been dumped. Hodges listened for six hours and decided this was just the greatest con man he'd ever seen. Medlin, who portrayed himself as a tough hood, a cold-blooded murderer, said he wanted $200 for his story so he could skip parole and go to Mexico. The paper couldn't do that, Hodges said, but suggested that Medlin go "underground" while he and his boys checked out the story. Medlin couldn't go for that. He'd have to be with them at all times. When Medlin walked out of the smalltown newspaper office, Hodges told himself he was 95 percent sure he had made the right decision.

The nagging feeling that the heavy-set ex-con just might be telling the truth kept Medlin and his story snowballing through North Carolina newsrooms during the last weeks of November 1975. Each time he turned to the question of money, however, editors and reporters shied away. On November 29, Medlin didn't show up at the former YMCA that served as the halfway house, and U.S. marshals in Greensboro reported him missing. The story grew, however. To *Winston Salem Journal* reporters he said he had been "roughed up" by local hoods and needed $150 to get out of town. After some wrangling, during which Medlin convinced the newspeople he was a sonofabitch by tearing up their notes, they agreed to give him the $150 and a fifth of bourbon for his story. Their editor, however, killed the story.

Aiming for higher literary stakes, Medlin ended up in the corridors of the English Department at the University of North Carolina at Greensboro, talking tough and saying he needed a writer who'd help him with a book on Jimmy Hoffa. A secretary referred him to Robert Watson, a poet in residence. "I got a best seller that will make half a million dollars if someone will help me write it," Medlin told the poet. Watson referred him to Patrick O'Keefe, a part-time teacher and freelance writer who had recently left a reporting job on the *Greensboro Record* and whose wife worked in the university library. Fellow newspeople at the *Record* described O'Keefe as an odd combination of con artist and naïf who became involved in a charismatic religion and wrote an article for the *Record* describing how the spirit of the Lord came to him while he was having a hamburger at Shoney's.

O'Keefe let Medlin tell his story to his writing class, and the next day the unlikely pair were off to New York. By failing to report to the halfway house, Medlin had been classified as missing. By leaving North Carolina, he became an escaped parolee.

The air fare was paid for by *Harper's* editor Lewis Lapham, part of an $800 advance to O'Keefe for a magazine piece on Medlin. When the two Carolinians showed up, Lapham took one look at Medlin and said, "I think I know a guy at CBS who might be interested. Name's Hewitt." While O'Keefe and Medlin took a cab uptown to West 57th Street, Lapham called Don and suggested CBS really check out the convict. As for O'Keefe, the editor reported the Greensboro writer had handled two assignments for *Harper's* and seemed competent.

Medlin knew how to lay it on. Federal psychiatrists had diagnosed him as a schizophrenic, a psychopathic killer, he told Hewitt, Safer, and Joe Wershba. He had killed a number of people and had been implicated in seven murders. When Don asked *how* he knew where Hoffa's body was buried, the convict leaned forward and whispered he had put a .38 down a professional killer's throat and gotten the man to tell. Don and Morley were both terrified and fascinated. Joe was skeptical. That evening, they paid Medlin $1,000 to do a short videotape for them. He was going to lead *60 Minutes* to the body, he told Safer on camera, because he wanted to have the satisfaction of calling Hoffa's murderers and telling them the body had been found. Then he wanted to have an hour in which to flee before CBS called the authorities. And where was Hoffa's body? It was encased in concrete, lying on the ocean floor in twelve feet of water two and a half miles off Key West. Wershba did some fast checking. Medlin and Hoffa had indeed been at Lewisburg federal penitentiary at the same time, but Wershba didn't like the whole thing and asked Don to let him check some more.

Hewitt went to Dick Salant. To skirt the news division policy forbidding payments for news interviews, O'Keefe was hired as a consultant. All dealings would be with O'Keefe, who was made to sign an agreement stipulating he would receive $9,000 upon the discovery of Hoffa's body, although it was understood that O'Keefe and Medlin would split the money. This arrangement, however, wasn't good enough for Medlin. He threatened to drop the whole thing and, according to O'Keefe, had just about everyone terrorized. The money up front, Medlin insisted, or he'd take his story to *The New York Times*. Suddenly, the $9,000 appeared on the table in front of O'Keefe and Medlin.

Because of the heavy New York to Florida Christmas-New Year's traffic, the two North Carolinians got on a flight that stopped in Tampa. Wershba and crew took another flight, and it was decided they would all rendezvous at the Holiday Inn in Key West the next day. In their Manhattan hotel room, Medlin had decided he would have $6,000 and his partner could keep $3,000. He also persuaded O'Keefe to let him carry the money. Ten grand was a lot of cash but Medlin was tough and mean. There was little chance that a mugger would try to mess with him. On the plane, he began telling O'Keefe that Hewitt and CBS were trying to screw them out of Medlin's rights to the story and to the possible film rights. O'Keefe was half convinced Medlin might be right. Movie rights might be worth a lot more than a one-shot on *60 Minutes*. When they landed in Tampa, they got off and checked into a Holiday Inn. That night Medlin began to drink. He called a woman he said was his cousin. She would be their secretary and bookkeeper. When she came to the room, Medlin got obnoxious and she left in a huff. At 4 A.M. and, with about $10,000 in his pocket, Medlin announced he was going to look for her. Ten hours later, O'Keefe called Hewitt in New York to say Medlin and the money had disappeared.

Don was furious and accused the writer of being in on the con. Remembering Medlin's repeated threats to kill everybody, Hewitt eventually advised O'Keefe to take refuge with Tampa police. O'Keefe joined Wershba and crew in Key West the next day. Wershba chartered a boat, hired a scuba diver, and spent the weekend and Monday checking for concrete slabs in twelve feet of water two and a half miles from shore. On Wednesday, FBI agents picked up Medlin at the Holiday Inn French Quarter in New Orleans, after receiving information from the *New Orleans Times-Picayune* that Medlin had tried to peddle his story about Hoffa's body and made the mistake of telling the city editor he was staying at the Holiday Inn. Medlin handed over the $3,100 that was left and was jailed for violating parole. Newspapers had a field day. The front page headline in *The New York Times* read: Hoffa Tipster Gone CBS Out $10,000. The *Greensboro Record* had a reporter recap the caper, knowing that editor Hodges on the *Sanford Herald* had smelled the con, and headlined: Small Fry Media Nibbled; Big Fish Swallowed Bait. The *Record* also called Medlin's mother in Sanford for an interview. She had quite a story about her son and the underworld figures he knew, and she'd tell it for $500. The *Record* politely declined.

*60 Minutes* had had its own fun with colleagues in televised and newspaper journalism. At the height of the Ken and Barbie Dolls fad for bland newscasters, Mike Wallace had done a piece on "happy talk" journalism and news teams in matching blazers and blow-dries, cueing in "action reporters" from behind *Star Trek* desks. The 1974 segment focused on an all-out news ratings war being waged in San Francisco and zeroed in on the high-powered consultants whom station managers hired to teach them the high art of cloning speech patterns, teeth, and hairdos. This television self-poke got the newsmagazine to take a look at junketeering: going on trips paid for by the people about whom the freeloading journalist is ostensibly writing an unbiased report. Wallace trailed automotive reporters to an Indian reservation out West, where the gentlemen of the press got to test drive a new jeep called the Cherokee for a couple of hours before they gave themselves to the amenities American Motors Corporation provided for them at a dude ranch. He listened to a journalist defend his integrity, then established through an interview with AMC that if such freeloading didn't yield favorable reviews for the Cherokee, the junkets would be scrapped. Mike noted that reporters got 18 percent discount when they bought cars directly from the company. Next, he went on a Ford Motor Company trip to California with 100 reporters, found out that IBM sent thirteen women editors to Washington to look at a new IBM supermarket checkout counter and that sportswriters' expenses were sometimes paid by the teams they covered.

Hewitt and Wallace had turned the heat on Washington's liberals for pushing busing while sending their own children to private schools. Now they could hardly do less than inquire about CBS newspeople going on junkets. After showing Pittsburgh *Post-Gazette* reporter finding a pair of ten dollar bills with his press kit (supposedly a CBS taxi reimbursement) when he checked into a Los Angeles hotel for a CBS gala, Wallace mentioned that even Walter Cronkite had gone on junkets and was "a sometime traveler on the freebie circuit." Walter was furious. Gossip columnists picked up the tiff. Cronkite said his trips were of personal nature, made with friends, and had nothing to do with his CBS assignments. Wallace didn't back down but wrote in a letter to inquiring *New York* magazine that "there is room for a difference of opinion between two colleagues."

The news side quite possibly had its sweet revenge the night Medlin was arrested in the New Orleans Holiday Inn. *The Evening News with Walter Cronkite* featured an interview with O'Keefe explaining how Medlin had bilked *60 Minutes* out of $10,000.

Morley Safer's most controversial story caused shivers in the precious metals market in November 1978. *Limited Editions* was an inquiry into the questionable value of commemorative coins and plaques issued by the Franklin Mint Company as collectibles. "There's one area of collecting in which you almost certainly would have lost your shirt," Morley intoned, "and that's in the materials sold and advertised by the Franklin Mint." The segment focused on the private mint's coins and plaques, many of which were originally advertised as "limited editions," but turned out to be limited only by the number of people who wished to order them. Morley claimed that more than 75 percent of all Franklin Mint issues had slumped massively in price and showed Franklin Mint commemorative coins go into the melting bucket in a New York coin ship to be sold for their bullion value.

A number of coin dealers and specialists, not to mention Franklin Mint itself, claimed the *60 Minutes* show set off panic selling. *Numismatic News,* a leading coin collector's magazine, called the segment "a shallow and distorted impression of an intricate subject" and said that, ironically, the exposure caused additional collectors to dispose of their coins. "If they go into the melting pot, as CBS contends, that would make the remaining specimens scarcer, causing a commensurate advance in prices."

Prices did advance, because of the surge in silver (it was the year the billionaire Hunt brothers were speculating in silver bullion futures), but the higher prices themselves led to increased sales to dealers who merely melted down the coins. *Numismatic News* editor Arnold Jeffcoat said that people who had watched the November 12, 1978, broadcast had been scared into selling prematurely and, as a result, lost money, whereas people who missed *60 Minutes* that evening were less likely to have lost their shirts.

Franklin Mint Chairman Charles Andes didn't sue. Instead, he handed media critics transcripts of the videotape his staff had made of his meeting with Safer. The interview came to twenty single-spaced pages. The transcript of the on-air Andes-Safer interview ran less than two pages.

The Consumer Federation of America gave Don Hewitt an award in 1980 that said his newsmagazine had done more for consumerism than the federation itself. "It isn't that I'm looking to be a consumer advocate," Don said. "It's just that those are good stories, and they're stories that are interesting to do and can be told well on television."

Toxic waste was the newest environmental scourge in the late 1970s, and *60 Minutes* raised questions about business ethics that put profits before human safety and about federal and state governments arguing, stalling, and passing the buck when it comes to paying for waste cleanups. Produced by Harry Moses, *The Hooker Memos* was broadcast in December 1979 and featured Hooker Chemicals and Plastics Company President Dan Baeder answering some tough ones from Wallace. An environmental company engineer in Lathrop, California wrote a first memo in 1975 and, for the next three years, kept warning management they were contaminating the ground water and creating "a time bomb."

Baeder said the California Water Quality Control Board knew all about it, but Mike had other memos up his sleeve. Yes, Hooker had made the pesticide DBCP, Baeder said, but in 1977 when National Cancer Institute studies showed it to be a very potent carcinogen, Hooker stopped making DBCP. And had no intention of going back into the DBCP business? Wallace asked. When Baeder confirmed this, Mike came up with a December 1978 interoffice memo examining the option of reentering the DBCP market. Baeder responded that the memo was just a study, that Hooker had no intention of starting to make the pesticide again, that before being a corporate president, he was a human being.

BAEDER: We would not have gone back into it. Again, you're—you're dealing in studies that people make. We make a lot of studies. Why do you hammer us on something that might have happened but hasn't happened?

WALLACE: The only reason I'm hammering it is: Is this the way that America does business?

BAEDER: America looks at many options in doing business. It looks at many options.

WALLACE: And one of the options is, can we afford . . .

BAEDER: No, no, Mike. There is a risk in making almost an . . . there's a risk in making drugs. Mike, your drug people look at this same thing in every pharmaceutical drug they put on the market. There is a risk. There . . .

WALLACE: Do you know how this—this memo—ends up? It says, "Should this product"—DBCP—"still show an adequate profit, meeting corporate investment criteria, then the product should be considered further." That's the bottom line.

BAEDER: Mike, I tried to tell you that profit is not the preliminary consideration.

Six months later, *60 Minutes* zeroed in on the original Love Canal horror story as governments began asking themselves and each other who should pay for genetic "time bombs," relocations of residents, and buy-outs of their homes. *Warning: Living Here May Be Hazardous to Your Health* was researched by newcomer producer Esther Kartiganer and filmed before the Environmental Protection Agency issued the results of its tests of residents for genetic damage and aired the week the EPA announced that eleven of the thirty-six people examined suffered chromosome damage.

Over 200 families that lived close to the toxic waste dump had been evacuated in 1978, and the tests were intended to provide evidence for the government's case against Hooker. The segment opened with Reasoner standing at "ground zero," the school built over the filled-in chemical dump. It showed him visiting the ghostly perimeter of evacuated and now fenced-off homes, explaining how New York state had bought 230 homes and permanently moved out the first two rings of houses; how officials in Albany were worring about setting precedents for who knows how many other potential hazard sites; and about the cost of moving and buying out still more Love Canal residents. There had been more miscarriages, birth defects, and low birth weight babies outside the first two rings. We saw a clip of residents reacting angrily

to State Commissioner of Health Dr. David Axelrod, telling them that
with the exception of pregnant women and children under two, extensive environmental data showed there was no reason for anyone to be
removed. Showing he could be as tough a customer as Wallace, Reasoner got Axelrod to admit that his refusal to recommend evacuation and
buy-outs of homes in a wider ring around the toxic pit might have some
connection with the fact that there might be several hundred other potential hazard sites around New York. The commissioner insisted, however, he had made his recommendations on the basis of scientific information.

Going after the big fish was tricky. Not only do powerful corporations have the means to hit back with awesome lawsuits, but it is pretty
difficult to duplicate the phony auto repair sting in the executive suites.
As Mike Wallace told *Mother Jones'* Jeffrey Klein in 1979, "If you have
a company president with his hands in the till, then you have a character
on whom to focus. But other kinds of money pieces are sometimes quite
hard to tell on television because they are complicated." Companies are
looted through predatory mergers, but to do a story on hostile take-overs,
Wallace added, demanded the participation and cooperation of the principal players in the take-over and perhaps in the ensuing proxy fight.
"And that you do not get."

Still, there were stories on criminal indictments against Ford Motor
Company—a heavy *60 Minutes* sponsor—over exploding gas tanks in
its Pinto models; on the labor practices of Coors Brewing Company; the
sales pyramids of Amway Corporation and Mary Kay Cosmetics; corporate perks at Dupont and Rockwell International and, in pharmaceu-
ticals, Hoffmann-LaRoche pushing doctors to prescribe more Valium and
Eli Lilly's down-playing of adverse reaction to its arthritis drug, Ora-
flex. Upjohn's injectable contraceptive Depo-Provera was given double
exposure. A 1983 report dealt with the contraceptive's possible cancer-
ous side effects; a 1984 story showed its use to control rapists and other
sex offenders by chemically lowering their testosterone counts. Segments were devoted to Consolidated Edison, Illinois Power, and Pacific
Power & Light and these utilities' unhappy experiences with nuclear power
plants and, in the case of Washington Public Power Supply System
(Whoops), on how to live down $3 billion cost overruns on a plant.
(Former executive to Wallace: "You do your best and hope you come
out right.") Besides Love Canal and DBCP in California ground water,
there were stories on Dow Chemicals and dioxin contamination, on Vel-
sicol Corporation and its pesticide chlordane. The biggest horror story
was *Kepone*. One of the first stories reported by Dan Rather, the report

dealt with the irresponsibility of Allied Chemical Corporation toward its
workers in the making of the deadly insect killer. The case resulted in a
$13 million fine against Allied for its part in contaminating Virginia's
James River. The company pleaded no contest to 940 counts of pollution relating to the period when it operated a plant in Hopewell, Virginia.
Allied was cleared of charges that it had participated in the pollution of
the James with the defunct Life Science Production Company, which
had taken over the plant and supplied Allied with Kepone under contract. Allied and Life Science Products were among the defendants in
civil suits for damages amounting to nearly $200 million, filed by for-
mer employees of the plant who had suffered neurological distur-
bances—including tremors and visual impairment—as a result of exposure to the chemical, and by fisherman who had lost their livelihood when
the lower James was closed to fishing. It was feared that the long-lasting
chemical would eventually contaminate Chesapeake Bay. Rather was
proud of the story, writing in *The Camera Never Blinks,* his biography
written with Mickey Herskowitz, that the indictments might have happened without the broadcast, "but, at least we were able to make sure
the situation would not be ignored."


The most original challenge to one of *60 Minutes'* investigations was
*60 Minutes/Our Reply,* a forty-two minute film put together by Illinois
Power Company. The utility had had the foresight to have its own camera
crew on the scene when producer Paul Loewenwarter and Harry Reasoner filmed Illinois Power's embattled Clinton nuclear energy plant in
September 1979. *Who Pays . . . You Do!* was a blistering attack on
Clinton's pyramiding costs. "The American nuclear power program is
in trouble, and not only because of Three Mile Island and the presidential commission's report on hazards," Reasoner began. "It's in trouble
because the cost of building the plants has gone crazy—a *China Syndrome* of costs." Aired nine months after the Three Mile Island accident
in Pennsylvania, the November 25, 1979 broadcast told of a $430 mil-
lion project estimated to cost $1.3 billion but likely to cost still another
billion. It was the complex story of a mid-sized utility not knowing what
it was getting into when it started building the plant. Clinton was IP's
first nuclear plant and the first for its contractor, Baldwin Associates.
Reasoner told how IP was asking the Illinois Commerce Commission
for the right to raise its customers' bills by 14 percent to pay for Clinton. A cost engineer said management had never had a written report on
schedule and costs before he was hired. When he submitted his, he was

fired. A construction foreman said there was no pressure from management to control costs, that he increased his own estimates by tens of
millions. Another superintendent said that if he ran out of something to
do, the rule ·was to waste the rest of the day rather than getting involved
in another work area. Reasoner summed up the report by saying a utility
company, its customers, and a nation wouldn't solve the energy crisis
by going broke.

The next day, Illinois Power's stock fell a full point on the New York
Stock Exchange in the busiest trading day IP had ever seen. Eight days
later, IP had completed its counterprogram. *60 Minutes/Our Reply* included the original Loewenwarter-Reasoner segment and documentation
of what IP claimed were seven outright CBS errors and several misleading statements. The company film was available to anyone willing to
send a blank video cassette in exchange, and 1,300 copies were shipped
within a month. Mike Wallace made two corrections on the air four weeks
after the original broadcast. The 14 percent rate increase IP had asked
for was not only to cover the Clinton cost overruns but general infla-
tionary increases, he admitted, and the Commerce Commission hadn't
recommended against the rate boost, only against the part that was to
cover the Clinton costs. By the end of 1981, 2,500 copies of *60 Min-
utes/Our Reply* had been given to General Electric, General Motors,
chambers of commerce, other utilities, and journalist schools in the U.S.
and overseas. A bid to air the film on WTBS, Ted Turner's Atlanta superstation, was turned down at the last minute because of copyright
problems. By the mid-1980s, of course, nuclear power was a failed industry, and if Loewenwarter, Reasoner, and *60 Minutes* had wanted to
top the Illinois Power reply with an update of their own, they would
have had the last laugh. By 1984, Clinton 1 was due to go into service
in November 1986 at an estimated total cost of $2.85 billion, a mere
half billion dollars above the Reasoner figure that had provoked IP's ire
back in 1979.

Pacific Gas and Electric tried to go Illionois Power one better when
*60 Minutes* wanted to do a story on PG&E's Diablo Canyon nuclear plant
in California. A company with a long-standing record of challenging the
media, PG&E not only demanded the right to tape all interviews independently but to select any subject raised in the program and comment
on it on the air unedited. Hewitt acquiesced to the utility's cameras filming alongside *60 Minutes* cameras, but refused the demand for unedited
comments, and the story of Diablo Canyon was never aired.

Av Westin proved more accommodating in the wake of a Geraldo
Rivera report on *20/20* that accused Kaiser Aluminum & Chemical Cor-

poration of intentionally marketing unsafe aluminum wiring and of withholding information about the product's performance. Kaiser demanded a retraction from ABC and asked Congress to consider hearings "to examine the implication of this increasingly insidious and dangerous practice." Broadcasters were appalled when Westin offered Kaiser Aluminum four unedited minutes on *20/20* in 1980, calling this an outright capitulation. ABC went back on the promise, saying *Nightline*, not *20/20*, was the forum for "a full airing of both the subject of aluminum wiring safety and the broader issues of 'response time' and 'access.' " Kaiser said nothing doing, filed a $40 million suit for slander and said it would ask the FCC to order ABC to provide response time. Nearly sixteen months after the offending *Hot Wire* broadcast, Kaiser's four minutes finally got on the air, not on *20/20* nor on *Nightline*, but on a brand-new program called *Viewpoint*, which Ted Koppel introduced as "an attempt to give a few of our critics a forum on network television in which they can respond to real or perceived injustices done to them by network television." Kaiser had to share the 10 P.M. spotlight with other aggrieved parties—blacks, Arabs, women against ERA, and big business represented by Dan Baeder, ex-president of Hooker Chemical, Chase Manhattan's David Rockefeller, and Mobil Oil's vice president and high priest of advocacy advertising, Herbert Schmertz. Geraldo Rivera followed Kaiser's four minutes with seven minutes of counter rebuttals, but Kaiser was delighted. It withdrew the FCC complaint against ABC and dropped the lawsuit.

Introspection was suddenly becoming trendy. On Christmas Eve, 1982, Dan Rather hosted CBS's answer to *Viewpoint*, an hour-long probe of the news process as seen from newsroom, boardroom, and other vantage points and, a month later, Koppel was back with a second *Viewpoint* examining how pressure groups manipulated television.

The Dan Rather hour was called the first of an *Eye on the Media* series. It distilled the essence of a November weekend at Princeton University, sponsored by CBS and the Columbia Graduate School of Journalism. In attendance were many of television news' leading lights. Barbara Walters, Rivera, and Westin were there from ABC, John Chancellor from NBC. Besides Hewitt and his tigers, CBS fielded Rather and Leslie Stahl, its White House correspondent. Business was represented by Schmertz, of Mobil, and the presidents of Bendix, Chevron, and Southern California Edison: William Agee, George Keller, and Howard Allen. There were journalists from major newspapers, judges, lawyers, and public figures. Moderated by quick-witted Harvard law professor Charles Nesson, the debate lasted nine hours.

Illuminating points were scored all around. Chevron's Keller said television investigations had a way of leaving other people's truths on the cutting room floor. Roger Colloff, the CBS News vice president and lawyer overseeing the legal aspect of each *60 Minutes* segment, said it could not be otherwise, that no network could allow outsiders to substitute their editorial judgment for its own. Hewitt observed that anybody in his shop who deliberately distorted a story to make it unfair would be fired. He also said the public had the right to know what was behind a corporation's carefully tailored PR image.

Nesson invented Zuber, a hypothetical manufacturer of kerosene space heaters, and a television program called *The Investigative Hour*. He had the news stars and the *Fortune 500* executives act out their roles in a *60 Minutes*-type investigation of unsafe space heaters. The first tip-off, Nesson decided, came from a laid-off worker at Zuber's, who knew there were problems with the heaters, a man who cared but also a person out of work and perhaps in need of money. "If I'm gonna help you, it's gonna take time, it's gonna take effort, drawing on my knowledge of this business," Nesson said, pretending to be the former Zuber employee. "You people sell your advertising for a lot of money. How about it?"

Steve Glauber, the producer of *Highway Robbery* and a number of other hard-hitting stories, admitted that *60 Minutes* occasionally paid reporters who weren't themselves interested in a project. Nesson asked Wallace if he had any problems with Glauber talking to the laid-off Zuber employee. After a dramatic pause, Wallace said no, but he would want to talk to Hewitt and Colloff.

Moving the investigation along, Nesson assumed that the now hired consultant would reveal that one of the biggest problems was that consumers unwittingly used less than first-grade kerosene in their Zuber heaters. In its sales literature, Zuber made it perfectly clear that only top-grade kerosene should be used, yet a lot of grade 2 or 3 fuel was used, causing noxious fumes that were harmful to people suffering asthma and emphysema, and to pregnant women. Nesson imagined Wallace, camera crew in tow, marching into a service station selling inferior kerosene and confronting the attendant. Wasn't the payoff to have the salesperson squirm?

NESSON: Mr. Wallace, what you want to do is to go and have a one on one confrontation with another human being. You want it to be people. You want it to be a person who's doing something bad and being called for it.

WALLACE *(laughing with the audience):* No. The short answer is no. We're telling the public, "Watch out!"

Nesson said he wasn't suggesting that Wallace wasn't interested in conveying the broader picture. "What I am suggesting is that one of your ways of conveying it is to humanize the problem through a person to person confrontation."

"You reach people very well that way," Mike answered. "In a way— and I'm not afraid, not ashamed to use the word—in a very dramatic way, to say, 'Wait a minute. This fellow is selling something that is potentially dangerous.' "

When Allen was asked about his personal responsibility toward people who were injured because, predictably, they used the space heaters *not* according to instructions, the Bendix CEO said he couldn't be responsible for what people did if they were properly informed, not misled, and if Zuber exercised reasonable standards of care for its products. "Now beyond that if you want to drive a car without brakes and get killed, that's your problem."

Stonewalling was a favorite corporate ploy in dealing with investigative reporters. Leslie Stahl said she had had the same experience as Rather when it came to getting through to businessmen. "They don't seem to understand that we're only as good as the people who talk to us. We're only as good as our sources."

Hewitt cut to the core, saying business considered the press its adversary and for a very simple reason. "The businessman only wants two things ever said about his company: what he pays his public relations people to say and what he tells his advertising people to say. He doesn't want anyone ever to look above, beyond, or over that. That's understandable. I would love to go through life with everybody saying: '60 Minutes, The Quality Goes in Before The Names Goes On' or 'We're 60 Minutes, Doing What We Do Best.'

"If I were a car company, I'd be delighted if the whole world thought that everybody who worked for me was named Mr. Goodwrench. His name is not Mr. Goodwrench, his name isn't Mr. Badwrench. His name is Mr. Wrench. And whenever you do anything to play with this carefully tailored image that they have spent millions manicuring and tailoring, they don't like it."

An ironic confirmation came from Mr. Goodwrench's employer in 1984 when General Motors demanded unrestricted response time as a precondition for even talking to *20/20* about GM "lemons." ABC refused and the newsmagazine report, produced by erstwhile Cronkite investigative ace Stanhope Gould, went on to document that 1978 to 1981 model GM cars equipped with diesel engines represented the biggest collective case of automotive lemons in U.S. history.

The fear of *60 Minutes* and investigative reporting has spawned its own cottage industry. Executives dreading a call from Hewitt or one of his people can turn to a half dozen companies that will provide a crash course on how not to get sliced to ribbons by Mike Wallace and his colleagues. "I have yet to find one single client who wants to be on *60 Minutes*," says Virgil Scudder, the head of MediaComm, whose one-day coaching sessions, costing between $1,400 and $1,800, will teach a businessman how to come prepared, how to parry phoned-in listener questions on panel shows, the inconsistency trap, and Wallace's cajoling—his playing what-if, posing the A and B dilemmas, and the rest of the booby-trapped interview landscape. Jack Hilton and Peter Jacoby claim they coach half the executives on the *Fortune* 500 list, and Arnold Zenker, a former newsman, travels the country giving seminars to business people facing national and local investigative reporters. For those for whom these advisers' fees are a bit stiff, Hilton has coauthored *On Television! A Survival Guide for Media Interviews.* Hilton and Mary Knoblauch devote a chapter to *60 Minutes* and its methods ("60 Minutes Can Be a Lifetime") and warn, when the newsmagazine calls: "Check your closet for new skeletons, take a TeleCounsel course (hang the cost), and prepare yourself for the most telling examination of your life." The authors warn that the *60 Minutes* people will use every resource, from disgruntled employees to college students who apply for jobs and report what they see; that unlike many other shows, *60 Minutes* crews can't be stalled until they lose interest because they will pursue a story for a year or more if necessary. Hilton and Knoblauch explain that the editing process, which selects only the most telling moments of the filmed raw material, does have a silver lining. The winnowing also makes a person being interviewed look as colorful and interesting as possible. In *Mastering the Public Spotlight,* Boston media consultant Arnold Zenker teaches big business to be quick to request air time to voice opposing opinions and to produce and distribute their own programs free of charge to television stations.

*60 Minutes* had a look at the anti-*60 Minutes* phenomenon in 1984. Produced by Grace Diekhaus and reported by Wallace, *Camera Shy* featured corporate executives coached for encounters with Wallace by Zenker, Hilton, and Jacoby, and revealed that Leslie Stahl, NBC's Ed Newman, and *60 Minutes'* own Allan Maraynes had been paid by Hilton and Jacoby to coach government and business leaders. Newman and Maraynes found no conflict of interest in grooming people to face inquisitive reporters, but Stahl was less than happy. All this coaching wasn't done just to tell camera-shy executives not to scowl or to pretend to welcome criticism, but to train people to get away with saying as little as possible, "to train people not to be accountable."

# 10

# The Business of Religion

*Handling the rich loam of religion*

Forceful religious leaders like to think their causes are unique, and they resist comparison. But resurgent fundamentalism was not only sweeping Islam in the wake of the Iranian revolution, but because of its uncompromising stance against Communism, Polish Catholicism also had a fundamentalist tinge. In Northern Ireland, Protestant fundamentalism was one of many new voices in a drawn-out struggle that involved religious loyalties alongside economic and ethnic grievances. Israel had a fundamentalist orthodoxy demanding closer secular compliance with Judaic law. In Japan, a militant offshoot of Buddhism and the philosophical faiths of Taoism and Confucianism developed in the form of Nichiren-sho-shu, forcing uncompromising millions—especially the young—into a spiritual and political force. In the United States, new Christian voices rallied support through the "electronic church"—evangelistic television—and lobbied for the passage of laws it favored and for fundamentalist candidates for public office. The new Christian right insisted that we rally around a hard-line outlook of absolutes and total demands. A cluster of forces, among them the Moral Majority, took credit for having helped turn the country on a new conservative course in 1980, not only

139

by helping Reagan win the presidency but by defeating liberal senators
and members of the House of Representatives and various lesser office-
holders who might think moderation is not necessarily the first step to
surrender.

Criticism of religion is something of a taboo in the United States, a
nation that puts "In God We Trust" on its coins. Realistic evaluations
of men of the cloth shock both the faithful and unfaithful in America. It
is therefore a measure of *60 Minutes'* power that it has risked offending
just about every faith and denomination, from mainstream Catholics and
Jews to militant Protestants and followers of an Indian swami deep in
the hills of Oregon. Don Hewitt has remarked upon this fleetingly on a
few occasions, telling *Newsweek* in 1983, for example, that *60 Minutes*
is neither the darling of the liberals nor of the conservatives. "If you
don't believe it, ask the World Jewish Congress and the PLO, both of
which have at various times held us in contempt." How his program has
handled religion—and especially religion and money—is an area in which
the stories speak eloquently for themselves. As Harry Reasoner said in
reporting a Utah fruit processor's fight with the Mormon Church, "I
suppose the question comes down to the fact that, historically, whenever
any church has had extreme wealth and temporal power, it has usually
led to abuses."

Aired in December 1979, *Garn Baum vs. the Mormons* was broadcast the week after the Church of Jesus Christ of Latter-day Saints ex-
communicated dissident feminist Sonia Johnson for criticizing her church's
opposition to the Equal Rights Amendment, and the *60 Minutes* segment, produced by Richard Clark, focused sharply on the hierarchy and
patriarchy running the Mormon Church in Salt Lake City.

Garn Baum was himself a Mormon, but a Mormon who was trying
to win an antitrust suit against the Mormons in a state where the church
had enormous influence on the press, politics, business, even on the legal profession. At the bottom of Garn and Peggy Baum's trouble was a
whisper campaign telling Utah County cherry growers not to sell their
crops to Baum's processing plant because Garn was in financial trouble
and wouldn't be able to pay them. Baum's banker insisted Baum was
financially sound that year, but the growers apparently listened to the
rumors and took their business elsewhere, which prompted the lawsuit
against, among others, the Mormon Church. Baum could only speculate
that a few greedy people wanted his successful business. They were
Mormons, and they were paid employees of the church. To answer Reasoner, the church provided a public relations director who said the church
was not involved in any conspiracy against Baum, and that the man who

started the rumors was a consultant to the church on its church farm.

Clark and Reasoner dug deeper and found the Utah Department of Agriculture had gotten a law passed by the 90 percent Mormon state legislature, permitting it to raise Baum's required performance bond from $25,000 to $100,000, more than ever required from any processor. The department investigated itself for possible conflict of interest and found itself not guilty. The increased performance bond was too much for the Baums. The processing plant, valued at about $2 million, was sold at a sheriff's auction for $500,000. The buyer—the Mormon Church. And Clark and Reasoner found a Salt Lake City lawyer willing to say the church was a major financial institution, that for an attorney to have his name merely tied to a lawsuit against the Mormon leadership or against a corporation of the church was intimidating.

Four years earlier, Mike Wallace had reported what was to remain one of the most controversial stories of his career. For *Syria: Israel's Toughest Enemy,* he visited Jews in Damascus who told him, and led him to conclude, that they were better off under President Hafez al-Assad, the anti-Israeli hardliner, than they had been under previous regimes. The broadcast caused an uproar among Jewish viewers. The American Jewish Congress made a formal complaint to CBS protesting Wallace's "inaccurate and distorted" reporting. Letters from viewers objected to his alleged anti-Semitism. Promising another look, Wallace returned to Syria in 1976 to find that the situation was indeed as he had described it in February 1975. Wealthy Syrian Jewish businessmen, lively Jewish schoolchildren did not project images of fear and repression. A Syrian Jew living outside the country was interviewed and said President Assad was a good man, not only for the Jews in Syria, but for all the population, and a Damascus doctor noted that his new identification card no longer carried the special legend "Mossawi" ("follower of Moses").

Rabbi Arthur Hertzberg, the president of the American Jewish Congress, remained unconvinced and accused Wallace of trying to justify the initial report. "It is difficult to imagine a more deceptive and illusory portrait of Jewish life in Syria," said Hertzberg, pointing to the fact that the Syrian Jew interviewed abroad was filmed with his face in shadow, indicating the man feared reprisal. In reviewing the segment and the American Jewish Congress condemnation, *New York Times* critic John J. O'Connor noted that Assad was on record as supporting fewer restrictions on travel abroad for Syrian Jews, and gave the last word to Wallace, who in the second report said that to deny that these few gestures were an improvement, "is to deny what we have seen."

In January 1980, *60 Minutes* profiled Oral Roberts, "the granddaddy of the electronic preachers," as Morley Safer described the sixty-two-year-old Oklahoma evangelist. Produced by Joseph Wershba, *All About Oral* looked into the finances of Roberts' combined medical and faith healing center in Tulsa that the city didn't want, and his laying on of hands to get people out of wheelchairs. It quoted Robert Roberts, Oral's son and eventual successor, as saying his father talked to God, and quoted Vaden Roberts, the preacher's elder brother, who had been there during the days of tent crusades, as saying that Oral couldn't cure the lame and the halt.

Wershba and Safer found Jerry Sholes, a former writer of Oral's TV shows and fund raisers, who said getting people out of wheelchairs wasn't a rigged performance; it merely concentrated on individuals who used wheelchairs for comfort, people who could get up to go to the bathroom or get into a car. "These are the people in Oral Roberts' seminars who will get out of their wheelchair and they may be healed for as long as it takes them to get backstage and behind that back curtain and get back into the wheelchairs."

Just as Norman Gorin and Mike Wallace couldn't get past Stanley Rader to talk to Worldwide Church of God founder Herbert W. Armstrong, so Wershba and Safer couldn't persuade the Oral Roberts organization to allow them to ask the preacher himself a few questions. Martin Phillips and Wallace earlier had had a look at the telephone boiler room techniques a Los Angeles fund raiser used for the Southern Christian Leadership Conference (SCLC). Steven Blood used upwards of twenty telephone salespeople to raise money for the SCLC and himself by selling ads in the church magazines he published. The salespeople got 30 percent on everything they managed to raise, Blood took a 30 percent commission himself, and another 30 percent went to overhead—offices, phone bills, printing the magazines—leaving 10 percent for the SCLC. Roy Innes, the head of the Congress of Racial Equality, who had used Blood as a fund raiser for CORE, called him a shark, a bandit, and "a leech on the black community," but Bishop H. Hartford Brookins said 10 percent of something was better than 100 percent of nothing. Brookins hated *Blood Money,* which aired in March 1980, calling it "subjective, completely out of order" and charging that Wallace had not been objective about money raising.

A month later, Allan Maraynes and Wallace came up with *Scientology: The Clearwater Conspiracy* on this group's botched attempt at taking over the city government of the west Florida community. The segment aired just as founder L. Ron Hubbard disappeared and a bitter

THE BUSINESS OF RELIGION

internal battle over the control of hundreds of millions of dollars broke
out. Maraynes and Wallace told how the church—which its leaders call
a religion and its critics a highly profitable business with cultlike over-
tones—bought two downtown buildings under false pretexts in 1975 and
tried to smear the mayor and two women writers when they tried to investigate the deception. Girls began telephoning former mayor Gabe Ca-
zares with sexual innuendos, slandered *St. Petersburg Times'* Betty Or-
sini when she dug into the story, and tried to silence Paulette Cooper,
the author of a 1971 book, *The Scandal of Scientology,* by cooking up
a scheme to steal her stationery and make it appear she had sent the
church office two bomb threats. Cooper was arrested and spent $19,000
defending herself, finally taking a lie detector test before authorities
dropped charges. Another church plot against her was named Operation
Freakout and was intended to get her placed in a mental institution.

To the surprise of Maraynes and Wallace, a pair of church "elders"
agreed to answer the charges on camera. Kenneth Whitman, the thirty-
two-year-old president of the church in the United States, and David
Gaiman, the worldwide head of public relations, didn't try to defend the
wrongdoing but laid it to overzealousness of a few church members. The
founder of Scientology certainly had nothing to do with it, they said,
until Wallace read to them from a Hubbard policy letter telling his followers that in the face of a perceived threat, "you are to immediately
evaluate and originate a PR campaign to destroy the person's repute and
to discredit them so thoroughly that they will be ostracized." *60 Minutes* was to return to Scientology as the eerie similarities to the last years
of Howard Hughes were played out in a Riverside, California court drama,
where Scientology franchise holders claimed the seventy-one-year-old
Hubbard—who once insisted he had lived through a series of incarna-
tions and was in fact seventy-four trillion years old—was a captive of
former underlings, while his son tried to have him declared legally insane or dead.

Baghwan Shree Rajneesh was the next charismatic leader to attract
*60 Minutes'* scrutiny. He, too, was unavailable, but had an eloquent
spokesperson, a beautiful woman named Ma Anand Sheela, for on-camera
riposte. Unlike Hubbard's disciples in Florida, the followers of this Indian mystic were totally successful in taking over a community.

Hewitt's newest producer, Monika Jensen, researched Baghwan for
months in Oregon's scrubby desert hills, interviewing disciples and residents of Wasco County. The guru had entered the United States in 1981
on a tourist visa and, like the Scientologists in Clearwater, his followers
had been less than above board in moving in on Antelope, a community

of fewer than 100 people 350 miles southest of Portland. The locals were at first amused by the "Baghwan people," most of whom were educated and affluent young Americans and Canadians. Calling themselves "sannyasins," the disciples wore crimson-hued clothes, leaned toward encounter therapies, indulged in what some called free sex, and prided themselves on combining the profit motive with environmental concerns. Antelope's attitude changed when the sannyasins grew to 800 in number, when they took political control of the town and won the right to incorporate part of their 64,000-acre ranch as Rajneeshpuram, Oregon's newest city. Rick Cantrell, a Wasco County commissioner and former judge, cast the favorable vote in the 2 to 1 decision. He was charged with conflict of interest for selling $17,000 worth of cattle to the Baghwan people just before the vote.

The Baghwan, who could be seen driving serenely along a rusty road with a young woman at his side in one of his twenty-seven Rolls-Royces, would not comment on his situation, including Immigration and Naturalization Service efforts to deport him. Jensen's camera crew was reduced to shooting the lineup of Rolls-Royces and to listen to Sheela, as his top aide was called, saying the luxury cars were just a whim. Sheela drove a silver-blue Mercedes-Benz herself, with a bumper sticker saying, "Jesus Saves, Moses Invests, Baghwan Spends." Frances Dickson, the wife of Antelope's postmaster, likened the commune to a working country club for the rich. "These are very affluent people, but they can't cope," she said. "They love it down there because they don't have to make any decision—not even what color clothes to wear." Former Antelope councilman Loren Reynolds said, "They've taken over our town, harassed us, and everybody here is just about ready to shoot them." Reynolds was going to move, he added, as soon as he could find someone other than a sect member to buy his house.

A report on the battle for the hearts and minds of mainstream Protestants after the Moral Majority took credit for having helped elect Ronald Reagan got *60 Minutes* into trouble with traditional church leaders. This time the producer was Marti Galovic, a young woman who had just joined Hewitt's producer stable. The manipulator was the Institute on Religion and Democracy, one of several small advocacy organizations bankrolled by conservative foundations such as the Scaife Family Charitable Trust and the Smith Richardson Foundation. The target: The National Council of Churches, made up of thirty-two member denominations that include 36.6 million Protestants, 52 percent of the U.S. total. The charge: collection plate donations were being misused by the Na-

tional Council of Churches, which had become unduly partisan on behalf of leftwing, even Marxist, causes in poor countries. In a scene that
church leaders were to denounce as unrepresentative, cameras panned
down the pews with the alms plate in a Methodist church in Logansport,
Indiana, while Morley Safer intoned that such donations were being spent
"on causes that seem closer to the Soviet-Cuban view of the world than
Logansport's." *The Gospel According to Whom?* cut quickly from the
collection plate to stock footage of Fidel Castro and marchers in Moscow's Red Square. The point, as Morley suggested repeatedly, was that
officials of the National Council of Churches (NCC) might be using
Sunday offerings to promote Marxist revolution in the Third World. The
1983 broadcast came on the heels of an overwrought *Reader's Digest*
attack that mixed innuendo, misleading statements, and selective quotes
from NCC documents. "The *Reader's Digest* article was expected and
predictable," said Methodist Bishop James Armstrong (no relation to the
Worldwide Church of God patriarch), "but the *60 Minutes* show could
do us great damage." Church spokesmen scored some telling points
against *The Gospel According to Whom?* It was true that substantial church
money had gone to a Nicaraguan government literacy campaign that was
suffused with revolutionary propaganda, but producer Marti Galovic and
Safer omitted the fact that the U.S. government had supported the same
program with far more money. At least one letter to *60 Minutes* called
the broadcast a piece of born-again McCarthyism. More soberly, *Newsweek* called the conflict between a church council trying to be a voice
for the voiceless by responding to oppression in the Third World and
mainline Protestant denominations' increasingly aging and reactionary
middle-class flocks a sign of the times.

Was *The Gospel According to Whom?* another piece of *60 Minutes*
entrepreneurial investigation? Galovic said the idea was hers, that she
had become interested in the subject when she heard Richard Ostling,
religion editor of *Time,* discuss some of the activities of the World Council
of Churches on a CBS radio broadcast. Two months later, however, Ostling wrote that the Institute on Religion and Democracy had come to
*Readers's Digest* and *60 Minutes* with the story. "The IRD's success is
a classic of neoconservative activisim. Adroitly gathering synergistic boosts
from like-minded groups and individuals, the institute has prepared a
number of hard-hitting research reports," the religion editor wrote.
"Rather than submitting them to obscure academic journals, it has sought
the interest of media outlets like *Reader's Digest* and CBS's *60 Minutes*
to give its conclusions mass exposure." The Federal Communications

Commission asked CBS to respond to complaints about *The Gospel According to Whom?* and to elaborate on why it believed the episode didn't come under the personal attack rule.

To the churches' chagrin, however, the FCC eventually concluded they were not entitled to invoke the personal attack rule because *The Gospel According to Whom?* had not addressed a "controversial issue of public importance." Officials of the United Church of Christ, who took the lead in filing the complaint, condemned the ruling. "If religion is not an issue of public importance in today's society or any society," said Beverly J. Chain, director of the church's Office of Communication, "I wonder by what definition an item does become of public importance."

*60 Minutes* made Catholics uncomfortable with a 1983 report on the marriage annulments that so scandalized Pope John Paul that the Vatican tightened the rules on the American Church.

With Paul Loewenwarter as producer, *Divorce Catholic Style* centered on Jane Frinzie, a middle-aged Milwaukee woman, whom Dominic Frinzie had divorced in 1979. To allow his new wife to partake in Catholic Holy Communion, Dominic asked the Milwaukee archdiocese to annul his first marriage, in effect declaring his long union with Jane never to have existed. No representative of the archdiocese would speak to Mike Wallace, but a couple of Catholic priests tried to explain. One of them admitted the psychological criteria had been broadened so much that practically any Catholic marriage could be declared null and void. Jane Frinzie's lawyer and most ardent supporter was her son, Joe, who said the dispensation, if granted, would also make him a bastard. Despite the efforts of mother and son, the annulment was granted in 1982. Because of the Vatican's opposition to the ease with which American archdioceses granted annulment, however, the Frinzie case was submitted to Rome for review.

A look at activist church leaders smuggling Salvadorans and Guatemalans into this country drew the wrath of the political right that year. Called *Underground*, the segment showed Quaker Jim Corbett bringing illegal aliens across the Mexican border, and telling Ed Bradley he wasn't sure how many—"it could be 250 or 300"—he had smuggled across.

Accuracy in Media accused *60 Minutes* of being sympathetic to the smuggling and of telling only half the story. The missing half, AIM asserted, was the proof that behind this effort to undermine the enforcement of immigration laws was no Christian charity or Quaker pacifism, but extreme left ideals out to "challenge U.S. foreign policy." But Bradley did ask the head of a California detention center for illegal immigrants why the detainees came to this country. "Strictly economic," the Immigration and Naturalization Service officer said. "That's all?" Bradley asked. "That's all," came the reply. A Salvadoran, whom Bradley interviewed through the chainlink fence, said he had come, "Because everything in my country great persecution, you know, because the situation politic is no good for us, you know. Besides, this country can give us an opportunity."

# 11

## Honorable
## Mention
### *Getting people out of jail*

The stark, probing spotlight of *60 Minutes* has not only caused punishment to rain down on polluters, sent hypocrites scurrying for cover, and put crooks behind bars; it has opened jail doors, built reputations, and shown us good guys we'd never suspect. Lenell Geter walked out of the Coffield Unit of the Texas Department of Corrections eleven days after Suzanne St. Pierre and Morley Safer spent half the December 4, 1983 broadcast telling his story. Earlier that year, Florida authorities released a Canadian financier after Monika Jensen and Ed Bradley reenacted his kidnapping by a pair of Sunshine State bounty hunters on the streets of Toronto; and California prosecutors blew hot and cold after Grace Diekhaus and Mike Wallace told the story of two Los Angeles doctors who, with the family's consent, turned off a terminally ill patient's life-support system, only to be charged with murder, tried, acquitted, and charged again after their acquittal was overturned. And support, fame, and money poured into 3819 West Adam Street in Chicago after the airing of Marva Collins's Cinderella story.

The conviction and sentencing to life imprisonment of twenty-six-year-old Geter for a fried chicken restaurant holdup that netted its perpetrator $615 were the stuff Texas gothic was made of.

The Geter whom Safer introduced to his viewers in a prison interview was a lanky, studious, reserved, and bespectacled type. He was a newcomer to Texas, one of six black South Carolina State College engineers who, in 1982, went to work for E Systems, a military and electronics contractor in Greenville, fifty-five miles northeast of Dallas. Geter became a suspect when a white woman in Greenville noticed him in a park near her home and complained to the police. The Greenville police sent his photograph to area police departments as a possible suspect in a rash of area robberies. In August, Greenville police arrested Geter and his roommate, Anthony Williams, while investigating the area stickups and robberies. Williams was acquitted of charges in a separate robbery arising from the investigation, but Dallas County prosecutor, Gerald Banks, brought his case against Geter to trial.

Defended by a court-appointed attorney who put together his defense in little more than a day, Geter was convicted by an all-white jury after five witnesses picked him out of a series of police photographs and after a Greenville police lieutenant testified that a South Carolina sheriff had told him Geter was "probably an outlaw." Nine E Systems workers testified that Geter was at work in Greenville, fifty miles from the Kentucky Fried Chicken outlet in the Dallas suburb of Balch Springs the day of the robbery, but none placed him at work at the precise time of the midafternoon crime. No gun, clothing, fingerprints, or other physical evidence was found. Despite the fact that Geter had no criminal record, he was given a life sentence.

Safer interviewed the principals, who said the obvious things. Prosecutor Banks was sure justice had triumphed, that Geter was a Jekyll-and-Hyde personality lawbreaker. Defense lawyer Edwin Sigel said the prosecutors had refused to interview witnesses who, he said, could prove Geter was at work when the robbery was committed. "In the initial stages this was a matter of racism—he wouldn't have been arrested if he wasn't black," Sigel said of his client. Safer interviewed E Systems workers, who had become determined crusaders to right a wrong, including two employees not among the group gathered by Sigel for the trial. One, draftsman Debra Cotton, said she had talked to Geter twenty minutes before the crime took place fifty miles away and another, senior designer engineer Dan Walker, said he could place Geter at work some twenty-five to forty minutes after the 3:20 P.M. robbery. And Safer and crew went to South Carolina, where Bamberg County Sheriff Ed Darnell said he had never told Greenville police that Geter was "probably an outlaw," that, on the contrary, he had said Geter had no criminal background. *In Jail* brought pressure on Dallas County District Attorney Henry Wade to reopen the case, and angry swipes from Wade, who claimed that the defense was trying the case through the media. As the local and national press picked up the story, Prosecutor Banks called the Geter affair a frustrating media circus but, by midweek, Texas Governor Mark White said he was "very concerned" about Geter's sentence and asked the Texas Court of Criminal Appeals to hear the appeal as soon as possible. Ten days after the broadcast, Geter was granted a new trial and released from prison on $10,000 bond posted by a coworker. Four days later, Wade said he would drop all charges if Geter would take and pass a lie detector test. Geter had so little confidence in the fairness of a polygraph test administered by Dallas County officials that he refused. The prosecution, in turn, refused to drop charges, and April 9, 1984, was set for the start of a new trial.

Two weeks before the trial date, Wade announced that his office had found another suspect in the Balch Springs robbery and asked that all charges against Geter be dropped. In what Mike Wallace said everybody at *60 Minutes* hoped would be the last Update on Lenell Geter, he revealed that four of the five eyewitnesses who had picked out Geter now identified the other man as the robber. A pained debate began in Dallas over what had gone wrong and how often the same thing might happen. Attorneys not involved in the case told reporters Geter was the victim of law enforcement people and of a D.A.'s office less interested in finding the truth than in getting a conviction. One lawyer who had tried many similar cases wondered how many other Lenell Geters the nation's prisons held.

That *60 Minutes* had this kind of power was first evidenced in 1979 when producer Leslie Edwards and Dan Rather began calling local and state officials in New Jersey about the thirty-year sentence for kidnapping handed down a year earlier against a high school teacher named Mims Hackett. Within a month, authorities began calling *60 Minutes* back, saying it had been decided the thirty-eight-year-old Hackett should be considered for parole. Before *Equal Justice?* was aired that December, Governor Brendan Byrne had paroled the teacher.

It was one of those stories that had come through the mail. Hackett's wife, Bernice, wrote to 555 West 57th Street asking for help. They were skeptical on the eighth floor. They were reluctant and doubtful, as they told her, especially since a jury had already spoken. But the facts were weird, and Edwards went to Orange, New Jersey, a community of tree-lined avenues, family-owned businesses, and row houses less than fifteen miles from Manhattan. Orange was 50 percent black, but the power structure, as Rather said in introducing the story, had remained white. Hackett, a father of six, active in the Parent-Teacher Association, youth groups, and church, had never been in trouble with the law until he decided to run for the city council. When Rather asked Bill Cook, a man long active in local politics, what Hackett's mistake might have been, the answer was to the point: "His fatal mistake probably was being born black, which he couldn't do anything about, and being black and running for political office in Orange, which he could have done something about."

Edwards, himself a twenty-eight-year-old black New Yorker who had come to *60 Minutes* from PBS after producing an eerily prescient documentary on Iran, spent months in Orange and nearby Union City where Hackett had taught. As the schoolteacher had moved into his council campaign against four white candidates in early 1976, the local white authorities tried to get him indicted for kidnapping one Larry Moss. A grand jury declined, but when it appeared certain Hackett would win the election, police again went before the grand jury. One week before the vote, they got the indictment and quickly leaked it to newspapers. Hackett lost by eighty votes. In November, he was charged with atrocious assault and battery, two counts of threatening to kill, and kidnapping. According to police, Moss told them he had been abducted, beaten, taken to East Orange and severely beaten by three men, one of whom was Hackett. Police made a major point of the fact that Hackett's car definitely was involved. The teacher maintained he was home the night Moss claimed he was abducted but that he had loaned his car to a relative to go looking for belongings taken from his apartment in a burglary and that the relative had in turn loaned the car to somebody named Clarence Williams. A few days into the trial in Newark, Hackett's attorney dropped the case and went on vacation, leaving the defense to an assistant. On the witness stand, Larry Moss, his brother Anthony, and a friend all identified Hackett as the driver of the car the night of the crime. The teacher was found guilty and sentenced.

Edwards' first coup was tracking down Larry Moss, also known as Little Dude, a sometime police informer who was willing to say on camera that the idea of the abduction had been dreamed up by Orange detectives, that they had harassed him, picked him up, and threatened to bust him if he didn't cooperate in the scheme, but that the kidnapping had never taken place. At the trial, the prosecution had questioned whether Clarence Williams, to whom Hackett's relative had loaned the car the night of the alleged crime, ever existed. After nine months, Edwards found Williams. He, too, said there had never been any kidnapping.

Hackett was paroled after having served eight months of his thirty-year sentence. By the time *Equal Justice?* was broadcast, he was back teaching science at Union City High School, but as a convicted felon, on parole, he could not run for public office.

Stanley Jaffe was neither young and black nor a threat to the local political status quo, but when *60 Minutes* aired his story he was serving a thirty-five-year sentence for land sale irregularities, plus one count of failing to appear for a pretrial hearing in rural Putnam County, Florida. Florida legal authorities were baffled at the harshness of his punishment, but as the man who prosecuted him told Ed Bradley on camera, the county sure didn't like outsiders coming in and swindling people.

The trouble began in May 1981, when fifty-six-year-old Jaffe failed to appear for a pretrial hearing in Palatka, the county seat fifty miles south of Jacksonville. The prominent Toronto land developer was facing charges involving criminal violations of the state's Uniform Land Sales Practices Law by a Florida real estate firm Jaffe owned. Faced with the loss of $137,000 it had posted in bail, the Accredited Surety and Casualty Company decided not to wait for a formal extradition request and instead sent Tim Johnsen and Daniel Kear to Canada to bring Jaffe back. Like most modern bounty hunters, Johnsen and Kear figured they would get 10 percent of the bond, plus expenses and a bonus.

Jaffe's daughter reenacted the scene in front of a Toronto highrise for Bradley and producer Monika Jensen's crew. Her father was returning to his condominium from an afternoon jog when the two freelance deputies stuck what looked like a suspiciously un-Canadian police badge in his face, hustled him to a car, handcuffed him, and sped the seventy-eight miles to the border at Niagara Falls. Alerted by his daughter, Niagara Falls police refused to intervene when Jaffe appealed to them at the airport. Johnsen and Kear took Jaffe aboard a chartered jet, waiting to fly to Florida.

Thirty-five years was a stiff sentence for violating the 1963 Florida Uniform Land Sales Practices Law, especially since no one else had ever been charged under it. But beefy prosecutor Stephen Boyles had no apologies. The law was there to deter; Jaffe should have thought of the consequences when he jumped bail.

In Ottawa, a government spokesman told Bradley that bounty hunting might be a quaint relic of frontier justice in Florida; in Canada you would call it kidnapping. More than any other nation, Canada had scrupulously cooperated in complying with U.S. requests for the extradition of fugitives. Under the 1971 U.S.–Canada treaty, Florida Governor Robert Graham could have requested Jaffe's extradition. When *Time* looked into the story, it discovered that Boyles never provided the governor with the necessary documentation.

*Bounty Hunter* aired February 6, 1983. Florida authorities' initial re-action was to hang tough. The State Parole and Probation Commission rebuffed State Department requests for Jaffe's parole. When it appeared parole officials might yield, Boyles filed new charges against Jaffe, this time alleging organized fraud, which carried a maximum sentence of thirty years. Governor Graham refused to intervene. Canada made legal moves in the U.S. district court in Jacksonville and charged bounty hunters Johnsen and Kear with kidnapping. The dispute got so hot that Attorney General William French Smith and Secretary of State George Shultz sided with Canada. Wrote Shultz, "As no good reason appears why the extra-dition treaty was not utilized to secure Mr. Jaffe's return, it is perfectly understandable that the government of Canada is outraged by his alleged kidnapping." Jaffe was paroled.

*Charged with Murder* was a Grace Diekhaus-Mike Wallace inquiry into the flip side of high-tech medicine, a case closely followed by the medical profession because it was the first time criminal charges were brought against doctors for stopping the treatment of a terminally ill pa-tient.

Los Angeles prosecutors alleged that Drs. Robert Nejdl and Neil Barber misled the family of Clarence Herbert. After routine surgery, Herbert had fallen into irreversible coma. The doctors huddled with the elderly patient's wife. They had stopped all extraordinary efforts to save Herbert, but he still had some slight brain activity. Now they wanted permission to cut off all food and water to allow him to die in dignity. Herbert lived for another eleven days, as Wallace explained, and the prosecution charged Nejdl, and Barber had urged the wife to agree to cutting off the life support in order to cover their own malpractice. In March 1983, Los Angeles municipal court judge Brian Crahan dis-missed murder charges against the two physicians, branding the allega-tion of malpractice sheer speculation. Judge Crahan said if doctors found themselves facing jail for unhooking patients, they might be discouraged from ever trying to save them.

And there were other instances of dubious justice. Three weeks after *Bounty Hunter,* producer Jim Jackson and Harry Reasoner presented *Open and Shut Case,* the story of William Jackson, who was identified by two women as the black man who had raped them in 1977. Jackson was tried, convicted, and put away, but the rapes continued and a second Jackson, also black, confessed to the crimes in 1982. In October 1979, Reasoner reported the story of a twenty-year-old girl who stole a five-dollar bill and got seven and a half years, and an additional five years for burning the mattress in her Florida cell.

"Few people ever would have heard of Terry Jean Moore if she hadn't ended up pregnant by a prison guard and sharing her cell with her baby," Reasoner said, introducing the story. Produced by Drew Phillips, *The $5 Bill* and the outcry it provoked when Terry's baby was born at the Florida Correctional Institution, made the parole board release mother and baby a few weeks after the broadcast. "I think that maybe knowing *60 Minutes* was coming might have added a little pressure," said Jackie Steinberg, Terry's Legal Aid Service lawyer.

A federal grand jury in Denver dismissed indictments against the law man hero of the April 27, 1980 segment called *Walking Small in Pitkin County*. Sheriff Dick Kienast had incurred the wrath of the FBI and the Drug Enforcement Agency for believing that upholding the Constitution was slightly more important than using borderline undercover tactics to snoop on suspected drug traffickers.

Pitkin County is ski country: Aspen, Snowmass, Ashcroft, and Buttermilk Mountain; three-room condos selling for half a million; and old miners' cottages selling for the same. The FBI and the DEA said the county had become a major center for the so-called recreational drugs of the upper middle classes and that Sheriff Kienast was a cop gone wrong. In crimes of violence, robbery, traffic safety, drunk driving, even open drug violations, the forty-year-old sheriff was as tough as anyone enforcing the law, but when it came to people's rights of privacy or undercover police operations, he refused to cooperate with the Feds.

Morley Safer described Kienast's department as "a very relaxed, unmacho atmosphere. No badges of rank, no rank at all. Very much a beansprout and friends of the earth look" and went on to show Kienast not only had the backing of the fast après-ski set, but of Aspen's more solid citizens and of Mayor Herman Idell, who believed the FBI and the DEA were going after Aspen because it was glamorous. "There's a lovely town down valley about fifty miles," Idell said. "It's called Silt. Silt, Colorado. Now, I don't suggest the DEA is ever going to go into Silt. Yet I assure you there are drugs in Silt." An FBI investigation of Kienast was terminated shortly after *Walking Small in Pitkin County*, produced by Greg Cooke, was aired. Three years later at the height of the John Z. DeLorean affair, the Reagan administration admitted it was Justice Department policy to concentrate drug enforcement on seeking highly visible convictions of celebrities and glamour people.

Corporate underdogs have profited from having their David-versus-Goliath struggles with bigger competitors publicized. A. H. Robins

Company saw its earnings increase on its Sergeant flea collars and pet-care products after Mike Wallace told how the Hartz Mountain Corporation had tried to muscle the Sergeant products off supermarket shelves. (Without admitting or denying guilt, Hartz agreed to pay $42.5 million to settle an antitrust suit brought by Robins.) Individuals and institutions who have benefited from *60 Minutes'* attention include researchers working in difficult areas of medicine, from Reye's syndrome and Alzheimer's Disease to Huntington's Disease. The latter was the subject of *Time Bomb,* a wrenching Barry Lando-Mike Wallace inquiry into the incurable genetic disorder that generally is detected only in midlife. The 1982 story explored the emotions of children who are the potential time bombs, concentrating on two English families in which the mothers had developed HD. *Time Bomb* was praised by Dr. Nancy Walker, the administrator of federal grants for research into the disease, and by HD organizations. A year later, Lando and Wallace took up the subject of children fathered by American servicemen in Vietnam and the Pearl S. Buck Foundation's attempts to find, document, and bring to the United States some of the 4,000 Amerasian children. Called *Honor Thy Children,* the segment told of the herculean task the Buck Foundation was undertaking in the absence of even diplomatic relations between Washington and Hanoi and of U.S. naturalization statutes demanding not only that the foreign-born prove American parentage but that the American father actually recognize his paternity. The broadcast showed Wallace in the streets of Ho Chi Minh City talking to youngsters with traits ranging from half-Nordic to half-Negroid, and to their mothers holding up dog-eared snapshots of long-departed men. "Ours is a reluctant, narrow audience," said Foundation director Don Shade, Jr., a year after *Honor Thy Children* was aired. "We had expected a modest response. Instead, we got ex-servicemen, deep into new lives, call up and ask us to help find their children."

Support for Dr. Jerry Jampolsky and his Center for Attitudinal Healing in Tiburon, California skyrocketed after the December 1979 airing of *Helping,* an Al Wasserman-Morley Safer piece on children suffering from advanced cancers. "It is not a hospital that treats the body, it's a place that treats the spirit—that part of medicine that doctors often ignore," said Safer in introducing us to an eleven-year-old boy with bone cancer helping a fourteen-year-old brain cancer victim transcend his self-pity and come to realize that without sharing—even pain—life is a waste. Dr. Jampolsky was to call *Helping* the media event that "got the message across." Four years later, there were thirty-five attitudinal healing centers.

Bob Meehan's Palmer Drug Abuse Program in Houston was unknown for eight years until *People* magazine reported that the fifteen-year-old daughter of Carol Burnett and TV producer Joe Hamilton had kicked the drug habit. The Philip Scheffler-Dan Rather story, *PDAP*, that aired in January 1980 was less than kind to Meehan, quizzing him on his apparently inflated success figures, the $10,000 parents paid to place their teenagers in his program, his $100,000 a year salary and consultant fees, and the PDAP detoxification methods, which, critics charged on the air, merely shifted the young people's dependency on drugs to a dependency on Meehan. A week later, a viewer wrote, "Drug pushers are making billions [and] you dare to knock Bob Meehan for making a hundred thousand dollars a year saving our children from the pushers?" Within a year there were PDAP centers in several other cities.

An unforgettable strip of *60 Minutes* film showed chubby Dr. Jerold Petrofsky puffing to keep up with a young woman on a tricycle with electrodes attached to her hip, knee, and ankle joints as she tooled across the Wright State University campus in Dayton, Ohio. Nan Davis was totally paralyzed from the waist down in a car accident and in 1982 became the first of Dr. Petrofsky's patients to stand up on her own with the help of his electronic prothesis that attached one end of the electrodes to the limbs and the other to a microcomputer programmed to transmit an intricate series of impulses to the muscles. In 1980, there was a sympathetic portrait of Dr. Lawrence Burton, a fiercely independent cancer researcher rejected by the American Cancer Society, and a compassionate look at football players crippled by injuries sustained on artificial turf.

Hewitt and Company rang out the Seventies with an inspiring fairy tale. The Cinderella story was so marvelous it was made into a movie of the week and years later would still bring smiles of fond recollection to the faces of *60 Minutes* aficionados.

*Marva* was about a teacher in Chicago—black, fortyish, tall, angular, and passionately concerned with underprivileged children who have been deemed "unteachable" by the system. Marva Collins runs the Westside Preparatory School, a storefront school dedicated to the proposition that learning isn't dictated by race, neighborhood, or money. "When life gives you lemons, make lemonade," is one of Marva Collins's adages posted on the orange walls of the former bank building. "I'm no superwoman. Everything works when the teacher works."

As a teacher for fourteen years and a mother of three, Marva had understood the effects adult expectations have on children. So often, she would say, white children were taught they could accomplish everything; black children were taught they couldn't. White children were praised; black children were rejected and humiliated. And when black children failed, the failure was chalked up to race, culture, and income. "I tell my students a different story," she said. "They hear over and over again that they are the smartest children in the world. I demand that they perform. In fact, I tell them they either have to learn or die—and I haven't lost a student yet. All my children read *Self-Reliance* by Ralph Waldo Emerson. You see, we can't believe we can't achieve."

Marva Collins quit the Chicago school system in 1975, utterly disillusioned with the rules, the unions, the failure, and outraged at teachers preferring to go on "easy" student outings rather than do some hard work in the classroom. Using $5,000 saved from pension funds, she started her school, with ten students who met at her house to study hand-copied textbooks and old books she retrieved from trash bins. Supported fully by her husband, Clarence, she created an atmosphere of discipline and love that worked miracles. In her class, the students didn't break for recess in the winter. Many were too poor to afford hard-soled shoes, so she turned a disadvantage into a source of pride by making them feel they were too busy working to play outside. When most second-graders were singing "Jingle Bells," Marva's class was performing an operetta she had written, or re-creating the musical, *Don't Bother Me, I Can't Cope.* "Because I taught a different way and demanded more, I used to find hate notes in my mail from black teachers," she told *Essence* in 1981. "Once I was standing up in assembly and a black teacher actually knocked me down. She was screaming, 'Everybody thinks you're some kind of god.' And I guess to prove she wasn't afraid of me she bowled me over."

The Marva Collins story, first picked up by the *Chicago Sun-Times,* had producer Suzanne St. Pierre enthusiastic from the beginning. When Morley Safer arrived to start filming, he, too, was captivated. "Who is Marva Collins and why is everyone saying those wonderful things about her?" he began, standing among the urban blight, the winos, and drug addicts of West Garfield Park and inviting us to come with him inside 3819 West Adam Street.

In the classroom, he explained there were no frills, that the thirty children had no art classes, no music, no gym, not even recess, and no discipline problems. A boy named Cyrus told Morley he liked to read in bed so he could dream about what he read, that his favorite authors were Booker T. Washington and Hans Christian Andersen. Marva explained it all had to do with the standards people set for children when they first begin, that the attitude in her one-and-a-half room school was that once kids learn how to learn, they kind of live to learn. She took to St. Pierre, Morley, and the film crew and found the final broadcast totally positive. Viewers loved it, too. "Could you please clone Marva Collins for every school in the United States," a viewer wrote, "and send the first one to Great Falls, Montana."

It almost happened. A publisher offered her a cool million to open 100 Marva Collins schools nationally. The catch: she would have to use his materials exclusively. And the newly elected Reagan administration put out feelers to nominate Marva Collins Secretary of Education. Instead, the *60 Minutes* exposure opened a financial spigot that allowed her to make plans for accommodating some of the children on the waiting list that now swelled to 700 students. Almost $50,000 in contributions rolled into Westside Prep and another $75,000 came from Hollywood for the rights to her story and the school. Cicely Tyson was cast as Marva and came and sat in Marva's classroom for three days in preparation for the role. The TV movie, which aired on CBS in 1981, provoked a backlash from some Chicago public school teachers. A newspaper published by an organization of substitute teachers charged Marva and her school were " a media hoax," that she was not taking in the rejects of public schools but middle-class children hand-picked for high ability. Two Chicago radio and television reporters did their own investigative reporting, contending Marva had misrepresented her credentials; that she had plagiarized another educator's ideas; that she refused to release her students' test scores; and that Westside Prep teachers mistreated children. Morley Safer stood by his original reporting when the controversy became a national story and told *Newsweek* the reports aired in Chicago were "outrageous" and "loaded with inaccuracies."

Meanwhile, Marva used the contributions, the TV movie income, and money earned from speaking engagements to rent space on the second floor of an old bank building, a few blocks away on Madison Street, and increased her enrollment to 200. Westside Prep, she said in *Marva Collins' Way,* the book she wrote with Civia Tamarkin, was not a "one-room fairytale." She was going to show that good education could happen on any scale.

# 12

## Affairs of
## State
### National issues

Barry Lando and Mike Wallace were in Damascus and on the air with Syrian foreign minister Abdel Halim Khaddam and Lebanese Druse leader Walid Jumblat Sunday, January 8, 1984, four days after the release of downed flier Robert O. Goodman signaled Syrian restraint. The two Moslem leaders' perspective and minimal requirements for a lasting solution to Lebanon were far from the White House position, but neither the White House nor the State Department was willing to provide *60 Minutes* with a spokesman.

Providing air time for the other side has irritated successive occupants of the White House and State Department policymakers since Jane Fonda and a film crew went to Hanoi in 1972, but it was only with the Iran crisis and the expansion of satellite transmission facilities to Third World capitals that such instant "global village" communications were possible. World War II and Korea were covered from only one side. No Allied network correspondents in Berlin or Pyongyang relayed the Wehrmacht and Kuomintang point of view (German members of the Washington press corps were interned as enemy aliens after 1941). Vietnam was the first television war and the first conflict in which TV news-

159

men tried for the "reverse angle"—in some cases quite literally, as when
Sean Flynn was killed in one GI combat engagement when he followed
his cameraman's impulse to run forward for the enemy's POV (as point
of view is abbreviated in film jargon). Hewitt was an early practitioner
of this television news instinct for getting the other side's POV. He sent
Reasoner and Wallace to cover opposite sides in fighting in Northern
Ireland, Nigeria, and the Middle East, as we have seen. It makes for
"value conflict" and exciting television. By telling the story in dynamic
terms, we understand better. "Our best hope to avoid war is to understand the enemy," wrote Sam Keen in *Faces of the Enemy* in 1984.

   But governments do not want us to understand the other side's POV.
The instinct of national leaders is to project hostile and divisive emotions on the outsider (in the paranoid imagination *alien* always means
*evil)* and in most countries television is a tool of government. Satellites
may expand horizons but when questions do not coincide with national
policy, to inquire may be unpatriotic. When Wallace asked Menachem
Begin about the second-class status of Arabs in Israel, the Prime Minister said, "How can you ask me these questions?" Answered Mike,
"I'm a journalist." Television crews had tape of Russian soldiers patrolling the streets of Kabul during the first days of the Soviet invasion
of Afghanistan in December 1979. Soon the Western journalists were
put on planes and shipped out of the country. The Thatcher government
severely restricted TV coverage of the Falkland War, and the Reagan
administration banned the media from the invasion of Grenada. In the
aftermath of the invasion, the Joint Chiefs of Staff asked Winant Sidle—the former public affairs officer at the Pentagon who helped Lando
and Wallace get to officers who could contradict Lieutenant Colonel Anthony Herbert's assertions of murder of Vietcong suspects—to develop
guidelines for TV coverage of future military actions. Sidle's problem
was not secrecy—the press had always been willing to respect agreed-
upon security strictures—but that coverage is too negative. "They are
always looking for somebody to hit over the head," he said. Or television is being "used" by the other side. When the 444-day Iranian
hostage crisis was over, Walter Cronkite's executive producer Sanford
Socolow was asked whether the American networks hadn't been used
by the supporters of Ayatollah Ruhollah Khomeini. "We get used all
the time," he replied. "Presidential news conferences—we're used."

   Four months into the hostage crisis, the Carter administration brought
extraordinary pressure on CBS to suppress a Lando-Wallace piece, which
tried to examine the root causes of the seething hatred of Americans that
television cameras captured every day on the faces outside the occupied

embassy. White House press secretary Jody Powell pleaded with Don Hewitt not to run the story, appealing to his patriotism. President Jimmy Carter got on the phone to CBS News President William Leonard to tell him not to broadcast the segment, while Secretary of State Cyrus Vance and presidential counsel Lloyd Cutler called Lando and Wallace. Jody Powell kept asking Don what he cared for in life, what he believed in, what he loved. At the end, Hewitt recalled, he had had enough: "Listen, you . . . If you're saying what I think you're saying, I loved and cared about this country before you were born. I think all you care about is the Massachusetts primary, if you must know!"

Lando and Wallace had prepared a long, painful segment for Sunday, March 2, 1980—the 120th day of captivity for the hostages in Teheran. The piece tried to come to grips with the big "why." Why did Iranians hate Americans so much? Lando and Wallace had been in Iran a number of times and, as Wallace was to tell Stephan Lesher two months later, this was not a coup d'etat by a handful of colonels or the triumph of far left partisans coming down from the hills. Perhaps two-thirds of the Iranian people supported this revolution.

The embassy had been seized November 4, 1979—three days before Massachusetts Senator Edward M. Kennedy announced his presidential candidacy—and since then the Carter White House had tried to obtain the release of the hostages. Spirits were lifted briefly in late January when the Canadian government announced that six Americans working at the U.S. embassy had been sheltered by Canadian embassy personnel after the takeover and secretly flown out of Iran, but on February 11, Iran's new president, Abolhassan Bani-Sadr, laid down the conditions for the release of the hostages: the United States would have to acknowledge "past crimes"; promise not to interfere in Iran's internal affairs; and recognize Iran's right to obtain extradition of the deposed monarch. Twelve days later, a U.N. commission arrived in Teheran to review the Iranian grievances, but nothing came of the mission.

Simply called *The Iran File,* the Lando-Wallace piece would remind *60 Minutes* viewers (there would be 40 million of them that first Sunday in March): that it was the CIA that had restored the exiled Mohammed Reza Pahlavi to his throne in 1953; that according to Senate Foreign Relations Committee reports, the CIA had helped set up the Savak, the Shah's hated secret police, which tortured tens of thousands and, during the chaotic last months of the regime, murdered thousands. The program would say that there had been plenty of warnings that if Washington allowed the ailing Shah, in exile in Mexico, to enter the United States for medical treatment, the reaction in Teheran would be furious; that the

State Department had spelled out the risk of mob rule and hostage taking; that suggestions of beefed-up security around the embassy compound in Teheran had been ignored.

*The Iran File* would be the second *60 Minutes* piece on the crisis. Hours after the embassy take-over the previous November, Lando had flown to Teheran. He knew Sadegh Ghotbzadeh from a still earlier piece he and Wallace had done on Khomeini while the Ayatollah was in exile in France. Ghotbzadeh refused to see the *60 Minutes* producer, but Lando managed to pull enough strings to make Mike Wallace the first American reporter to be granted an interview with Khomeini. The ground rules had been stiff for the November 18 interview at the Ayatollah's residence in Qum, 100 miles from Teheran. All questions had been approved in advance, and Khomeini would answer no others. It was a turbulent Sunday in Iran. Three of the hostages were put on display pending their promised release, and rumors were flying that the remaining Americans would be put on trial.

Sitting in his stockinged feet next to the imam, Wallace had learned from Khomeini's lips that unless the Shah was returned, the hostages would not be freed. There were two reasons for this, Khomeini said through his interpreter: the Shah and his family had plundered the country; and, more important, "we want him back to show the extent of the crimes committed by this person during thirty-seven years of his rule." Mike tried to break the ground rules, asking if there was no room for compromise. The Iranian interpreter refused to translate. Mike persisted, "If the President says he refuses to return the Shah and if the imam says he will not free the hostages, then what—what can be the answer?" The interpreter said this was not in the submitted questions, but Wallace made him ask in Farsi anyway. The answer was that Khomeini wouldn't even listen.

Wallace was bold enough to ask—and obtain—Khomeini's permission to go to the embassy and see the hostages. When he and his crew got back to Teheran, however, they were not allowed into the embassy. The militants claimed to be students loyal to Khomeini but, as the world was learning, the degree to which he controlled them was unclear. At times they disagreed openly with the Revolutionary Council. The Khomeini interview was nevertheless sent to New York via satellite and, thanks to the eight-hour time difference, *The Ayatollah* was the lead-in story that evening.

Nothing but frenzied hatred came out of Iran during the next two months. Every night, Walter Cronkite ticked off the number of days the hostages had been held, constant reminders that kept the nation's attention focused on the crisis and tried to buy time and patience for Chief of Staff Hamilton Jordan's cloak and dagger dealings with Teheran. Through a pair of French lawyers, Jordan had met secretly in Paris with Ghotbzadeh, who was fast becoming a fixture on American television with his almost daily press briefings (later, he would be arrested, tried, and executed for treason). To show good will and good intentions, Ghotbzadeh suggested the Carter administration arrange for the timely demise of the Shah in his Panamanian hideaway.

For Lando and Wallace, the projected background on the whole Iranian tragedy began to fall into place in the third week of February when Joseph Sisco, the twenty-five-year State Department veteran whose last post before retirement had been undersecretary to Henry Kissinger, agreed to see them.

Lando and Wallace flew to Washington where Sisco was now chancellor of the American University. The former diplomat tried to paint a balanced picture of American-Iranian relations since the early 1950s, but when pressed by Wallace had to admit the United States shared a measure of responsibility. Turning to Bani-Sadr's three-point demands—admission of past wrongs, a pledge not to interfere in domestic affairs in the future, and agreeing not to block Iranian efforts to get back the Shah and the wealth he allegedly embezzled—Wallace asked, "Are those demands in your—I mean you're a trained diplomat. Are those unacceptable?" Sisco sidestepped the question, saying that in the present situation there could be only one negotiator, President Carter. Did Sisco think *60 Minutes* would be wrong in bringing out this agonizing backgrounder at this time? On the contrary, the university chancellor answered. It was important that this material be evaluated by the American public.

The White House was well informed by Sisco and, perhaps, by the FBI, which had helped *60 Minutes* to locate the Shah's chief of police hiding out in California. What did the White House object to? To the airing, at this time, of the Iranian grievances against the Shah and the United States. More specifically, the President feared that exposing the CIA-Savak connection and the names involved might play into the hands of the militants holding the hostages.

Strong stuff. But CBS News had not been through the Watergate upheavals without learning a few lessons on how to handle White House muscle. Leonard suggested the President make a spokesman available to comment on the CIA-Savak link. The White House came back saying that could be done "later." On Friday, when Hamilton Jordan's French go-betweens to Ghotbzadeh threatened to resign because Carter was leaning too heavily on them, Wallace learned from Vance that twenty-four hours before the ailing Shah had been admitted to the United States the previous October 22, the Secretary of State had assured the President the embassy in Teheran could be protected.

The White House press corps learned of the administration efforts to delete *The Iran File*. When *The New York Times*' Les Brown called Leonard to confirm the story, he was told the White House complaints were "framed in relation to concern about the delicacy of the state of the arrangements with the hostages."

*The Iran File* was unique. Never had a television news story inflicted so much national pain.

The segment began with a clip of Mike Wallace interviewing the Shah in his Teheran palace in October 1977. The monarch was at the height of his power and was supremely self-confident. In the Organization of Petroleum Exporting Countries (OPEC), Iran was teaching the West a lesson. The Shah's army was the most powerful in the region. The Shah was the driving force behind efforts to raise the living standards of his country's rural poor. Communications by road and air were improved, and outlying areas, which had formerly been ruled by local magnates, were brought under the control of the central government. Some underground opposition continued, inspired by disgruntled vested interests, partly by the banned Tudeh Party, and partly by what the government described as "Islamic Marxists." But all opposition movements were defeated by the vigilance of the security agencies, which operated not only in Iran but also in some of the Iranian diplomatic missions abroad. This was an irritant in some host countries and aroused unfavorable comments in sections of the Western media, which accused the Shah of violating human rights in his suppression of dissidents.

Mike asked the Shah about torture and was told that such practices might have been used in the past but police no longer tortured people.

WALLACE: I talked just today to a man, whom I believe, who told about torture.
SHAH: How many years ago?
WALLACE: Within—I want to be very careful. Not yesterday.
SHAH: Ah, well, maybe. I don't know.
WALLACE: The word has gone out to stop it?
SHAH: To stop what?
WALLACE: Torture.
SHAH: But a long time ago, yes.

Next, Wallace introduced us to the man who had told him about torture back in 1976. Raji Samghabadi was an Iranian journalist now writing for *Time*. Samghabadi's brother had been tortured by the Savak the
very week Wallace interviewed the Shah. Still more painfully, Samghabadi told how his brother had been hospitalized with aftershocks from
torture in December 1977 when President Carter was in Teheran. To ring
in 1978, Carter was with the American press at the Teheran Hilton. The
President gave a speech saying America had never had such a good friend,
that he had been profoundly touched by the way the Shah took care of
his people. Samghabadi had dashed from the Carter press bash at the
Hilton to his brother's hospital bed.

Wallace got Max McCarthy, a three-term Democratic congressman
who in 1976 had been the embassy press officer in Teheran, to confirm
the story. Now Washington bureau chief for the *Buffalo News*, Mc-
Carthy remembered Samghabadi's brother and the torture that left him
like a zombie.

From there, *The Iran File* introduced us to Jesse Leaf, who in the
early 1970s had been the CIA's Iran analyst and who could confirm that
interrogation techniques were part of the training CIA operatives gave
Savak recruits. And part of intensive interrogation classes included torture methods, although Americans had little to teach Iranians in this do-
main. "They have a long, long glowing history in that part of the world
of torture," Leaf said.

After talking about Savak attempts to murder an Iranian newspaper
editor living in Paris, Wallace turned to the Shah's secret police activities in the United States, specifically the Savak's checking up on Iranian
students. How did Wallace know the Savak had been operating in the
United States? Because he had asked the Shah in that 1976 interview.
Was the Savak in America with the knowledge and consent of the U.S.
government? Mike had asked. "I think it is," the Shah had answered.

The Shah's response had caused intense embarrassment for Secretary of State Henry Kissinger, who had categorically denied U.S.
knowledge of Savak activities in America. Wallace maintained Savak
operatives had kept spying on dissident Iranian students in American
universities, sometimes relying on FBI information transmitted via the
CIA. And the activities had continued during the Carter years. According to a 1978 *Washington Post* report, then Deputy Attorney General
Benjamin Civiletti warned Zbigniew Brzezinski that Savak was involved
in significant police, security, and nondiplomatic activities. Why had the
U.S. government tolerated this?

For an answer, Wallace turned to a 1977 interview he had done with the Shah's ambassador to Washington, Ardeshir Zahedi. It was a tit for tat, the ambassador had maintained. "If the United States government does not want it, we are not going to insist and we shall ask them to leave," Zahedi said. "At the same time, we shall ask your people to leave my country." Washington had not been ready to pay that price. Iran was a vital listening post for the CIA, with a thousand miles and more of border with the Soviet Union. This meant turning a blind eye to the excesses of the Shah's regime. Even worse, perhaps, Kissinger ordered American diplomats in Teheran to cut themselves off from opposition parties, from popular forces, former CIA officer Richard Cottam told Wallace.

To reconstitute the chaotic last months of the Shah's regime, Lando, with the FBI's help, tracked down its chief of police, Reza Razmi, living under an assumed name in Fresno, California. As the Shah had fled Iran, Razmi had entered the United States in New York, asking for CIA protection. The revolutionary government in Teheran wanted to try Razmi for crimes against humanity and lodged an informal protest with the State Department, and Secretary Vance had promised to look into the matter. In the meantime, the CIA referred Razmi to the FBI. The FBI office in San Francisco referred Razmi to the local police.

Lando tried to talk to Razmi in Fresno, but the former police chief refused. *The Iran File* ended with the Joseph Sisco interview. There was to be one last stab of pain here. Wallace read to Sisco from a Senate Foreign Relations Committee report about CIA-Savak collusions in the United States, and about one instance when the Savak had planned to murder an American. The information came from a man who had told the CIA he had been asked by Savak operatives to kill a U.S. citizen. The diplomat didn't know what to say. "Well, you can't possibly condone anything like that, and I don't think—I don't think of anyone who does," he finally said with a sigh.

Wallace summed up. It was the decision of President Carter and Secretary Vance to allow the Shah to enter the United States that triggered the seizure of the embassy in Teheran, "a decision about which they'll have some tough questions to answer once the hostages are free."

Neither Carter nor Vance was to answer those questions. Were the White House eyes on the election primaries? A month after *The Iran File,* forty minutes before polls opened in the Wisconsin and Kansas primaries, Carter and Powell summoned reporters to the Oval Office to announce a "positive development" concerning the fifty-two hostages—a development, as Stephan Lesher would underline in *Media Unbound,* that, sadly, dissipated after the polls closed. Jimmy Carter's

*Keeping Faith: Memoirs of a President* claims he resisted pressures for months from David Rockefeller, Kissinger, and others to grant the Shah asylum because he feared the revolutionaries in Teheran might harm the American diplomats in retaliation. He relented, he writes, only when advised that the cancer-stricken monarch was in imminent danger of death. But given his concern for the diplomats in Teheran—a concern he belatedly transmitted to Leonard—why did he not evacuate the embassy before admitting the deposed ruler? The question is left unanswered in the Carter memoirs. Vance, who resigned his office during the hostage crisis, was to have even less to say. Two dry pages of *Hard Choices: Four Critical Years in America's Foreign Policy* are devoted to the event.

Lando and Wallace came back to the subject in 1983. Reported from Paris where Bani-Sadr was now heading a government in exile, *The Khomeini Years,* as the update was called, said Iranians were worse off under the aging Ayatollah than they had ever been "under the brutal rule of the Shah." In three years, Wallace reported, 50,000 Iranians had been executed by the Revolution, and if Khomeini relaxed his grip, as the Shah had done toward the end, he would do so "at his own peril."

The coverage of America's opportunism and blind spot at the height of the Shah's haughty rule and of its humiliation in the hands of the zealots who followed him was riveting television of the kind that comes with success. It was television built on a reputation for fearless exercises in controversy by articulate and self-confident professionals who seemed sure of where they were and where they were going and were not afraid to step on a few toes to get there to get the story. Critics of *60 Minutes* liked to say the show didn't go far enough, that the coverage generated into rivalry of who would be the first to interview Khomeini, and that *The Iran File* in particular was little more than a Watergate exercise that could be subtitled: What did American officials know about torture in Iran, and when did they know it?

If *60 Minutes* covered the Iran tragedy with seminal authority, its approach to those earlier national traumas, Vietnam and Watergate, was less vigorous, because of both a lesser degree of self-confidence and deliberate policy. In the 1970s, the newsmagazine had not yet developed the following and power it possessed in 1980 and, in the case of the Watergate especially, CBS had reason to fear the White House. Still, Lando and Wallace delivered the controversial *Selling of Colonel Herbert* when *60 Minutes* was barely three years old, and there were reports on the South Vietnamese army, on its politicians—Nguyen Cao Ky and Doung Van "Big" Minh—on cluster bomb manufacture, POW wives, antiwar activists and draft evaders, but CBS News and Hewitt also believed the program should be an antidote to the daily news clips of war.

Hewitt's policy on Watergate was to have it both ways—to be both part of the running story and a relief from it, but preemptions ruined his chance to be in on the final drama. *60 Minutes* drew close to the fire a first time interviewing Clay Whitehead, but the segment was a dud. The White House communications director talked about "the priority totem pole" in news and managed to hide behind rhetoric. "There is an unhappy combination of disdain and insecurity about him, a fatal desire to displease," *Newsweek* wrote in a review of Whitehead's *60 Minutes* appearance.

In 1973, the unraveling scandal seemed never to end. The White House displeasure with the networks reached a new high in October when President Nixon, in a televised news conference, branded network news as the most "outrageous, vicious, distorted reporting I have seen in twenty-seven years of public life." It was on this occasion that Dan Rather asked Nixon "to tell us what goes through your mind when you hear people who love this country and people who believe in you say, reluctantly, that perhaps you should resign or be impeached?" The President answered, "Well, I'm glad we don't take a vote of this room, let me say." The following Sunday, October 28, *60 Minutes* was preempted by the New York Philharmonic's Young People's concert. On November 4, it was a 1939 Tyrone Power movie, *Jesse James* and, a week later it was *JFK: One Thousand Days and Ten Years.* On November 18 when Nixon declared he didn't profit from public life, the San Francisco-Los Angeles football game ran through the entire hour. On January 13, 1974, when special prosecutor Leon Jaworski's indictments began raining down, the Superbowl game washed out the entire *60 Minutes,* but on January 27, when Vice President Gerald Ford declared he would stay aloof from the evidence the White House claimed would clear Nixon, *60 Minutes* was on with an interview with Egil Krogh, the head of the so-called plumbers' unit that both Charles Colson and John Ehrlichman had used.

As a restorative, Hewitt sent Wallace to bob in the medicinal waters of various European spas. There was Mike explaining that in a world knee-deep in additives, tensions, pollution, and post-nasal drip, "there is something therapeutically old-fashioned about places like these— Birchner-Benner, Carlsbad, Evian, Vichy, Montecatini, names that roll off the tongue." They reran the Safer piece on Gibraltar. Wallace did a portrait of Maria Callas, Safer did western author Louis L'Amour. A further distraction from Watergate and the role the news media was playing in its unraveling were Wallace's successive looks at journalism's own warts: first the invasion by speech therapists and drama coaches of newsrooms to jazz up local newscasts; then the practice of junkets. On March 1, a federal grand jury in Washington indicted seven former Nixon aides—John Mitchell, H. R. ("Bob") Haldeman, John Ehrlichman, Charles Colson, Robert Mardian, Kenneth Parkinson, and Gordon Strachan—for conspiring to hinder the investigation of the original June 17, 1972 break-in at the Democratic Party headquarters. By midsummer, the Watergate events moved quickly after the House Judiciary Committee began televised hearings on whether to recommend that the full House vote to impeach Nixon. On Sunday, August 4, when Vice President Ford admitted House support for Nixon was eroding, *60 Minutes* aired a piece on where the whole probe had started—*The Washington Post* newsroom. Nixon resigned the next day, and the following Sunday the 6 P.M. slot was preempted by Stanhope Gould's much-delayed investigative report on the rock music industry, but *60 Minutes* itself preempted the 9:30 slot to deliver a Nixon retrospective.

Hewitt and Company kept after the Watergate principals and CBS News' old nemesis, Charles Colson, was to claim that his *60 Minutes* appearance was one of the prime factors that led him to plead guilty. In 1972, Colson had told Frank Stanton that the Nixon administration was going to bring CBS to its knees. He tried to resist Wallace's personal and persistent wooing, but the former Nixon hatchet man finally gave in. On the air, Wallace confronted Colson with some of his delinquencies and asked how he planned, as a born-again Christian, to make amends. "Have you tried to make up to those you hurt?" Wallace asked. Colson dodged the question, but as he was to write in his book, *Born Again,* he was dismayed by his own evasiveness.

Wallace's two-part interview with Haldeman not only made headlines because of what the former White House chief of staff didn't say but because of the fact that CBS News paid him for it. Checkbook journalism had its antecedents. In 1962, NBC had become involved in a piece of private cold war propaganda. Piers Anderton, the network's Berlin bureau chief, got permission from New York to pay a group of West Berlin students $7,000—they had originally demanded $50,000—for the TV rights to their tunnel boring under the newly erected Communist Wall. Using NBC equipment and film, the students filmed the escape of twenty-six people, including five babies, but the Cuban missile crisis and off-year elections postponed the showing of the tunnel documentary for six months. The payment to the tunnel leader had become known to East Germany and was now used as anti-American propaganda. NBC was roundly criticized by the State Department. At CBS, Edward Murrow,

Eric Sevareid, and Walter Cronkite had, after considerable controversy, drawn up policy guidelines and made a clear distinction between news and historical memoirs. The network would never pay for the former and only under great scrutiny occasionally consent to recompense the latter.

The news division first defended their paying Haldeman on the ground that the interview was more like "memoirs" and that the payment to the Watergate coconspirator was "in the neighborhood of $25,000" for two one-hour interviews with Mike Wallace and some Haldeman home movies. Soon word began circulating that much more money was involved. CBS News issued a clarification: Haldeman would receive $25,000 for each of the one-hour interviews. Then came a revision upward to a flat $100,000 and, still later, an acknowledgment that paying Haldeman probably was a mistake.

When Gordon Manning, the executive producer of the *CBS Evening News,* and Wallace flew to Washington for preliminaries during Haldeman's trial, the former Nixon chief of staff made one comment that seemed to promise the interview of the century. Standing in the ceremonial chamber of the U.S. Courthouse, Haldeman at one point looked across toward the White House and said Nixon was one of the weirdest men ever to have occupied the executive mansion. When it came time to roll the cameras, however, it was another story. Mike was well armed with questions, but Haldeman deftly turned the situation to his own advantage. At the start of each tape reel before the actual "Roll camera!" command, Wallace would say, "All right, Bob. I want to talk about this and this." Haldeman would say, "Okay, Mike, we'll get to it on the next reel." The alloted two hours were up before they got to those juicy parts. *Haldeman, The Nixon Years* was broadcast March 23 and 30, 1975, in successive *60 Minutes* time slots.

> WALLACE: You loved Richard Nixon, didn't you?
> HALDEMAN: No, I didn't—and I don't.
> WALLACE: I'm not sure I understand.
> HALDEMAN: It's a very concise answer.

The more accusatory Wallace's questions became, the softer were Haldeman's answers. Mike never broke through the frosty politeness of this former advertising man and renowned media expert. CBS was roundly criticized for this expensive molehill, and Wallace was to call it the worst interview of his career. In *Esquire,* Nora Ephron speculated that Wallace had come overprepared. "He spent fifty-five hours in preliminary talks with Haldeman—a period of time so long as to make me suspect he left the fight in the locker room—and when he sat down to tape, for over six hours, he found out firsthand why H. R. Haldeman used to be called the Berlin Wall.'' On the *CBS Morning News* eight years later, Wallace told Diane Sawyer, "We got nothing. Nothing."

Nine years later, they tried again. This time CBS News bought 38 hours of conversation with Richard Nixon and spread 90 minutes of what was billed as the former President's "memoirs on videotape" over two successive editions of *60 Minutes* plus one edition of the new midweek newsmagazine *American Parade*. Hues and cries went up in the press over this new instance of checkbook journalism and over the fact that it wasn't Mike Wallace or any other journalist who was doing the interviewing, but former White House aide and Nixon loyalist Frank Gannon. Both CBS Broadcast Group Vice President Van Gordon Sauter and Don Hewitt defended paying $500,000 for the video memoirs. Sauter's comments came in a speech in Los Angeles, where a *Los Angeles Times* cartoon had satirized the purchase. Said Sauter, "I recall no such cartoon when *The Los Angeles Times* purchased the print memoirs of Jimmy Carter. I recall no such column of indignation when *The New York Times* purchased the print memoirs of Winston Churchill, of Joseph Stalin's daughter or, for that matter, Nixon himself." In a letter to *The New York Times,* Hewitt pointed out that no one raised the question of ethics when newspapers paid for famous people's memoirs.

But Bill Moyers, CBS's own commentator, assaulted the network's decision. On the *CBS Evening News* the night after the first installment aired April 8, 1984, Moyers said the salient point was that journalists, not a long-time associate of the former President, should have been asking the questions. In introducing the memoirs, Morley Safer said that Nixon talked with "astonishing candor," on the videotapes, but there was nothing new. Watergate was "wrong," "illegal," and "a very, very stupid thing to do," Nixon told Gannon, going on to make it appear that the break-in of the Democratic Party Headquarters was more an error of judgment than a case of corruption at the highest level of his administration, as the audio tapes stowed at the National Archives show it to be.

Checkbook journalism is a gray area for major news organizations, but only *60 Minutes* has been charged with paying fugitives from justice to tell their story.

Ten thousand dollars bought interviews in 1981 with a pair of American gunrunners holed up in Lebanon and gave CBS vice president and director of public affairs broadcasts Roger Colloff something to explain when a New York district attorney's office went public with the information two years later. In court papers filed in September 1983, Manhattan Assistant District Attorney Matthew T. Crosson said Barry Lando and Mike Wallace had been involved in negotiating payments to Frank E. Terpil and George Gregory Korkala six months after the New York Supreme Court convicted the pair in absentia on conspiring to sell machineguns, ammunition, and poisons to undercover police officers posing as South American terrorists.

That November 1981 segment was morbidly exciting. There was Mike in Beirut, coaxing the two cocksure fugitives to explain their business. Terpil was a former CIA agent, nicely wired into the old boys' network of retired CIA operatives, including Edwin P. Wilson, Libya strongman Muammar el-Qaddafi's one-man weapons procurement agent. Terpil had operated a training school for terrorists in Libya and had been the right-hand man of deposed Ugandan dictator Idi Amin. In June, Terpil and Korkala had been convicted in absentia of international trade in weapons with terrorist organizations and each sentenced to seventeen to fifty-three years in prison. In passing sentence, Justice Thomas B. Galligan said that because the two were "so offensive to the norm that civilized people respect," it was perhaps a blessing that they were not in New York. He added, "But they are so devious and their thinking so warped that while they are at liberty, civilized people are in jeopardy." Terpil remained at large, but less than a year later, Korkala was extradited to the United States. It was in preparation for his retrial that the Manhattan attorney's office sought the outtakes of the Lando-Wallace tapes in Beirut with the two fugitives. When CBS asked the State Supreme Court to quash the subpoena for the unused portions of the *60 Minutes* report, the district attorney disclosed the network had paid $12,000 to an intermediary, knowing that $10,000 of the money was for the fugitives.

Wallace acknowledged the payment to the intermediary, but asserted he had no knowledge of Terpil and Korkala receiving any of the money. Colloff said he would not have authorized the payment if there had been suspicion money would have gone to the two men. Assistant District Attorney Crosson, who claimed he had written and tape-recorded statements from Korkala and the go-between that Wallace and Lando had negotiated with Korkala about paying for the interviews, said, "For CBS to say they didn't know the money was going to Terpil and Korkala strains the imagination."

Economic developments dominated the early years of the Reagan administration as the country suffered through its deepest recession since World War II, while foreign initiatives were largely limited to relations with the Soviet Union, Latin America, and a frustrating search for peace in the Middle East. The Candy Factory produced acidulated bonbons on the Reagan White House preoccupation with defense, its foreign affairs, and one of its controversial appointments.

The arms buildup came under attack by former Secretary of Defense Robert McNamara in *Dear Mr. President,* a January 1983 segment produced by Elliot Bernstein and reported by Harry Reasoner, in which the Johnson administration's Pentagon "whizkid" and later president of the World Bank said Ronald Reagan was mortgaging America's future to the tune of $7 billion. When President Reagan called for a research and development effort to provide a futuristic defense against intercontinental ballistic missiles in April 1983, Hewitt ran a 1978 segment called *Space Wars* again. As Reasoner said in introducing the story, the sense of urgency had not been there five years earlier. Now, chemical lasers and particle-beam weapons were suddenly taken very seriously. The European opposition to the nuclear buildup was focused on Petra Kelly, the powerful and attractive spokesperson for Germany's Greens, interviewed by Safer.

*60 Minutes* was out front on a controversial Reagan administration appointment. The White House didn't appreciate *The Thomas Reed Affair,* a quickly assembled William Willson-Mike Wallace report on the President's special assistant for national security. The segment aired March 13, 1983, when the White House was still saying the President had "full confidence" in the San Rafael, California business executive and former Air Force Secretary serving as vice chairman of the newly created National Commission on Strategic Forces. A long-time friend of Reagan and of National Security Adviser William Clark, Reed had been charged with making a $427,000 profit after obtaining insider information of a proposed $4 billion take-over of AMAX, Inc., by Standard Oil of California. Two days after *The Thomas Reed Affair* was broadcast, Reed was allowed to withdraw as Reagan's special assistant for national security affairs.

There were reports on Cubans still in U.S. prisons two years after the Mariel exodus, on Titan missiles, nuclear devastation, and Japanese-American trade wars, but there were no stories on San Salvador, Yuri Andropov, Marines at Beirut airport, or the aftereffects of invasion on Grenada. Unlike ABC News, *60 Minutes* did not attempt an independent inquiry into the 1982 massacre of Palestinians in the Shatila and Sabra camps. Nor did it delve into the attempted assassination of Pope John Paul II. When *TV Guide* asked Hewitt about this in 1983, he said he didn't think such criticism was valid. "I don't label myself as news;

I'm reality," he said. "The evening news deals with news. We deal with reality."

The reality that was selling in the mid-1980s, as the media found out when they protested the Grenada news blackout, was less confrontational, less controversial. When the Reagan administration excluded reporters from the scene of the Grenada action, journalists argued impassionately that the press' freedom and the public's right to know were at stake. But the public sided with the government. In letters and phone calls to the networks, viewers supported the press ban in Grenada, 5 to 1. Letters to editors of daily newspapers were only slightly less hostile, running 3 to 1 in favor of the Reagan administration's exclusion of the press. *Time* magazine's letters on the issue ran almost 8 to 1 against the press. Print and electronic journalists discovered that people didn't like them, that they were considered rude and accusatory, more interested in what sells, in scandal, than in reporting the news, and too quick to hide behind the First Amendment. Big-city newspapers had to admit to embarrassing stories about fabricated people and made-up quotes, while on television the news too often seemed to be reduced to microphones thrust into grieving people's faces and reporters and cameras lying in wait at subjects' homes. The dispute over Grenada seemed to uncork a pent-up public hostility, *Time* reported, to reinforce a popular perception that journalists regarded themselves as detached from, and perhaps even hostile to, the government of their country. The mistrust was heightened by several celebrated libel suits, particularly by General William Westmoreland and Los Angeles physician Carl Galloway against CBS, Mike Wallace, Dan Rather, Steve Glauber *et al*, that raised questions not only about objectivity but the techniques used to shape a story.

# 13

## Shaping It
### *The editorial process*

*60 Minutes'* editorial process was put on trial in Los Angeles in 1983. In a libel suit growing out of a Steve Glauber-Dan Rather piece called *It's No Accident,* about false auto insurance claims, the plaintiff's lawyer got to see the outtakes, or unused portion of the broadcast, and concluded that a substantial number of the interviews were staged, rehearsed, and contrived. Film clips introduced in court showed Glauber, Rather, and crew repeat questions for those being interviewed, badger one interviewee, and flatter another. Questions were stated in a leading fashion and words were suggested. The trial was given extensive publicity as Dan Rather was cross-examined on the witness stand for two days, fighting to retain the most precious components of *60 Minutes* journalism, his present anchor stardom, and credibility and integrity.

*It's No Accident* was about the filing of bogus claims for property damage or personal injuries. Talking directly to the camera, Rather explained it this way: "In the cases we're talking about there are no accidents, just setups. A lawyer, who is in on the setup, sends the alleged victims to the crooked doctor—sometimes an M.D., usually a chiropractor—and they conspire to file phony claims. The insurance company usually is glad to settle for $3,000 or under, because it's cheaper to settle than to investigate.'' Rather interviewed several people: an investigator for the insurance companies; a so-called ''capper'' who finds claimants and sells their bogus cases to doctors and lawyers; an attorney who used to buy cases from these cappers; a doctor who admitted he used to conspire with fifteen different lawyers to commit these frauds; and a law school teacher. The identities of the capper and the doctor were protected, but the lawyer—who had been suspended and faced possible disbarment—was introduced by name. The doctor told of dealing with one attorney involved in these frauds who was an important member of the California governor's Select Committee on Narcotics Enforcement. He was not asked to name that individual.

The only person implicated by name was Dr. Carl A. Galloway, a doctor from the L.A. community of Lynwood, who was never interviewed by *60 Minutes*. Represented by lawyer Bruce A. Friedman, the doctor sued Dan Rather, Steve Glauber, and CBS for $30 million. (Friedman dropped Hewitt's name from the suit, saying he had no evidence tying the executive producer to the disputed broadcast.) The suit claimed Dr. Galloway had been slandered because *It's No Accident* named him as the physician who signed phony medical reports to back up fraudulent insurance claims. The ''patient'' in the segment, Rosa Bravo, was actually a private investigator's assistant who, on camera, described how the receptionist at the Manchester West Doctors' Office agreed to provide her with back-dated medical bills for treatment she supposedly received after suffering a minor car accident. She had paid three visits to the clinic, she explained. On the first visit, she was told that the back-dated bills could be provided. The second time, she was given a ninety-second treatment and, at the third appointment, she picked up her medical report, which listed nineteen visits and billed her for $892. On the air, Rather said this report ''was signed by Carl A. Galloway, M.D.'' Dan and crew went to the clinic and confronted Glenda Wynn, the receptionist, with the fact that she knew Rosa Bravo had been given a false set of bills. He didn't ask Wynn or anyone else, however, *who* had signed Dr. Galloway's name on Rosa Bravo's medical report.

In pretrial testimony before Superior Court Judge Bruce A. Geernaert, both Rather and Glauber admitted they took no steps to ascertain that the signature was actually that of Dr. Galloway. The doctor, Rather said, was not ''a major focus of the story and our investigation. The focus was the Manchester West Doctors' Office, not Dr. Galloway. Therefore, when you said, 'Did you not think it important to demonstrate this or that about Dr. Galloway,' it's in that context that I say, No it wasn't.'' In what was to be a crucial point in the trial, both Rather and Glauber said they had each left two telephone messages for the doctor to call them back and that he had never tried to reach either of them. ''My experience with guilty people is that they don't call back,'' Dan said in the pretrial testimony. ''They usually get a lawyer.''

Friedman scored a major coup when the Supreme Court of California upheld Judge Geernaert's ruling that he be allowed to see the *60 Minutes* outtakes. The plaintiff's lawyer was ordered to keep the unused portions of the broadcast to himself, but after examining the tapes and transcripts, Friedman claimed they showed *60 Minutes* was ''a fraud on the public.'' He asked the court to lift the order of confidentiality.

CBS switched lawyers and vigorously opposed Friedman's motion, arguing there was no Freedom of Information Act question involved here because outtakes constituted unpublished press material and the First Amendment shielded such material from public scrutiny. The court neither accepted CBS's defense nor granted Friedman's motion. Instead, it said there might be a valid public interest in the way *60 Minutes* put together the program, and the judge issued an open invitation to ''any legitimately interested party, particularly a member of the press, to ask for the outtakes.'' Bruce Herschensohn, a news commentator on KABC, ABC's owned and operated Los Angeles outlet, petitioned the court to release the production tape and, a week before the trial, the court ruled Friedman could refer to the outtakes in trying the case.

The trial before Superior Court Judge Jack W. Swink was painful for *60 Minutes*. *It's No Accident* showed private insurance investigator Milton Crawford questioning Montennette Johnson, who has emerged from the clinic with a phony claim purportedly signed by Dr. Galloway. At first, she maintains she did have an accident. Then Rather, on screen, says, ''After some hard questioning [she] changed her story.'' In the next scene, Johnson indeed admits she was not in an accident. In court, Friedman established there was no ''hard questioning'' by showing the entire Crawford-Johnson interview to the jury. On the witness stand, Crawford testified he had obtained Johnson's signed confession that her claim was a fraud five days before she ''confessed'' for the *60 Minutes* cameras.

From investigator Crawford, Friedman elicited the admission that he had never had any knowledge of Dr. Galloway's receiving any payments in connection with fraudulent claims portrayed in the *60 Minutes* broadcast. The rest of Crawford's testimony, however, was less complimentary to the plaintiff. Manchester West Doctors' Office was owned by Walli Shamsuddin, who had originally been hired as bodyguard and operator of the clinic by the former owner, a chiropractor who had moved to Las Vegas. Shamsuddin was a capper, Crawford testified, and Dr. Galloway was related to Shamsuddin by marriage. CBS lawyer Robert Vanderet told the court Shamsuddin was currently in jail for killing his wife with a submachine gun.

Dr. Galloway, a slim, bespectacled man in his forties, spent a day on the witness stand, testifying he didn't sign the phony medical reports obtained by Rosa Bravo, Crawford's assistant. A graduate of Amherst College and the University of Rochester Medical School, he said his first contact with Shamsuddin was his brother's marriage to Shamsuddin's sister. Galloway and Shamsuddin became friendly, he said, and began discussing Shamsuddin's request that the doctor help out at the Manchester clinic. Dr. Galloway testified he had never ordered any stationery for the Manchester West with his name on it, that his involvement with the clinic had been limited to one afternoon a week while had been on the staff of one hospital and engaged in his own private practice. He had resigned his position at Manchester West a month before Glauber and Rather began investigating. In fact, the first time Shamsuddin called to see if *60 Minutes* had contacted him, he thought the Manchester West owner was "joking."

By the time Dan Rather was called to testify, the trial was its own news event. While Judge Swink permanently barred a KNXT camera crew on the ground that its parent network was the defendant (and after Friedman told the judge in chambers he had overheard a CBS lawyer instructing KNXT reporter Bill Sternoff on how to present the story), Cable News Network (CNN) covered the court proceedings live. Ronald E. Guttman, CBS associate general counsel, was in court every day and, to underscore the importance of the case to the network, he was joined by Gene Mater, CBS senior vice president of communications and news practices. Awkward at best for CBS, the trial stretched into, and past, the annual convention of CBS affiliates held in Los Angeles. The media kept the delegates abreast of the latest from downtown (the wire services played up the fact that Rather refused to talk to fellow reporters outside the courtroom), and Bob Schiefer, who substituted for Rather on the evening news, had Dan Rather-testifies-in-Los Angeles-trial items in the lineup, once including a snippet of a jerky camera chase of somebody's back from the outtakes.

Crudely, CBS executives stalked the hallways trying to influence the press coverage. *The Los Angeles Times'* Peter Boyer was openly insulted with loud suggestions that he should give attorney for the plaintiff Friedman a byline because he was so partial to his case. *The New York*

*Times* reporter had her paper thrown angrily at her feet and her coverage subjected to criticism in a letter to her editor. CBS lawyers complained to Judge Swink when Friedman talked to CNN reporters in an area outside the courtroom where the jurors would pass.

In the corridors at the affiliates' convention, the traditional we're-the-greatest backslapping was mixed with can-*60 Minutes*-beat-this-rap? speculation. Van Gordon Sauter strolled the convention floor explaining that the spate of litigation hitting CBS News and other news organizations would, like all phases, eventually fade away. The media should be happy that corporations such as CBS had the money to handle such litigation, which he termed "very expensive." The suits (as he spoke, a 1984 trial date was set in Manhattan in the General Westmoreland case) had not intimidated CBS for its news evaluation and judgments, he said.

On the stand, Rather had to admit that, after trying twice to reach Dr. Galloway, no further attempts were made. Addressing the jury directly, he said he had left his phone number with the Manchester West receptionist, had called again after leaving the clinic, and felt confident the message had "gotten through" to the physician. Dan had left Los Angeles November 17, 1979, and, he testified, "we worked as quickly and as hard as we could to get it on the air." A December 2 deadline had been missed, and *It's No Accident* was broadcast the following Sunday. Characterizing the segment as "the kind of story *60 Minutes* likes," he defended Glauber as "one of the premier investigative reporters," while conceding "that doesn't mean he nor I are incapable of making errors."

"I never doubted we had a phony report, and that report was signed by Dr. Galloway," Rather testified, citing, among other things, an appointment card and the notice on the Manchester West wall, both bearing Dr. Galloway's name, in addition to receptionist Wynn telling him the doctor was in his office three days a week, as evidence that the office *was* Dr. Galloway's. Friedman kept questioning the news star about the accuracy of *It's No Accident,* and at one point asked if there were any major errors made. "No, this was a home-run ball," Dan replied, adding, "what you're saying is that you disagree with the way we swung at it."

Away from the control of his anchor desk and without the flattering key lights and stage makeup, Dan looked his fifty-one years. Much of the time he was confident and articulate, but there were moments when he was taut, evasive, and looked haggard. ABC and NBC had Dan Rather-testifying-in-Los Angeles items in their nightly lineups, complete with tape of him in the witness chair. On days when he testified, *Entertain-*

*ment Tonight,* the half-hour showbiz news program, offered roundups. Besides the daily press, *Time* and *Newsweek* weighed in, and in addition to its live courtroom coverage to 20 million viewers, CNN offered commentary by a pair of lawyers specializing in First Amendment law. "I am frustrated that the coverage has been sporadic," complained Sauter. "There has to be continuity. And our basic concern is that some misrepresentations have become part of the lore of the trial." His own news department's coverage was less than continuous, and NBC's Reuven Frank and ABC News Vice President Richard Wald didn't think they had to apologize. "Dan Rather is a household word, and every week Nielsen tells us how many households," said Frank. "He is being sued for a large amount of money, and people are interested in coverage of television." Wald said that if the story had been about an agricultural reporter on a rural newspaper in Northern California, ABC probably wouldn't have covered it, but if there was a principle at stake and if Dan Rather had *not* been there, ABC would still have reported it.

The first break for Rather, Glauber, *60 Minutes,* and CBS came in the fourth week of the trial when Judge Swink ruled Dr. Galloway could not seek punitive damages because malice and ill will had not been proven as required under California law. In his closing arguments, Friedman asked for $4.5 million for Dr. Galloway, citing "humiliation" and "loss of professional reputation and integrity" for the doctor. Rather was in the courtroom as Friedman called him "arrogant" in assuming the messages had gotten through and that the doctor was guilty because he had not returned the calls. Friedman accused CBS of manufacturing an appointment card bearing Dr. Galloway's name and of using this as "the cornerstone of its case." In response, chief CBS counsel William Vaughn asked the jurors to focus on whether reckless disregard for the truth had been proven. Dr. Galloway, Vaughan said, "was not defamed or unjustly accused—he was caught. He chose to associate himself with this clinic, chose to put himself in a position where he was open to criticism; that wasn't anything CBS did. Dr. Galloway's assertion of innocence, of naïveté, that he didn't know what was going on, is roughly equivalent to the piano player in a bawdy house who says he didn't know what was going on upstairs."

CBS won. After three days of deliberation, the nine-woman, three-man jury voted 10 to 2 in favor of the defendants. Under California law, a nine-vote majority is required for a decision in a civil case. "We were trying to figure out what was in Dan Rather's mind at the time of the broadcast," said jury foreman David Campbell after the verdict. "Most of us didn't feel he had acted in reckless disregard for the truth." Dr.

Galloway said he felt vindicated because of the vast news coverage the case received. "My patients," he said wistfully, outside the courtroom, "are all behind me."

In New York, Fred Friendly put the philosophical perspective on the victory, saying CBS, *60 Minutes,* and Rather had grown in stature—the network and its newsmagazine for being accountable, for being willing to defend themselves, and Rather for showing himself in a new light, "a good light, not just the talking end of a Teleprompter, but as someone who is able to cope with a very difficult problem, willing to face his accusers."

Five weeks later, Dr. Galloway and his attorney petitioned for a new trial. Following a legal step that Friedman admitted resulted in new trials in only one case out of twenty, the motion claimed CBS had been "devious and deceptive" in shifting the thrust of its defense during the trial. Friedman alleged juror misconduct and, referring to the 1964 *New York Times v. Sullivan* ruling, contended Dr. Galloway was not a public figure and therefore should not have had to prove *60 Minutes* had acted recklessly, merely that *It's No Accident* was false and its incorrectness had injured him.

A rich man's bride is raped by a bandit; the rich man is murdered, or possibly he is a suicide. Four times we see what happened, as told by the three people involved and a fourth time, as told by an involuntary witness. The world of film received a thunderbolt at the 1951 Venice Film Festival when *Rashomon* was premiered. Directed by Akira Kurosawa, this striking and often disturbing inquiry into the nature of truth continually reconstructs the double crime. One by one the woman, the bandit, the rich man's ghost, and the woodcutter-witness in tenth-century Kyoto tell what happened that fateful day in the forest, each giving an account that enhances her or his conduct. But at the end, we can only ask: What can we ever be sure of?

Tantalizingly, they have thought of "doing a Rashomon" on *60 Minutes,* of taking a story and showing that the power is in the editing, that by editing in several different ways anyone can convey any picture, any bias. "Let's say we took the Reserve Mining story, a piece about a company that was polluting the water up in Lake Superior," Mike Wallace told *The New York Times* in 1979. "We could do it from the point of view of the mining company, from that bias; or we could do it with a bias toward the environmentalists; or with a bias toward the townspeople. All we'd have to do is use different parts of the same interviews."

Editing is the most controversial aspect of the newsmagazine. Residents of Polo, Illinois and business executives are not the only people to claim that *their* truth ended on the cutting room floor. Most people interviewed for *60 Minutes* express surprise at how their on-camera interview comes out. They are unnerved by the film-to-air-time ratio, usually 10 to 1, and often claim to have been worn down or lulled into a false sense of security. They are startled when the interview ends and the camera is turned around to shoot "reverse questions." With the camera aimed at the correspondent, he rerecords all his questions so they may later be spliced together with the answers. Although all the networks insist these reverse "cutaways" match the original questions as closely as possible and that news department guidelines mandate that editing with reverse questions must reflect accurately the spirit, tone, and intent of the interview, there is no denying that the reporter is allowed to polish his performance while the subject's answers must stand as first delivered. When Wallace interviewed Jerzy Kosinski for the Roman Polanski profile, the novelist noticed Mike and crew were as interested in the reverse questions as in his answers. "The process is very studied and very precise," Kosinski remembered. "Mike assumed an expression that was at once that of a man who already knows and a boy who wants to find out, a fascinating mixture of the inquisitive and the inquisitional."

It is in the editing that interviews conducted at different times and places are spliced together and it is in the editing that, in the lingo of the trade, a story is given "hook" (dramatic premise), "pipe" (the history of the characters), and "top spin" (what propels the viewer into the next scene). More fascinatingly, editing allows the construction of wholly synthetic confrontation that can generate tremendous "heat" (dramatic tension).

The confrontation device, says Bill Brown—a producer who left *60 Minutes* for NBC's *Weekend* newsmagazine after being responsible for such early heavy-hitters as the interviews with ITT's Dita Beard and novelist-hoaxer Clifford Irving—is so heavily weighted in favor of the reporter as to be intrinsically unfair. "On one side you have professionals, people accustomed to dealing with cameras and the rest of the technical side of it; on the other is someone who might never have been close to a TV camera before. Then they get a tight shot of his face, and of course he doesn't look comfortable. He doesn't know about eye contact with the camera, so his eyes are shifting. And all the while Mike Wallace is talking to him, and Mike is a very imposing character." Walter Cronkite is another critic of *60 Minutes'* camera techniques. "The extreme closeup would make almost anybody look guilty," says the former anchorman. "Under hot lights, perspiring, the slightest eye movement appears to be furtive.'' There is an in-house joke that parodies the Mike Wallace loaded-question style. It has him interview a girl scout: Let me get this straight. I just want to be sure that we all understand what's going on here. You come home, take a bath, and get all prettied up. You put on your newest training bra and your best uniform and go out—at night—to houses where you've never been, and you ring the bell, and when some man comes to the door, you say, "Would you like to buy my cookies?" Now, are you really selling cookies? Author Clark Norton spoofed Safer retelling *Romeo and Juliet* in a 1982 *TV Guide* piece. "Our story begins here in the picturesque town of Verona, Italy, a few hundred years ago. It is a saga of teenage romance gone horribly wrong—a tragedy that some say should never have happened at all . . .''

In 1976, producer Joe DeCola discovered an authentic "dog of war," a British-born naturalized American mercenary with an impressive Vietnam record as a specialist in sabotage, kidnapping, and assassination. John Dane was awarded twelve medals, including a Bronze Star, plus U.S. citizenship, and had since hired himself out in Zaire, the future Zimbabwe, Guatemala, and the Middle East. He was holed up in Mexico, on the lam from the United States for driving a stolen car with a trunk full of dynamite. The thirty-four-year-old Dane told DeCola that he had been approached by a young Los Angeles member of the Jewish Defense League about killing Yasir Arafat for $250,000. To back up his story, he played a tape of one of his meetings with the JDL's Irv Rubin. For his own protection, Dane explained, he always made such surreptitious recordings. There were just too many imponderables in his line of work.

With Dan Rather, DeCola flew to Mazatlán. On camera, Dane established his credentials, his marksmanship, and professionalism and repeated the JDL proposition. DeCola's crew filmed him shooting near bull's-eye at a target with a weapon he was handling for the first time and, to Rather, Dane explained he "worked" only on military or political targets. "If you want your wife knocked off, your grandmother in an accident, or your mother-in-law to be deceased suddenly, that's— you can go down to Los Angeles and get those all you want. That's not my style." To assassinate Arafat, he had demanded half in advance, half once the mission was accomplished. With this interview safely in the can, DeCola called Rubin in California and said he and Rather were "doing a story on the JDL," would he mind being interviewed. "Gosh, no, come on over," said Rubin, who turned out to be an eighteen-year-old still living with his mother. On camera, Rather confronted the young radical with a copy of Dane's recording and with what the mercenary had told them in Mexico. On the May 1976 airing of *Hired Gun,* the two interviews were dramatically "cut together," beginning with Rather playing the tape recording for Rubin:

RATHER: . . . I know this is a tape recording—made with a man named John Dane. Do you know Mr. Dane?

RUBIN: I've heard of him.

RATHER: That was your voice on the tape recording, was it not?

RUBIN: I would refuse to comment.

RATHER: Well, I know that that was your voice.

RUBIN: Yeah, okay.

RATHER: You were talking with Mr. John Dane. You were talking about an assassination attempt on Arafat.

RUBIN: We were fantasizing.

RATHER: Did he come to you or did you go to him?

DANE: He came to me.

RATHER: Tell me in brief what his proposition was.

DANE: Just as I've outlined. In exchange for a sum of money, I was to go to the Middle East and assassinate him.

A little later, Rather asked Dane if he had assured Rubin the murder could be done.

DANE: Oh, yes.

RATHER: If he came up with the money?

DANE: Absolutely. He was also made to understand that there'd be a lot of people that would be most upset should dear Mr. Arafat be suddenly demised and that the large sum of money would be required in order to hide from all of his friends and admirers and sponsors—mainly his sponsors.

RATHER: How many times did you talk to John Dane, total?

RUBIN: Might have been twice.

RATHER: Well, we know you talked to him more than twice. You talked to him at the restaurant, the Hollywood restaurant. Right?

RUBIN: No comment.

RATHER: You talked to him in the secret meeting at a private home just outside of Los Angeles, right?

RUBIN: No comment.

A piece of audio tape is what made *Looking Out for Mrs. Berwid.* With the tape recorder always plugged into their emergency telephone, police officers heard a terror-stricken woman scream for help before she was murdered. All producer Norman Gorin had to do was to film Morley Safer at the Nassau County, New York police station listening to the playback and telling us who is who. It is December 6, 1979; 5:07 in the afternoon.

EWA BERWID *(on tape)*: Olga! Call the police! Olga!

SAFER: She says, 'Olga!' Olga is the name of the oldest child. 'Olga! Call the police!' And then the 911 operator.

OPERATOR *(on tape)*: Stop screaming and tell me where you are. Where are you?

SAFER: The woman is shouting, 'He's killing me!'

EWA BERWID *(on tape)*: *(Indistinct . . . screaming).*

OPERATOR *(on tape)*: Ma'am?

EWA BERWID *(on tape)*: He's killing me!

OPERATOR *(on tape)*: Ma'am? *(Mrs. Berwid screaming).* Lieutenant. Lieutenant, I have this woman on this line. She's hysterical. Something's wrong there, but I don't know what. She's calling some guy's name. He don't answer.

EWA BERWID *(on tape)*: Oh! Oh, God!

OPERATOR *(on tape)*: Ma'am?

SAFER: The police could not get a name or address out of her. If they'd been able to, they say, they would have been there in three minutes. And then the line went dead. It was about ten or eleven minutes past five, the approximate time of death of Ewa Berwid.

As Safer said in introducing the March 1980 segment, *Looking Out for Mrs. Berwid* was about a murder that could have been prevented if psychiatrists at mental institutions relied a little less on their own evaluation of patients and paid a little more attention to lay people's warnings about returning insane minds to society.

Adam and Ewa Berwid were emigrants from Poland, both engineers who had found good jobs when they settled in suburban New York in 1969. He found American life difficult; she adjusted easily. She soon made more money than her husband. He became resentful, abusive. When she sued for divorce, a family court ordered him to stay away from her and their children. He did not. He was arrested eight times for threatening and attacking his wife at her Long Island home. He sent her letters telling her he was going to kill her and how he might murder her. He was committed, and a judge, who saw him on a number of occasions, took the unusual step of personally writing to the state Department of Mental Health to say he was convinced that if Berwid were given a chance he would kill his former wife. Berwid was sent to the Mid-Hudson institution housing the most difficult and dangerous mental patients in the state, ninety miles north of New York City. After nine months, he was declared well enough to be transferred to a less secure institution in Brentwood, Long Island. After a month, he walked off the grounds and was picked up at the home of Ewa Berwid, where he had tried to kill her. After a second escape, he was shipped back to the maximum security institution. Seven months later, doctors once more declared him well enough to be transferred back to the Brentwood hospital.

On December 6, 1979, he applied for a day's furlough to go out and buy himself an overcoat. The doctors granted him a pass until 4 P.M., but noted on his medical record that if he were to be reported missing, Nassau County police, Mrs. Berwid, and her lawyer were to be notified. Instead of buying a coat, Berwid bought a hunting knife at a sporting goods store. As Safer said, leading up to the replay of the police tape, "Ewa Berwid has only hours to live." Three months later, a judge ruled Adam Berwid mentally incompetent to stand trial for murder, and he was shipped back to the maximum security institution.

An interview device perfected by Wallace is to smile and encourage the subject to continue talking, only to insert cutaways in which he has a stern, doubting, or reproving expression. Even a fellow reporter like Daniel Schorr, totally conversant with the demands and pitfalls of taped interviews, has felt himself a victim of the Wallace cutaway. In 1976 when Schorr was the intense focus of a congressional investigation for being the recipient of choicy leaks from a 340-page House Intelligence Committee report on the CIA, Wallace asked his CBS colleague for an interview. "You're news," Mike told Schorr, who had been suspended from network duties by Richard Salant and was facing contempts of Congress charges. Schorr's lawyer, Joseph Califano, told him not to do it, but Schorr was a veteran; he knew how to handle himself.

In his autobiography, *Clearing the Air,* Schorr describes how Don Hewitt in the control room gave the "Roll tape!" cue and how Wallace began by saying, "Dan, you have my profound admiration and that of your colleagues here and elsewhere, I know, for the eloquent and persuasive case that you made for the protection of a reporter's sources." Because of technical problems, Hewitt had Wallace start over again twice. The hour-long interview was cut to twelve minutes. "Deletes were Wallace's thrice stated expression of admiration and the general discussion of secrecy and disclosure," Schorr wrote in his book. Mike resented the charge enough to tell *The New York Times* three years later, "Listen, I've heard Daniel Schorr on freedom of the press at B'nai B'rith dinners, in the newsroom, and at Sigma Delta Chi luncheons a million times. I was after a totally different story. It reminds me of Henry Kissinger. Kissinger doesn't like to be edited either.'' In 1980, Schorr said in a *Saturday Review* interview that he and Califano had pushed for a live interview, but that Hewitt had talked him out of it, saying *60 Minutes* never did that because too many things might go wrong and that, in any case, Schorr had nothing to be sorry about. Added Schorr, ''Well, my answer is that the man with the scissors is the man with ultimate control.''

It is no doubt significant that editors—the people with the scissors—get their names on *60 Minutes'* credit crawl while writers go creditless. Hewitt has been in a drawn-out fight with the Writers Guild of America (WGA), which represents all Hollywood and network screenwriters. The WGA contract with CBS specifies that if an on-air performer does his or her own writing, no credits are given, meaning that if Bradley, Safer, Reasoner, and Wallace write the lines they so eloquently and confidently say while looking into the camera, everything is just fine. In 1981, however, the Guild threatened to subpoena the four correspondents and just about everyone connected with the newsmagazine, past and present, to prove that lowly, anonymous scribblers actually do much of the writing that Ed, Morley, Harry, and Mike are popularly believed to do themselves. ''Producers, researchers, even outside freelancers do most of the writing,'' charged Guild attorney Mona Mangan. ''And we think we can prove it.'' The question of what anchors and correspondents can write for other on-air personnel besides themselves led to a threatened walkout by more than 300 WGA-affiliated CBS employees in 1984. ''If anyone can write for anyone else, who needs news writers?'' Mangan said at a critical point of the contract negotiations. The issue was solved in the Guild's favor. The WGA charges against *60 Minutes*, meanwhile, remained in arbitration. If the Guild wins, it will demand four years of retroactive writing payments to its members and four years worth of writing credits on the air. ''They may have to take an entire evening just to run the credits,'' said Mangan.

Hewitt is a superb editor himself and considers the selection of the clearest sound and the most telling picture, the saving of precious seconds at every point, and the sharpening up of poorly phrased questions as the essence of nonfiction television. The corridors of the ninth floor echo with the whirr of film running through Moviolas and Kem tables and of the disembodied voices of the tigers being run forward and backward in cutting rooms. ''In television, you can't edit something till you hear it,'' says Hewitt. ''I rarely look at the pictures when I'm editing a piece. I just listen. There are those who say I do too much dramatic coaching, but what I'm really doing is just editing writing. It's the pauses and inflections I listen for as much as anything." This attention can both damage and benefit potential victims of investigations. If *60 Minutes'* intent is to demean, embarrass, or let an interviewee hang himself, his false starts, repetitions, his "ahs" and "ehs" can be left intact. If producer and editor want to portray him as cleverer than he actually is, all such hemming and hawing is snipped out.

Juggling questions and answers is the secret weapon. Network news guidelines forbid separating questions from answers. An editor cannot take answer 7 and tack it into question 13, even if it seems to make a point much better, but as court transcripts of Dr. Carl A. Galloway's slander trial would show, that was exactly what *60 Minutes* did in the disputed insurance fraud segment. As aired, Dan Rather asks attorney Robert Petty, "If I were an attorney and I sought to specialize in these kinds of cases, could I make a quarter of a million dollars a year, half a million dollars a year?" Petty replies, "Yes." Nowhere in the transcript of that interview, however, does the attorney actually give that one-word "yes" to Rather's question. Instead, Petty's response is, "So long as you were successful," followed by a number of qualifiers to his answer. The actual recorded "yes" might have come in response to a crew member asking Petty if he'd like a cup of coffee before they start.

People conversant with the prestidigitations of the editing table usually want to go on the air live, but where Hewitt is adamant about refusing this, *20/20's* Av Westin can be tempted. When Richard Nixon was doing the author's tour in 1978 on behalf of his book, *RN: The Memoirs of Richard Nixon,* Hewitt turned down a *60 Minutes* appearance because the former President insisted on doing it live. Westin allowed Barbara Walters to do Nixon live. "If you do a recorded interview," she commented in defense of the decision, "one of the advantages for the reporter is that he always comes out on top; he's always right. You've never seen a *60 Minutes* interview, or any [taped] interview, in which the reporter gets the worst of it. Doing live interviews has credibility."

If Wallace encourages people he is about to interview with flattering intros, nods, and smiles, Safer's bag of tricks includes saying he is *not* Mike Wallace. "Think of me as Uncle Morley," he told Dr. Paul Shriver as they prepared to start a session in the assistant superintendent's office in the Indiana State Prison for Women.

It was one of those little awful tragedies that had originated with a viewer, a woman who wrote that her cousin, Joyce DeVillez, was serving fifteen to twenty-five years for arranging the murder of her husband Bernard. The woman wrote that if the whole story of this couple were known, it would be considered a case of justifiable homicide. Producer Martin Phillips, Safer, and crew had tracked down the story. They had interviewed Joyce DeVillez, a slim woman of forty-three who had earned a college degree while in prison. They had visited the murder scene in Evansville, Indiana, Bernard's grave, and the tract home in suburban Los Angeles with two grown daughters and a son who, for the cameras, had gone through the pain of their childhoods, their father's constant beatings, his threats and, in the case of the eldest daughter, his raping of her when she was twelve. The DeVillez children understood what their mother had done. The eldest daughter was only angry that her mother had been foolish enough to get caught. The son admitted he was pretty violent, that he, too, smacked his wife.

Bernard had been twenty-five years old and Joyce fifteen and pregnant when they got married. By the time her first daughter was born, Joyce was back in her parents' house, afraid to see her husband. But he came for her one night, beat the door down, and took her back to their apartment, knocking her senseless. By the time they had moved to Evansville, Bernard was unemployed. Joyce found work and had a couple of lovers he never knew about. The beatings continued—irrational, bruising poundings of her that could last days and eventually drove her to call a woman named Charlotte Hendrix, who had boasted to a relative of Joyce's that she could arrange just about anything. How about, you know, a contract? Hendrix said, Fine.

On June 5, 1974, a young man of about seventeen called at the DeVillez apartment, saying he wanted to buy Bernard's pickup. Terry Walker said he had left his money back at the Jackson House Motor Inn. They drove back there. Walker got Bernard to come to the back of the motel. Three shots were heard, and DeVillez's body was found lying behind a chainlink fence.

Walker was arrested in Detroit and led police to Hendrix who, in turn, led detectives to Joyce. Police tape-recorded Hendrix phoning the widow, who could barely conceal her sense of relief. Confronted with this police recording, Joyce pleaded guilty to second degree murder of her husband and was sentenced to fifteen to twenty-five years in the Indiana State Prison for Women, the first women's prison built in the country. Safer interviewed the police sergeant who investigated the case and the Indiana state's attorney who prosecuted Joyce and asked a few speculative questions. Suppose Joyce had picked up a gun herself, in the kitchen at home, for example, and shot her husband dead; couldn't she have claimed self-defense and gotten away with murder? Probably. But the prosecutor said society had to make a distinction between killing in sudden anger and cold-blooded contracting for murder.

Safer interviewed Dr. Shriver for two hours on camera in the assistant superintendent's office, trying the same speculative questions on the psychiatrist and his colleague Ron Branca. When it came to Safer's reverse questions, Dr. Shriver was invited to answer again although he was told his answers didn't really matter as they would not be recorded or reported. Safer's questions were different this time, the doctor noticed, and so were his own, now unfilmed, answers. When Safer and crew packed up, they had, at least on audio, two sets of questions and two sets of answers. Of the two hours, less than thirty seconds made it to *Justifiable Homicide?* as the November 25, 1979 broadcast was entitled. Dr. Shriver got a lot of hate mail, as an unfeeling chauvinist, not for what he said but for the way Safer introduced him and Branca.

SAFER: Dr. Paul Shriver and Ron Branca are psychologists at Indiana State Prison. They've seen Joyce and counseled other women who have killed their husbands, and they feel that, in most cases, the women tend to exaggerate their husband's brutality.

SHRIVER: When you begin to think of a person as "my problem" or "this monster" or "this abomination of my life"—if that's the perception—you're taking the first step in a line of logic that leads you to see something that needs to be gotten rid of.

SAFER: If this were a movie, I think this is the way it might end. We'd have Barbara Stanwyck or Joan Crawford walking out of the prison gates and the door would clang shut behind her and there'd be a huge grin on—on—on her face that would say, "I got away with it."

SHRIVER: In two years, that will happen. Whether she'll be grinning and feeling she got away with it is something we have no way of knowing.

BRANCA: But the irony is that the prison is inside her. She's her own jail.

SAFER: Forever?

BRANCA: Forever.

SAFER: Justifiable homicide or cold-blooded murder? You decide.

These remarks were all that survived the editing. Inevitably perhaps, given *60 Minutes'* affection for confrontation and drama, the doctor's more provocative comment that such tragedies might be prevented if people could learn to see each other in untheatrical, unsensationalized terms was dropped.

Joyce DeVillez did walk out of the prison on a work parole after serving seven and a half years. After the furor over the program died down, Dr. Shriver wrote a long letter to *60 Minutes.* He had cleared his participation with the ethics board of the American Psychiatric Association; he had followed its guidelines; Safer had promised they wouldn't try Joyce on television. Yet that was exactly what *Justifiable Homicide?* had turned out to do. By phone, he was told he would be given air time for a rebuttal, but he never heard from *60 Minutes* again. He later took a vacation in Florida, caught a six-foot black shark, had it stuffed, hung it on his office wall in the prison, and named it Morley.

To charges that *60 Minutes* omits some elements of a story while playing up others by editing the material, Hewitt answers, "What journalist doesn't?" Editing is used to express ideas, to improve audience understanding, and to shape a progression, a story line out of a complicated series of facts. As Schorr observed in *Clearing the Air,* putting city council and school board meetings, House of Representative and cabinet sessions on television—live and unedited—tends to turn such proceedings into simulations—"self-conscious, self-serving, and rarely self-effacing." Shaping a strong story out of complicated events and facts is as old as story telling. Homer knew how to give the *Odyssey* hook, heat, and topspin, and ideas and subjects become dynamic when they are "anthropomorphized"—turned into people, into people confronting each other. "You reach people very well that way," Wallace told the *Eye of the Media* roundtable. He might have added that without riveting faceoffs or stimulating plotlines, you don't reach an audience of 30 to 40 million every week. Making current events interesting is the big challenge. "The kind of thing we're looking for is something that evokes an emotional response," says CBS News President Van Gordon Sauter. And he isn't talking about *60 Minutes* but *The CBS Evening News with Dan Rather.*

Back in the heroic days when Hewitt and Douglas Edwards did the news, their fifteen-minute broadcasts were a tabloid news service. Television journalism still has a hard time covering complicated subjects, and the evening news is still more snacks than the full menu, but Walter Cronkite's long and forceful tenure gave television news authority. Under Sauter, the "that's the way it is" certainty is gone, and Rather and his executive producer, Howard Stringer, have moved the emphasis to "moments that, ideally, establish a relationship with the viewer. A moment isn't a State Department briefing on Lebanon, nor a picture of artillery fire destroying a house in Beirut," says Sauter. "It is a Lebanese woman screaming in the rubble of her kitchen. It is a deserted railway spur rusting away in the desert of Alamagordo, New Mexico, where the first atom bomb was exploded and it says, possibly, that our nuclear fears have aged. A moment is a visual reflection of a feeling.''

Hewitt has never been afraid of theatricality, of dramatic action, premise, and structure, nor of slightly larger than life story-tellers. He calls *60 Minutes* a show on which four reporters take the audience along with them on a story, almost sharing their notes with the viewer.

.

# 14

# Hanging versus Lynching
## "60 Minutes" and the law

Considering where the newsmagazine pokes its nose, it is surprising that there are not more lawsuits. It is even a surprise that no one has taken a swing at the correspondents or the crews. Threats of legal action come in every week, but only a handful of suits is actually filed every year. Lieutenant Colonel Anthony B. Herbert's $45 million defamation suit—still before the courts a decade after it was begun—is in many ways an exception, but ever growing numbers of libel actions are filed against broadcasters and publishers, a majority of them by American business, which shows increasing willingness to use libel suits, and the threats of them, as a tool against what it sees as unfair treatment in the press.

The cost of litigation caused the National Council of Churches to ask CBS News to submit *The Gospel According to Whom?* segment "to impartial and public" arbitration to determine whether the Marti Galovic-Morley Safer report violated network standards of fairness and accuracy. CBS News rejected the offer, and church lawyers were unsure what action to take next. "We could afford the arbitration procedure, which we estimated would cost $10,000," said Harriet Ziegler of the

NCC. "Our lawyers think taking *60 Minutes* and Morley Safer to court could cost $2.5 million. We just can't afford that."

Four years before a Los Angeles jury found *60 Minutes,* Dan Rather, and Steve Glauber had not defamed Dr. Carl Galloway in *It's No Accident,* the network and *60 Minutes* fought a New York doctor. Long Island endocrinologist Dr. Joseph Greenberg charged he had been defamed in a segment on amphetamine abuse and sued for $30 million. *Over the Speed Limit* had featured an unidentified woman, appearing in a shadow, telling Mike Wallace how Dr. Greenberg had treated her for obesity. The woman, subsequently identified as Barbara Goldstein, said she had taken eighty pills a day under the doctor's direction, including four or six daily that were "amphetamine-type drugs." She expressed the belief the medication had caused her to become mentally disoriented and were connected with birth defects in her daughter. The Great Neck, Long Island doctor, who had refused to be interviewed for the 1976 segment, produced by Grace Diekhaus, cited his records, indicating he did not prescribe eighty pills a day for Goldstein. He asserted that some of the medication he was accused of prescribing was actually prescribed by the four or more doctors who were also treating her.

In a pretrial ruling, a New York appeals court found that Diekhaus and Wallace might not have met "the elementary standards of basic news reporting." The suit was discontinued by the plaintiff in the second week of trial in Mineola, Long Island. The discontinuance of the lawsuit involved no money damages but, according to Dr. Greenberg's lawyers, an apology to him from the network, an assertion CBS associate general counsel Guttman disputed.

The ghost of the Vietnam War had CBS and Mike Wallace—but not *60 Minutes*—as defendants in the biggest defamation suit against the network. CBS faced a $120 million suit by General William C. Westmoreland over *The Uncounted Enemy: A Vietnam Deception.* Wallace set the tone of the ninety-minute special in the opening minute:

WALLACE: Tonight we are going to present evidence of what we have come to believe was a conscious effort—indeed a conspiracy—at the highest levels of American military intelligence to suppress and alter critical intelligence on the enemy in the year leading up to the Tet offensive.

The documentary charged that while commander of the U.S. forces in Vietnam, Westmoreland joined in this conspiracy to misrepresent enemy troop strength to make it appear that his own forces were stronger and were winning the war. A few months after the 1982 broadcast, Van Gordon Sauter admitted the documentary, produced by George Crile, had violated some of CBS's journalistic ground rules, and that the claim of conspiracy was "inappropriate." He rejected Westmoreland's demand for forty-five minutes of rebuttal time, though he made an eleventh hour offer of fifteen minutes' air time.

Four months after the broadcast, a *TV Guide* cover story pronounced *The Uncounted Enemy* a "smear," accused CBS of distorting facts that might have contradicted its thesis and of leaving out rebuttals from officers challenging the idea that Westmoreland had underreported enemy strength to avoid stirring up domestic protest over the war. Sauter ordered former Cronkite executive producer and now senior news department executive Burton Benjamin to conduct an in-house probe and, two months later, issued a memorandum that said *The Uncounted Enemy* had violated some journalistic procedures. The memo added, however, that the network stood behind the documentary and cited the Benjamin Report as supporting this conclusion.

Benjamin's sixty-eight-page report became an issue in itself, and lawyers debated whether it deserved the protection of the New York "shield law," which prevents journalists from being forced to disclose sources. Along Broadcast Row, the Benjamin Report's revelations of how Crile had put the broadcast together were regarded as possibly incalculably embarrassing to CBS no matter what its conclusions on the accuracy of *The Uncounted Enemy*. In an early skirmish, CBS lost its bid to keep the report secret. By issuing the Sauter memo, Judge Pierre N. Laval ruled in the U.S. District Court in Manhattan, CBS destroyed any constitutional priviledge it might have had to keep the document secret. "CBS cannot at once hold out the Benjamin Report to the public, as substantiating its accusations and, when challenged, decline to reveal the report contending it is a confidential internal study utilized solely for self-evaluation and self-improvement," Laval ruled. CBS said it would appeal the decision.

Earlier, the network had won a plea to have the venue of the suit shifted from South Carolina, Westmoreland's home state, to New York City. Before the trial, *The Uncounted Enemy* became the subject of a thirty-minute PBS documentary on Hodding Carter's news media watch program, *Inside Story*. This investigation of the investigators was produced by former CBS producer Rose Economu, who had worked on complex CBS documentaries, including a piece on the use of the defoliant Agent Orange in Vietnam. She interviewed Westmoreland, CBS lawyer Roger Colloff, and Don Kowet, coauthor of the *TV Guide* article

(Sally Bedell, the other half of the *TV Guide* writing team, was now an entertainment writer on *The New York Times* and her bossess at the *Times* wouldn't let her be interviewed on the air). Realizing that stonewalling PBS and Economu might do CBS more harm than good, Sauter and Crile let themselves be interviewed. Wallace was interviewed for three hours but declined to appear on camera. Economu came away impressed with Crile's research into the murky areas of military intelligence at a time of war and with his candor. "He met with us and we asked him the hard questions and he answered them all with a great deal of consistency," she said. "I don't think the word 'smear' is appropriate." Carter was not so kind. "History may yet decide that there was indeed a conspiracy in Saigon to fake the numbers," he summed up on *Inside Story*. "But at this point the evidence is less compelling, the witnesses more contradictory, and the possible conclusions less obvious than the documentary suggests."

That, too, was the essence of the Benjamin Report. A week after Judge Laval's ruling, CBS surrendered and made public the internal inquiry. Less embarrassing than a lot of broadcasters had feared—or wickedly hoped—the report nevertheless provided details of inside disagreement over how to prepare *The Uncounted Enemy*. In his tough summary, Benjamin counted eleven principal flaws, including coddling sympathetic witnesses, choosing to interview people supporting the conspiracy conclusion and, indeed, failing to prove that there had been a plot at all. A month later, Crile was suspended for surreptitiously tape recording several telephone conversations with former Defense Secretary Robert McNamara. The suspension forced the cancellation of a news special Crile was preparing on Nicaragua and what forces inside that country the CIA claimed to be representing.

Nine months before the fall 1984 trial, both sides disclosed sworn testimony at twin press briefings in Washington. General Westmoreland charged the documentary had tried to portray an internal intelligence debate as a conspiracy and criticized CBS for continuing to reaffirm its conclusions that his command purposely underestimated enemy troop strength before the 1968 Tet offensive. In his corner was testimony from former Defense Secretary NcNamara denying any "faking of the data." In the network's corner was Gains B. Hawkins, the army officer who in 1966 and 1967 was responsible for estimating the enemy strength in Vietnam. In the spring of 1967, his testimony revealed, he presented Westmoreland with an analysis indicating far higher enemy strength than had previously been reported, but the general refused to accept the updated figures. "He voiced concern about the political impact these higher enemy strength figures would have in the United States, 'and told me to take 'another look' at the figures,'' Hawkins testified.

In May 1984, Kowet published *A Matter of Honor: General William C. Westmoreland vs CBS,* a purported behind-the-scenes account of the making of the documentary, which so blistered the network that it mobilized all its public relations resources to discredit the book. According to the former *TV Guide* reporter, Crile knowingly victimized the general, and Wallace was so unprepared when he interviewed Westmoreland that he had to read from cue cards written by Crile. CBS News countered with a barrage of letters and rebuttals written by Crile, Wallace, and others, to book reviewers and reporters covering television charging that Kowet was Westmoreland's "wholly owned subsidiary," that the writer had reported more than one hundred conversations without actually talking to any of the CBS principals involved, and that he had fabricated an alleged telephone call in which Wallace was said to have enlisted the help of *The New York Times* executive editor A. M. Rosenthal in downplaying critical coverage. "That program was a public lynching brand of journalism,'' Kowet answered back in Los Angeles while on a book tour. "It could have been a good program. Then there wouldn't have been a suit. And there wouldn't have been a book.'' As the Westmoreland suit moved toward its day in court, it was widely believed in broadcast and legal circles that besides CBS and the controversial broadcast, the Vietnam War and its participants would be on trial.

News organizations and lawyers specializing in First Amendment issues followed the case with concern. The court's order to make the Benjamin Report public was especially disturbing. Acknowledging that everybody in broadcast and print journalism was afraid of having newsrooms "overlawyered,'' James C. Goodale, a New York attorney specializing in free press issues, said internal probes could generally be kept confidential if they were performed by the news organization's lawyer or as a preparation for defending a suit. More ominous for *60 Minutes,* Barry Lando, Mike Wallace, and the network, Jonathan W. Lubell, the New York attorney representing Colonel Herbert, suggested Judge Laval's ruling might be a nice precedent when it came to trying *Herbert vs Lando.* Lubell likened the Benjamin Report to Ford Motor Company's studies of safety defects in its Pinto automobile. Those studies were finally made public and "I'm not sure why CBS should be treated any differently.'' More neutral observers tended to believe the public would be the ultimate loser because the result of hundred million dollar libel suits will not be only that the media will be more careful, but that they will be less willing to take up controversial issues.

In the face of adverse libel verdicts and the economic pressures they bring to bear, many news organizations have turned away from disclosures of individual corruption or exposés of private business. "Journalism is getting to be a cautious business," said Jerry Uhrhammer, a reporter for the *Press-Enterprise* in Riverside, California, and former chairman of the 1,200-member Investigative Reporters and Editors. At ABC and CBS, investigations are concentrated on *20/20* and *60 Minutes,* and newsmagazine producers are under increasing scrutiny by the network legal departments.

Truth without facts is unacceptable on *60 Minutes.* This may seem elementary in nonfiction television, but a sizable body of documentarians, most of them freelancers on the fringes of network and PBS production, say they are not journalists at all, but film-makers with an independent point of view. Their "advocacy" argument goes something like this: All nonfiction is slanted, most notoriously in profiles and biographies, whether written or filmed. What is important is not evidence, but the *way* things are said. Honesty also has to do with the story's angle of attack, and with frankly advocating a point of view. It has to do with letting contradictions happen. A person working on a documentary is not a puppeteer pulling character strings and railroading audience responses, but someone with a story line loose enough to let reality impose itself. Sensationalism is inherent in television "because you're not talking about it, you're showing it." Judgments are provisional and tentative, and nonfiction documentaries shouldn't be afraid of saying so.

This attitude makes for often thoughtful documentaries that nip their audiences in surprising ways, specials that have more style than substance, but when it comes to hanging someone, a documentary must make sure the hanging is fair. It must lay out the facts and examine the pros and cons, if the hanging is not to be a lynching.

Hewitt's credo that anyone may be hanged on *60 Minutes* if the data are there to support the conviction is enforced on the producers by CBS lawyers. Each segment is fine-combed, and if it is considered dicey or borderline, or other network attorneys insist the producers show they have enough proof so that, if sued, CBS has the goods to meet—and beat—a lawsuit. On rare occasions, affiliates are given an early Thursday satellite feed instead of the normal Sunday transmission of *60 Minutes* so they can fret over whether or not they should carry the upcoming edition. One such instance was *Kiddy Porn,* a 1977 Barry Lando-Mike Wallace collaboration that featured sleazy characters and Barry himself, filmed with a hidden camera, buying an illicit "chicken film," or child pornography movie, in a Los Angeles porn shop. *Kiddy Porn* was scissored even more than Hewitt had wanted.

CBS attorneys will work overtime and on Sundays to protect *60 Minutes*. On the afternoon of Friday, January 14, 1983, U.S. District Judge Adrian Duplantier blocked the coming Sunday broadcast of a Mike Wallace segment dealing with seven New Orleans police officers charged with violating the civil rights of blacks during a police murder investigation. Judge Duplantier took the action after CBS disobeyed an order he issued three hours earlier that he be allowed to see the script of the upcoming *60 Minutes* piece. He was acting on a motion by attorneys for the seven policemen due to stand trial in Dallas. The defense contended the *60 Minutes* exposure might prejudice jurors and should therefore be banned.

With few exceptions, the courts have refused to block publications or broadcasts, holding that prior restraints on the press are unconstitutional. On Saturday, CBS lawyers had Judge Duplantier's ruling overturned by a federal appeals court. Duplantier then issued a second order, blocking the segment in the Dallas area, but that too was overturned by the appeals court. The attorneys for the policemen then went to the U.S. Supreme Court Justice Byron White and Chief Justice Warren Burger. Justice White declined to block the broadcast; Justice Burger wouldn't review the matter, and there was Mike Wallace on Sunday at seven, leading off with the complicated story. Two months later, three of the seven cops were convicted in Dallas.

A year earlier, CBS had turned over transcripts and tapes of an interview from a Mike Wallace piece on a fast-food franchise fraud after a federal judge in Newark, New Jersey threatened the network with "a terribly large fine." Judge Herbert J. Stern said he needed the *From Burgers to Bankruptcy* material because the evidence already presented was unclear. Next, he said he was obliged to make the partial transcripts available to defense attorneys who had argued that unused portions of the 1978 segment could help the six men accused of defrauding investors in the defunct Wild Bill's Family Restaurant chain. Citing the so-called Brady Standard, which requires prosecutors to turn over material that might clear defendants of charges or guilt, Judge Stern said he believed portions of the unused *60 Minutes* segment "would materially aid the defendants." Chandler was furious. The decision, he said, "opens a veritable floodgate which will permit future 'fishing expeditions' by defendants in criminal trials. What is at stake is whether the courts can, without limitation in terms of relevance of admissibility, require the press to turn over unpublished materials in criminal cases. Should this view prevail, the independence and integrity of a free press will be seriously threatened.'' CBS appealed.

Eventually, a federal appeals court ruled for CBS and against Judge Stern, saying defendants in the fraud case could not have the full transcripts and tapes of interviews used in preparing the *60 Minutes* broadcast. The defense, the appeals court ruled, was entitled to unbroadcast portions only when these segments could be used directly to impeach the testimony of prosecution witnesses. Judge Stern had erred both in compelling CBS to give him full transcript of the *From Burgers to Bankruptcy* material and in saying he was required to give all that material to the defense so it could decide what use it wanted to make of it.

The issue of unpublished materials was decided against a tiny newspaper (37,000 circulation) in Illinois in a stinging blow to news organizations. At issue was a memo to a federal prosecutor written by two reporters on the *Alton Telegraph*. The pair had wanted the prosecutor to help them verify a tip that a savings and loan association in their St. Louis suburb was laundering Mafia money, then loaning it to a local real estate developer. The tip was never confirmed and the *Alton Telegraph* never published anything about it, but the reporters' memo was passed to federal S&L regulators, who found other irregularities in the savings and loan bank's dealings with its biggest customer. The developer's credit was cut off by the S&L, and he allegedly went broke as a result. Years later, the developer learned of the reporters' memo and filed a $10 million libel suit. Eleven years after the reporters passed along their tip to authorities, a local jury slapped the *Telegraph* with a $9.2 million verdict, a judgment nearly four times the newspaper's net worth. Two years later the matter was finally settled, with the *Telegraph* paying $1.5 million.

A year before *60 Minutes'* editorial process was put on trial—and vindicated—in Dr. Galloway's $30 million suit over *It's No Accident*, CBS News tried to grapple with the thorniest of issues: How do we define the individual's right to privacy as opposed to the public's right, or at least wish, to know. With the help of Columbia University's Graduate School of Journalism, CBS assembled a symposium at Princeton University. With cameras rolling and Arthur R. Miller, a Harvard Law School professor to stir up the debate, a dozen bright people in journalism, the legal profession, the arts and business discussed private lives versus public rights to know for nine hours.

Miller offered hypothetical cases: of a congressman snorting cocaine and cheating on his wife; of a right-to-life activist who in her teens had

had an abortion; of a movie star with a mother in a mental institution; and of a German-born American who, as a seventeen-year-old Wehrmacht recruit, had been a guard at Auschwitz concentration camp, and provoked the panel to decide what journalists and with them, the public, should be allowed to know, and where the line should be drawn. CBS fielded its news president Van Gordon Sauter, Morley Safer, Ed Bradley, and Bob Schieffer. Barbara Walters was there from ABC, Sally Quinn from *The Washington Post*. The law was represented by Floyd Abrams and Wyoming's formidable barrister—winner for the heirs of Karen Silkwood in the $11 million suit against Kerr-McGee Corporation over plutonium contamination—Gerry Spence, himself a subject of a *60 Minutes* profile. There was a good deal of oneupmanship in this *Eyes on the Media* roundtable, but forceful points were also made. Lauren Bacall scored for individuals pursued by the news media, saying the fight was uneven, that huge news organizations determined to go after someone's life story was no match for that person, whether an unknown or a celebrity. Abrams spoke for the press, saying "the truth is the absolute defense in libel." William F. Buckley notched one for privacy when he said the question was not to define the lengths of newspeople's curiosity, but the lengths of their "licit curiosity." Walters scored for television news stars when she said it was not the questions that damaged people but people's answers. Spence spoke for ruined reputations and savaged Abrams' defense of unidentified sources and 99.9 percent accurate research as not good enough when the issue is the possible assassination of someone's character.

With Dan Rather narrating, a one-hour distillation, *Eyes on the Media: Private Lives, Public Press,* was aired, to paltry ratings, on Academy Awards night in 1983. The broadcast showed that self-interest and personal conviction are at least as important as the constantly redefined reaches of constitutional law. The way we define libel decides what we read and watch and hear.

# 15

# A Judgmental
# Business
*Self-criticism, watching
the watchdog*

❧ "Is it right to confront reluctant witnesses with cameras and microphones?" Mike Wallace asked. "Should we withhold vital information from a prospective interviewee? Is it proper to pose as someone other than a reporter to get the story? Is it fair for us to set up our own enterprise—a bar, a clinic, a 'sting' operation, in effect—to lure unsuspecting subjects before our cameras? Is it appropriate, is it fair, to infiltrate a factory, a labor union, to find out what is really going on inside?"

The questions came in the opening edition of the 1981–82 season. The entire hour was given over to a panel discussion of *60 Minutes* and its practices. In addition to Don Hewitt and his angels, CBS's television commentator Jeff Greenfield, and media pundits from *The Boston Globe* and the *St. Petersburg* (Florida) *Times,* the past president of Investigative Reporters and Editors, and Fred Friendly was there to lend gravity and possibly give perspective to the proceedings. After showing an excerpt from *Fake ID,* the famous undercover segment in which a *60 Minutes* researcher falsified her identity to prove how easy it was to get a U.S. passport, Wallace was asked if he believed that in the pursuit of deceit, deceit was okay? Weren't there other ways of doing the story?

202

Didn't the Passport Office, for example, have case histories? A clip showing a *60 Minutes* soundman posing as a wealthy cancer victim in order to infiltrate a phony California clinic provoked Eugene Patterson of the *St. Petersburg Times* to say it was great television but terrible journalism. The way to go with a story like that, he said, was to find people who had been victimized by the cancer clinic. Why couldn't you make your story out of those people?

Because, to be convinced, viewers want as much documentation as possible, Hewitt answered. Later he summed up. "I think this probably all comes down to a very simple proposition: Does the end justify the means? Are we in the business of providing our viewers with documentary evidence of wrongdoing, misdeed, and can we do it better this way than if Mike Wallace gets on camera and says, 'Let me tell you what happened to me last week in Chicago?' "

But Jeff Greenfield wondered how Hewitt would take it if the tables were turned. "If I, as a sometime media critic, hired a camera crew to infiltrate and put a camera in the offices of *60 Minutes* to show how you guys got a story and you found out, I really don't think that you would accept this as investigative entrepreneurial reporting. I think you guys would hit the ceiling . . . You go in to cover a story, it's your camera, it's your microphone, it's your producer, and ultimately, it's Don Hewitt, you, and whoever else is responsible. You guys decide what gets on the air and I guess the question is: How would you like it done to you? How would you like somebody to point a camera at you and you didn't know it was there, confront you with embarrassing material, perhaps about a life you once led or something you once did?"

Mike said, "I wouldn't like it," drawing one of the program's few laughs when he added, "which is why I lead a life beyond reproach."

The idea of this very special edition, Don said, grew out of *60 Minutes'* popularity. "I think we have an inordinate amount of influence in this country. We tend to do stories about people and places and things that the American public talks about, and we'd be deaf, dumb, and blind if we didn't acknowledge that they talk about *60 Minutes*." Much criticism was raised during the hour, but no single investigative method was either uniformly decried or endorsed. Hewitt stopped short of saying the program would eliminate any reporting technique, even if some controversial techniques had been abused. Fred Friendly called *Looking at 60 Minutes,* as the special edition was called, a breakthrough. Like every other big institution, he said, "Journalism is under surveillance and attack, and this is constructive. For any news organization to say, 'We are accountable only to ourselves,' is ridiculous. If you listened carefully to this program, you could almost hear broadcast journalism grow up.''

Six months earlier, *20/20* and CBS's owned and operated Chicago station WBBM had investigated each other. With huffs of self-righteousness, each had found the other's investigative methods appalling. On April 20, 1981, WBBM preempted an hour of its prime time to air the result of its investigation of a Geraldo Rivera piece, *Arson for Profit*, which had just been awarded an Emmy for investigative reporting. The *20/20* segment purported to reveal how a Chicago landlord and his associates had bought and burned buildings to collect on the insurance. Twenty-nine fires and ten deaths, according to the ABC newsmagazine, had resulted.

The accusations were grave. Not only was *Arson for Profit* inaccurate and misleading, CBS's Bill Kurtis said in *Watching the Watchdog*, but the manner in which *20/20* producer Peter Lane and correspondent Rivera had gathered and presented their facts was questionable. The techniques Kurtis tore into included the use of undercover reporters, misrepresentation, invasion of privacy, and the so-called ambush interview. Kurtis showed Rivera surprising his target landlord as the man came out of a restaurant, bombarding him with questions, and getting a deadpan denial of any guilt. Kurtis also showed Lane misrepresenting himself as a potential buyer of a derelict building and entrapping an insurance inspector by giving him $100 on camera in exchange for a favorable report. ''After a sixteen-month investigation involving six agencies, federal, state, and private; after agents reviewed thousands of real estate records, and the research material turned up by the Better Government Association and *20/20,* a federal grand jury did not find enough evidence of arson for profit for even one indictment,'' Kurtis concluded, adding for ironic effect that Lane had refused to be interviewed by WBBM.

*Watching the Watchdog* was broadcast in Chicago only, but ABC quickly labeled it ''irresponsible'' and ''scurrilous, shoddy journalism.'' A month later, ABC was back with its own reflections on the WBBM attack, an hour-long rebuttal in the *20/20* time slot on its owned and operated Chicago station. ''Tonight we will show that in fact . . . it was WBBM and Bill Kurtis who were wrong,'' intoned *20/20* host Hugh Downs. The program showed *Watching the Watchdog* producer Scott Craig doing an ambush interview of his own. Downs claimed Rivera had tried three times to get the aggrieved landlord to consent to a formal sitdown interview and, said Downs, the fact that a grand jury didn't find enough evidence for an indictment was not necessarily a criterion for a viable journalistic investigation. Finally, Kurtis and Craig had refused to be interviewed for ABC's rebuttal. Downs concluded, ''Tonight we have examined WBBM's work and we found . . . several factual errors and a number of partial truths and, as we showed, considerable selective editing. We found that the men who were watching the watchdogs, themselves deserved to be watched.''

Kurtis came back one more time. Shortly before he was made coanchor, with Diane Sawyer, of the *CBS Morning News,* he went over the Lane entrapment of an insurance inspector in a report for an annual survey of broadcast journalism. ''Filming from an unmarked van with hidden cameras and a wireless microphone, the *20/20* team caught an exchange of money between an insurance inspector and the ABC producer who had maneuvered the man into position before the camera,'' Kurtis wrote in the Alfred I. Dupont-Columbia University Survey. ''The television viewer thought he was seeing a bribe on camera, part of the arson for profit conspiracy. In fact, he was watching an insurance inspector with no record of bribe-taking receive $100 when it was offered. Did the television report reveal corruption that advanced its arson story—or create it?''

The question is as old as the cinema itself. By 1910, the pioneers knew the power and the thrills of montage. Take the same expressionless closeup of a famous actor's face, Lev Kuleshov suggested, and juxtapose it to shots of a soup bowl, a coffin, and a child, and viewers will marvel at the actor's ability to successively express hunger, sorrow, and fatherly tenderness. If you want to condemn someone, film him from a high angle. For hero worship, shoot up from a low angle. Before the introduction of sound, makers of features and newsreels possessed a remarkably fluid film vocabulary capable of expression such as D. W. Griffith's historical sweeps, Ernst Lubitsch's wry humor and the apotheosis of *homo sovietico* in the works of Sergei Eisenstein, V. I. Pudovkin and Kuleshov. In the 1930s and in World War II the art of propaganda on film was perfected, from Leni Riefenstahl's hypnotic Nazi propaganda to the U.S. Army Signal Corps' Pictorial Service movies about yellow-bellied Japs.

Television turned to newsreel organizations when it decided to broadcast news. Before switching to Fox Movietone, NBC hooked up with the Hearst-MGM News of the Day service and actually obtained its first film free from the Signal Corps and its first staff members from the Office of War Information. CBS had a contract with Telenews, a newly formed unit related to the Hearst-MGM news service, and Don Hewitt was a recently demobilized War Shipping Administration correspondent. The first guidelines on news editing were issued in the 1950s, with complete sets of do-and-don't rules following a decade later. The networks now keep their standards and practices in loose-leaf notebooks because rules are constantly being changed and updated to accommodate new news judgments on journalistic entrapment, trespass, the use of private documents, and outside organizations. As we have seen, *60 Minutes* has used the Los Angeles-based Community Informational Project to nail down medical insurance fraud. Besides collaborating with *20/20* on *Arson for Profit,* Chicago's nonprofit Better Government Association has helped the ABC newsmagazine investigate abortion clinics, shelter care homes for former mental patients, and unnecessary surgery.

Inevitably, perhaps, the series of programs and debates in which broadcast news organizations examine themselves and their brethern are not only self-serving, but actually fail to condemn any brand of reporting. Hewitt admits to reservations about certain reportorial techniques but thinks controversial techniques are valid when used with care. Westin says it is all a matter of individual judgments. "Sometimes shoving a camera in front of someone makes perfect sense," he says, "and other times it's sandbagging the individual." Making current events understandable is the primary concern of news programming. To give up *any* technique is just too hard.

However, such debate of confrontation journalism and how much news biz is really showbiz tends to obscure the basic assumption of broadcast journalism that there is no event, no story that can't be told. Cameras and microphones attract spectators, and news crews either pretend no one else is there (a panoramic view of Iraqi tanks rolling into Iran is invariably cut before we get to see twenty other news crews shooting the same scene) or make the crowd part of the story ("Below, at least two hundred people witnessed the suicide finally leap to his death."). Newspeople don't control events; they must improvise, adapt. To the people whose story they document, they often appear slippery if not downright deceitful, but that is because the journalistic allegiance is to the story, not to its component parts.

At the forceful level on which network newsmagazine journalism is practiced, there is a tendency to believe that facts somehow lie hidden in the fabric of life, that unearthing facts—and the truth—is a matter of using the right tools. The story of how a small town in western Illinois cut off the water to a family with a desperately ill little girl dictates an approach that is different from the one used to expose Chicago slumlords trading rundown tenements among themselves to inflate the insurance value before the buildings are torched. But in the midtown

Manhattan corridors and editing and screening rooms of *60 Minutes* and *20/20,* ambush interviews, journalistic stings, and trespass and entrapment are merely a part of the investigative repertoire. Techniques may be discussed, objections entertained, but there is little discussion of the newsmagazines' own dimension in the events they choose to cover. There is no consideration of the crew's physical presence in the telling, of celebrity Mike Wallace in Polo's Mason Street giving everyone eager to be on TV a chance to sound off; of whether showing the insurance inspector pocketing a $100 bill advances the arson story or helps create it, of the cumulative effect of shaping the facts into absorbing television.

Astute observers point to the truth on the cutting room floor, the ninety minutes of film that remains unused and the forty-five seconds' worth that is used, but the dangers implicit in the *60 Minutes* or *20/20* approach—the danger of turning reality, the fabric of life, into "stories," issues into theater—is not addressed. As Hewitt is the first to tell anyone, his program has had more spin-offs than any broadcast in television history. Besides *20/20* and the successive NBC newsmagazines, he also means *Sunday Morning, Real People, Entertainment Tonight,* and *That's Incredible. 60 Minutes* has been copied because it makes money, of course. But there are other reasons why it has become a prototype for a new sort of journalism.

# 16

## Imitations
### *The competition*

*60 Minutes'* most showbiz-oriented rival is neither of the other networks' current newsmagazines but *Entertainment Tonight,* the fast-paced celebrity show that is watched every weeknight by 10 million viewers. The biggest future threat is Roone Arledge's plans for a new prime time magazine for ABC, a project whose start-up costs he acknowledges may be a formidable $20 to $30 million.

The 1980s are a time of wrenching change for television. Entertainment comes from Hollywood, with the networks increasingly functioning as impresarios, schedulers, and feeders of programming to ever more powerful local stations. The much-heralded cable revolution is taking place and, as a double whammy to ABC, CBS, and NBC, the satellite revolution is being absorbed into humdrum station routine. Not only are stations building receiving dishes to pull down the seven o'clock news, but they are using the ''birds,'' as the satellites are called, to deal directly with the Hollywood suppliers. *Entertainment Tonight* is the first Look-Ma-No-Network success. The half-hour program is made in Hollywood by Paramount Pictures and ''birded'' to over 150 stations every day.

Satellite transmission is also eroding the networks' monopoly on national and world news. Live coverage of regional and national events by local stations and local news personalities began in earnest in 1980, and not only because it was an election year. Satellite costs were coming down dramatically, and satellite transmission was becoming an everyday newsroom tool in big, competitive markets.

And news and public affairs were making economic sense. The escalating cost of entertainment programming was of concern to ABC, CBS, and NBC, especially at a time when cable TV nibbled at the prime time ratings. At hour of prime time entertainment cost an average $800,000, more than double the price of an hour of *60 Minutes*. CBS and NBC tried to expand their evening news to one hour in 1980, while ABC turned its late-night specials on the hostage crisis into *Nightline,* a brand-new news half hour. Local stations resisted the expanded network news because they discovered not only profits can be made in local news, but that a top-rated local news show can give a significant boost to an entire schedule, no doubt because it is news that largely determines the public's image of, and confidence in, a television station.

Bill Leonard had become boss of the CBS news division at Dick Salant's retirement in 1979. The transition was orderly although Bill Paley had promised the news division presidency to Bill Moyers. The chairman had been appalled by the fact that Moyers would want to leave CBS for PBS and had offered lots of money and the CBS News presidency to keep him in the fold, but Paley had been unable to offer Moyers the one thing that would have made him stay: a regular prime time show like the one Ed Murrow once had. "I can't do that anymore," Paley told Moyers, "the minute is worth too much now."

Leonard's presidency was an interregnum, and he and everyone else knew it, but his two short years at the helm included the departure of Walter Cronkite. Roger Mudd was the favorite in the early innings of the slug fest for Cronkite's spot, but Mudd's patrician loftiness and Roone Arledge's miscalculations in wooing Rather to ABC finally made Dapper Dan the CBS evening news anchor.

The situation was tense in the fishbowl as Rather took over. The great debate was on what news actually was. And as viewers began switching dials, there were questions. Should they adopt ABC's tricky triple anchor format or should they somehow prevail on Paley to bring Walter back? Disillusioned viewers sampled the other networks in ever greater numbers, in search, it was said, of the certitude and comfort they had known with Walter for eighteen years. Six months after the Rather succession, the long-time ratings lead had eroded, and CBS News was at a virtual dead heat with ABC and NBC for the evening news. Were the megabucks that had secured Dapper Dan a big mistake? Sandy So-colow, who had been executive producer and guiding light behind the Cronkite show since the mid-1970s, suddenly found himself 3,000 miles from the fishbowl, heading the London bureau and replaced by Howard Stringer. William Self, the assumed heir apparent to Leonard, was suddenly gone.

The *CBS Evening News* was a vast operation, comprising 125 reporters, editors, executives, and researchers, and nerves were frazzled as the ratings sank and the slippage translated into a $10,000 erosion of the cost of a thirty-second commercial. In one fast week in November, CBS Broadcast Group President Gene Jankowski shuffled the news division executive suite and made a burly fifty-one-year-old individualist Bill Leonard's replacement.

Van Gordon Sauter came with a reputation. His favored sartorial style was straight out of an L. L. Bean catalog. While stationed in Los Angeles, he had lived aboard a cabin cruiser and commuted to work in a jeep. When visiting brass were due in from New York, he posted the office with a "full mogul alert." In Chicago, he had kept a parrot as a deskside pet. Everything became "zero based" as he took over. With the exception of Dan Rather, "nothing and no one has a given." Bearded, shrewd, and very much a sharply tuned television age intellect, Sauter quickly realized they were producing *The Evening News* as if Walter were still in the anchor chair. Sauter's first command was to use warmer production techniques (lavender turtleneck sweaters were tried on Dan) and to shake up the visceral look of all newscasts, he ordered "bumpers"—those COMING UP NEXT promos before commercial breaks—lasers, and graphics.

On the ninth floor, the *60 Minutes* organization watched the new broom with studied indifference. And, indeed, Sauter's aggressiveness, showmanship, and nonconformism, but consummate corporate gamesmanship didn't extend to tinkering with success (a stained-glass sign in his office proclaimed with mock reverence: "In Nielsen We Trust"). And a success it was. Through the 1979–80 season, *60 Minutes* was at the top of the Nielsens—followed by ABC's *Three's Company* and CBS's *M\*A\*S\*H* and *One Day at a Time*—and CBS charged advertisers $145,000 for a thirty-second spot. Hewitt was named the 1980 Broadcaster of the Year by the International Radio and Television Society. "I've got eight more years before retirement," he said. "I don't want anybody else's job. I don't want to broadcast. I want to stay right here and do *60 Minutes* as well as it is being done now. This is my dream realized."

In April 1979, he had married NBC's White House correspondent Marilyn Berger. Mike Wallace had introduced them and when they began dating, one of them would take the Eastern shuttle to the other's home until she joined WNET, New York's PBS station, as the UN correspondent for its short-lived *Special Edition*. She had been married one year right out of college and spent fifteen years as a single woman in journalism. The marriage—his third—took place aboard the yachts of socialites Bill and Hillie Levitt. They called each other their best critic. "I would like to believe that I am a successful enough male not to worry about my wife's successes in life," he told the New York *Daily News*. "I think they complement me. Would I mind if she made more money than I did? Not in the least. No, I'm not a feminist, nor am I a masculinist. I have an abhorrence of labels." She said she liked being married to the executive producer of the most popular show on television. "It had nothing to do with me, of course, but it's nice to know a man when he's at the top of his world." She moved to ABC and her duties took her to the Middle East on the Anwar Sadat peace initiative, and to Europe with the White House, but they preferred their Central Park South apartment with its spectacular view of mid-Manhattan and their Long Island weekend house in Southampton. On Sunday evenings, happiness for Don is to watch *60 Minutes* at home with a roomful of friends. "I like to observe when their interest flags and when they perk up," he said.

Sauter easily ratified the Salant-Leonard choice of Ed Bradley as Rather's replacement on *60 Minutes*. There was talk of getting a woman correspondent, and two years later it was wildly rumored that Diane Sawyer would become Hewitt's first tigress. To Sauter's greater satisfaction, however, her coanchoring of the *Morning News* with Bill Kurtis pulled the perennial breakfast show also-ran toward the ratings respectability of NBC's *Today* and ABC's *Good Morning, America*.

They tinkered with an afternoon news program on which the four *60 Minutes* stars shared hosting chores. Produced by Grace Diekhaus, *Up to the Minute* made its debut in September 1981 as a half-hour show running five days a week. Bradley, Reasoner, Safer, and Wallace each did a week's stint, sitting in a studio and chatting with assorted panelists about issues of the day: nuclear proliferation, school busing, abortion. It certainly wasn't Hewitt's kind of show (the assigned tiger never left his chair) but it was another way of getting more bang for the 120 million newsside bucks. Reasoner, who had once cohosted *Calendar,* was maybe the best. He chatted with Robert Walden, who played Joe Rossi, the pushy reporter on *Lou Grant,* and Bobby Riggs, the former tennis star and crank misogynist, on ''Aggressive Women: Turn-On or Turn-Off,'' and managed to get in a couple of barbs at their inane answers. Halfway through the fifteen-week trial run, everyone knew *Up to the Minute* would not be renewed. Hewitt and everybody except Diekhaus—the program was her idea—shed their obligatory crocodile tears as the flop was cancelled.

Despite their reputation for fearless investigative reporting, Wallace and Safer were involved in an embarrassing conflict of interest in 1981 that exploded in gleeful turning-the-tables news stories and splattered Hewitt with hard-to-duck questions of ethics. ''In no way will my judgment on whether this story is to be filmed for *60 Minutes* be affected by any consideration other than its newsworthiness,'' Don told *The New York Times* in early 1981. ''Personal considerations will have nothing to do with it.''

Morley had wanted to update a hard-hitting investigation of conditions in Haiti that Wallace had done in 1972. That report focused on what Mike had described as the ''bloody'' regime of François (Papa Doc) Duvalier and his son, Jean-Claude. The story had caused an infinite amount of distress to Lorraine Wallace. Her first cousin, Nancy Chenet, lived in the island with her Haitian husband and their children. Lorraine had had a gallery in Port au Prince. She and Mike spent part of every winter there, enlarging the house she still owned. Lorraine was also involved in Ambiance, a new family-run shop specializing in international wares.

Not much good had happened to the poorest country in the hemisphere since 1972. President Jean-Claude (Baby Doc) Duvalier had spent the better part of the decade ridding his regime of his late father's henchmen and consolidating his own power. Media censorship had been tightened once more, but 1980 had brought the ''boat people'' and international outcries as several thousand Haitians landed on the beaches of the Bahamas and Florida. Safer proposed a new look, at both Duvalier's harsh regime and the impoverished life that led these thousands to flee in barely seaworthy boats. Their arrival in the United States was a hot subject and an acute embarrassment to the outgoing Carter administration. Should the U.S. government lock them up and face accusation that it was doing so because the Haitians were black and fleeing right-wing oppression, or let them acquire legal refugee status as it had so generously done a year earlier for most of the 125,000 Cubans of the Mariel boat lift?

When Wallace heard of the plans to update, Hewitt was on a two-week tour of China and Japan. When Don got back, the two of them had lunch. Hewitt suggested Mike go to Morley with his problem. Safer heard Mike out and agreed to abandon the project. Was Morley's promise to lay off less than convincing? Did Wallace leak the in-house contretemps to make sure the nail stayed in the coffin? In late February, he acknowledged to Les Whitten, an associate of Washington columnist Jack Anderson, and to the Associated Press, that he had approached his colleague and asked him not to film the report in order to protect Lorraine's relatives in Haiti who might be subject to reprisals. CBS tried to minimize the damage. Hewitt announced the Haitian project would be put in the works, with Ed Bradley as the correspondent. Wallace took some of the blame. "My motive, the safety of my family in Haiti, was a decent one. But I shouldn't have brought it up in the first place. Having said that, Hewitt shouldn't have told me to go to Morley and Morley shouldn't have said okay." Safer voiced his own regrets. "Both Mike and I made a mistake," he conceded to *Newsweek*. "But I was caught off guard. This is the only time in my experience that someone tried to wave me off a story."

The brouhaha was too much for everybody's ego and in December 1983, Barry Lando and Wallace delivered *Haiti*, a faintly optimistic report that said the country was still a dictatorship, that the United States had poured in aid for decades and would have to continue doing that because there was no trust in the regime, therefore no foreign investments and no commitment by the Haitians themselves.

*60 Minutes* remained a national habit. It was no wonder that everyone else in television was trying to come up with a matching winner. *Entertainment Tonight,* or *ET,* was the surprise success.

From its rickety start in 1981, *ET* became the kind of slickly produced and expertly edited half-hour broadcast that was not many rungs below what Hewitt had in mind when he pitched his televised *Life* magazine idea to his bosses in 1968. *ET* had the potent young demographics that advertisers pay premium prices to reach.

*ET*'s Hewitt is George Merlis, the former executive producer of both *CBS Morning News,* which he is credited with reviving, and ABC's *Good Morning, America.* To accentuate its rise from pure puff and fluff, the program added an investigative team in 1983, starting out with a balanced and informative four-parter on the *National Enquirer* and a rundown on who gets what share of the average five-dollar movie ticket.

James G. Bellows, a former *Los Angeles Herald Examiner* newsman, as *ET*'s managing editor, steered the program toward harder news items in the entertainment industry. Halfway through his two-year contract, Arledge lured Bellows to ABC to work on the ABC News chief's most cherished project, a newsmagazine format that could supplement *20/20*. ABC News Vice President Richard C. Wald announced that this new, possibly ninety-minute program might go head-on against *60 Minutes* on Sundays in a 6:30 to 8 P.M. time slot. Yes, Wald added, the half hour headstart on *60 Minutes* was deliberate.

With the reverse logic argument that it makes sense to put a program in last place against something that is nearly impossible to beat, NBC went head-on against *60 Minutes* during the 1983–84 season. *First Camera* was the fifth newsmagazine incarnation for NBC since the peacock network had matched the every other week *60 Minutes* with its once a month *First Tuesday* in 1968.

It had been fourteen frustrating years for NBC and its on and off again news boss Reuven Frank. Frank had concocted *First Tuesday* and Frank was no slouch in the news wars. It was he who had beat Hewitt and Cronkite with his Huntley-Brinkley double anchor evening news. In an irresistible climb that paralleled Hewitt's, Frank had gone from news writer to executive producer of the evening news, followed by a tour of duty in the back of the book. In addition, he had spent a few years overseas before becoming president of NBC News. His back-of-the-book sting followed the quiet demise of *First Tuesday*. Like Hewitt's magazine, *First Tuesday* had languished opposite ABC's *Marcus Welby*. It had been moved to Fridays in 1971 with no better results. Two years later, Reuven began selling the network on another newsmagazine. Something new with someone new he had discovered over on the news side: NBC's young Paris correspondent Lloyd Dobyns.

Frank called his program *Weekend* and it was on weekends that he wanted it to air. In September 1974, he got the go-ahead for a once a month, ninety-minute newsmagazine to be hosted by Dobyns. The time slot was in doubt. The FCC was holding extensive hearings on its new prime time access rule, which barred the networks from the half hour between 7:30 and 8:00 P.M. Monday through Saturday. Reuven began assembling a team. What he was looking for, he let it be known, was producers and technicians "who hungered after movement and were suspicious of too much talk. Storytellers impelled by curiosity rather than by mission." Sy Pearlman was one of his first producers. One of Frank's first assignments for his new recruit was the story of a Texas school for the children of Hare Krishna devotees. When Sy came back from Dallas and they screened the footage, Reuven was appalled. "He had a judge talking for three minutes. He had this one talking, that one talking—all those damn experts," Frank remembered. "I said, 'Throw the judge out.' He said, 'What do you mean, throw the judge out? The judge talking is very important here.' I said, 'Not to me. Give me the picture. If it doesn't engage the audience, somebody talking is not going to help.' "

Fate would have it that the FCC prime time rule would not be modified and that *Weekend* got to replace *Saturday Night Live* in the first Saturday of each month in the 11:30 to 1 A.M. time slot. Heavy investigative reporting was obviously not what was called for, and with Dobyns and Pearlman, Frank went for offbeat material, curiosity for its own sake, delivered with a light, whimsical touch. Dobyns sat on an authentic park bench below a mock marquee and, with punches of wit and irony, hosted a potpourri of films, cartoons, and patter about killer bees, lighter-than-air flying machines, and the Reverend Sun Myung Moon. The cartoons, Reuven explained, were to keep viewers awake.

*Weekend* limped along at the bottom of the ratings, averaging 6.1 while *Saturday Night Live* in the same time slot drew an 8.1. Still, NBC began talking of shifting *Weekend* to weekly prime time in 1976. Reuven Frank was quoted as saying he didn't know how much change such a move would mandate, but others predicted the program would suddenly blossom with hard, investigative, issue-oriented pieces. The entire ninety minutes was given over to a single topic in May 1977. The trial balloon was a touchy subject and provoked a controversy inside NBC News, because Reuven managed to get the rest of the news operation to clam up about it. The subject was the family rehabilitation program of a California clinic specializing in father-daughter incest.

Producer Claire Crawford had worked hard with the Santa Clara Child Sexual Abuse Center doctors and staff to establish trust and respect. She had obtained a verbal commitment from the clinic not to grant interviews to other radio and television journalists, even those of NBC News, until the *Weekend* program had aired. As a result of that commitment, Tom Snyder's *Tomorrow* had to cancel a scheduled interview with the center's principals, and an NBC radio news reporter was denied the interviews for a series of reports on incest in the United States. Officials of the Santa Clara center also turned down requests for interviews from ABC and CBS until after the *Weekend* telecast. Hewitt was all for Reuven Frank in this instance. *60 Minutes* was not one of those turned down, but if there had been an attempt, he wouldn't have objected to being refused. "I would have understood and wouldn't have blamed them. Protecting an exclusive is a natural thing to do in journalism. It goes on all the time."

Frank felt frustrated because producers and correspondents too often failed to think their ideas through and because the format was too locked into the good guy/bad guy confrontation that looked sexy on the tube but contributed little to people's understanding of issues. Led by *60 Minutes,* the newsmagazines concentrated too much on what Morley Safer called the national disgrace stories and not enough on root causes. There might be tenuous links worth uncovering, and discussing, between a plant closing and the causes of unemployment, between one refugee family and the causes of war. Ironically, the constant emphasis on social sores had two contradictory results. On the one hand, people couldn't help feeling upbeat seeing a sore eloquently highlighted and therefore on its way toward healing. On the other hand, this concentration on social sores also made people shake their heads and ask, "What's the use?" The journalistic tool of dealing with issues by having clashing views expressed by "talking heads" in a studio discussion; or by Reasoner giving Ulster's Protestants' position and Wallace the Catholics' point of view; by doves and hawks quarreling about Vietnam; or by Israeli and Arab sympathizers exchanging rhetoric about Palestinians—usually ended up examining disagreement rather than areas of agreement. The way newsmagazines *packaged* issues, Frank felt, almost amounted to a bias against understanding.

While NBC fiddled in 1978, ABC launched *20/20.* Harold Hayes and Robert Hughes were the announced cohosts for the Thursday, June 6, debut. The hour-long newsmagazine would run through the summer and, depending on its ratings, might get a regular season slot. The fifty-one-year-old Hayes was the former editor of *Esquire* who, for one year, had hosted WNET's *Round Table,* a talk show dealing with the topics of the day, principally in the arts. Hughes was *Time* magazine's art critic, a thirty-nine-year-old Australian with a critic's knack for imparting knowledge offhandedly. He had appeared in fifteen documentaries for the BBC and was to gain notoriety in 1981 with his eight part BBC/*Time-Life* modern art series, *The Shock of the New.* After the summer trial run, *20/20* would become a monthly broadcast in the fall schedule to await the ratings verdict and the programmer's dictates.

For his Hewitt, Arledge reached beyond ABC's news division and came up with Bob Shanks, a West Coast entertainment producer. Shanks' credentials included *The Merv Griffin Show* and, in New York, *Good Morning, America.* Obviously ignorant of Hewitt's inspiration for *60 Minutes,* Shanks told *The New York Times* he was determined to keep *20/20* from being an outright copy of the CBS hit. The model for his newsmagazine, he said, wasn't *60 Minutes* but print magazines such as *Life* and *Look.*

The first outing was a disaster. The program offered investigative reports and news updates, kicky features, and instant self-improvement gimmicks. Among the latter was a section called Words, which taught audiences to pronounce and define such words as arcane and exegesis. *20/20*'s future star correspondent, Geraldo Rivera, waxed indignantly about jack rabbits being used as live bait to train racing greyhounds. Sander Vanocur, a former NBC foreign correspondent, had to use parts of a government film to juice up a story that kept insisting it was possible for ordinary crazies to make their own nuclear bomb but that the segment was certainly not meant to be alarmist. Sylvia Chase and Dave Marash were seen conducting interviews for a slight piece on California Governor Jerry Brown. There was an opening cartoon and a rapid week in review section called The Wayward Week.

The second edition featured a Rivera segment on urban homeless living under bridges and in train tunnels, a feature by Thomas Hoving on the making of the movie *Jaws 2*. Vanocur was back with a follow-up on his terrorists-building-nuclear-weapons report. The four pieces were presented "straight," without theatrical flourishes.

Av Westin became the executive producer of *20/20* and quickly whipped the broadcast into shape, although it would continue to be sensationalist and go for showbiz and celebrity profiles. Westin called this his trade-off. Pop culture pieces on music, movies, style, new books, and personalities were designed to keep the audience tuned in for the investigative reports, the geopolitical backgrounders, economic essays, and segments about crime, pollution, and energy.

Westin started with the assumption that audiences just weren't interested and that they had to be "lured into the tent," as Hewitt had said on a number of occasions. The rule Av imposed on his producers and correspondents was that they should assume their audience knew nothing about the subject at hand and really couldn't care less. This "zero knowledge and zero interest" postulate led to some sharp writing.

Geraldo Rivera became *20/20*'s fast-breaking star. He was the "beautiful ethnic" who managed to reach the goal of many of television's investigative journalists: to step out from under Mike Wallace's shadow and start casting shadows of his own. What Sidney Poitier did for the white middle-class idealization of blacks in 1960s movies, Rivera did for white middle-class acceptance of minorities on television newscasts in the 1970s. Rivera grew up street smart in the Long Island suburb of West Babylon and was a lawyer specializing in New York City petty criminals when WABC's Gloria Rojas called up and said the ABC flagship station was looking for a Latino. "I mean she didn't pull any punches," he remembered. "I had no experience, so obviously they didn't want me for that. The implication of this was that someone had sat down with a yellow pad and pencil and said, 'Okay, what do we have in New York? All right, we got a million of these, two million of those, three million of these, five hundred thousand of those. All right, we got to go after this, got to go after that, got to get these Italians. What do we have left? We have no Puerto Ricans! Well, we have got to get one. Who we gonna get? They can't talk English, they got kinky hair."

Starting with a 1972 documentary on conditions at the Willowbrook State School for the Mentally Retarded in Staten Island, which led to radical reforms in the hospital—and a Peabody Award for the long-haired, twenty-seven-year-old Rivera—he rose through a series of investigations into the plight of migrant laborers, prisoners, motorcycle gangs, and other stories not normally part of the evening news lineup. He kept his streetwise swagger, never entirely convinced that WABC had hired him in a flush of humanitarian concern. He created *Good Night, America*—not with the news division but the ABC entertainment division—was assigned to *Good Morning, America* to help improve its dismal early ratings. He moved in chic circles, was married for a while to Edith Vonnegut, Kurt Vonnegut's daughter, and almost ran for mayor of New York City. When Arledge reorganized the news division in 1977, Rivera was put into the mainstream of network news and, a year later, joined Westin on *20/20*.

Westin also had Sylvia Chase, the cagiest interviewer of them all. "Her subject won't know he's in trouble until she says with wide eyes, 'But didn't you just tell me . . .' " said NBC's crack investigative producer, Ira Silverman. She had come from the *CBS Morning News* after a stint as general assignment reporter for network news in New York. Dave Marash went back to anchoring the WCBS *11 O'clock News,* but Westin kept Thomas Hoving, the former director of the Metropolitan Museum of Art, who discovered a whole new career for himself as *20/20*'s celebrity interviewer. Westin added Tom Jarriel, a committed and convincing reporter with a yen for getting reluctant people to talk, and later got John Stossel, another CBS crossover. Av's off-camera talent included such heavies as Stanhope Gould, Walter Cronkite's young counterculture ace who, back in 1972, had produced the two Watergate reports that nearly toppled Frank Stanton and Dick Salant, and former Hewitt producers Joe DeCola and Marion Goldin. Gould had quit CBS for NBC over the way William Small had edited his investigative documentary on the 1972 CBS Records scandal. Goldin's stay with *20/20* was short-lived, as she later moved up to the futures editor's post on *World News Tonight*.

*20/20* went weekly in 1979 and grew in popularity on the strength of Rivera's reports on heroin use among children; private buccaneers like James G. (Bo) Gritz looking for Americans missing in Laos; Chase's harrowing insight into nursing homes making money by neglecting the elderly the government pays them to care for; Hoving's closet interview with Prince Charles' former valet (hotly entitled *Behind the Royal Doors*), and disquisitions on airline food; and Jarriel tracking fathers skipping child support payments, and Soviet deserters in Afghanistan. Occasionally, Barbara Walters weighed in with exclusives. ABC took good care of its magazine, providing it with a print advertising budget for splashy, full-page ads in *TV Guide*. When the program lost some of its younger, urban following to NBC's *Hill Street Blues,* the network persuaded Westin to do a couple of country-and-western features to attract a new "audience cluster." With its mix of investigative journalism, society profiles, surprise reporting, and its fresh material during the summer when *60 Minutes* relied on reruns, *20/20* climbed in the ratings. By the summer of 1983, it had become ABC's highest rating program for five weeks, beating out *Love Boat* on a few occasions. It acquired a number of distinct features: more women producers, even a producing couple, theme music and, as on a number of PBS public affairs offerings, viewers could send in two dollars and get transcripts of broadcasts.

In 1984, *20/20* slipped in the ratings, however, finishing the season in the No. 60 spot. This didn't prevent Bellows from finally announcing *Seven Days,* designed to be a flashy roundup of the news of the previous week. Scheduled for the 1984–85 season, the new newsmagazine, which included Jeff Greenfield, Sander Vanocur, and Pierre Salinger among its correspondents, was expected to have Kathleen Sullivan, coanchor of ABC's *World News This Morning* and one of the rising stars of ABC News, as its anchor.

Reuven Frank couldn't let *20/20* run away with whatever glory and ratings didn't belong to *60 Minutes* and, during the summer of 1980, he nailed together *NBC Magazine with David Brinkley*. NBC had some of the best investigative reporters on its roster, such people as Brian Ross and Jim Polk. Tenacious, and willing to dig up sources by being a pain in the neck, Ross broke the Abscam story and caused ABC and CBS to offer him the moon if he'd defect. He demanded that his producer Ira Silverman be part of the package, and NBC managed to hang on to both of them with what was called Fort Knox contracts. Jim Polk came to

NBC from the Watergate wars at *The Washington Star* and was nick-named a Junior League Ross, down to his preference for working with a steady producer, Charles Collins. NBC News had brought Dick Salant on board in 1979, and the former CBS News boss in turn brought his protegé William Self along. The reason was not charity toward super-annuated CBS executives but the dramatic ascendency of ABC News. Everybody at NBC was under the gun to stop the ratings hemorrhage.

From the inception, *NBC Magazine* was a veterans' showcase. There were no attempts at seducing Ross-Silverman or Polk-Collins to join the newsmagazine. Haughtily, disastrously, Brinkley set the tone. *NBC Magazine* wouldn't do rock stars like *20/20* and sure wouldn't chase crooked preachers as they did on *60 Minutes,* and the correspondents—veterans Garrick Utley, Betsy Aaron, and Jack Perkins—would be the cutting edge, not the field producers. He argued vehemently against letting producers set up the structure of a report and bring in the corre-spondent as a last-minute announcer. On *NBC Magazine,* the correspon-dents would devise the thrust and basic outline of a segment and call in the producers to work out the technical details.

Everything was going wrong for the peacock network and, in 1981, NBC President Fred Silverman himself was canned. Braving dismal rat-ings, pathetic profits, mutinous stations, and an audience that just wouldn't watch, the troubled RCA network made Grant Tinker the NBC presi-dent. Regarded as a talented programmer with taste, imagination, and a proven knack for delegating authority to able, creative people, Grant re-fused to panic and to shove shows on and off the air and into new time slots at a reckless clip (Silverman had moved NBC's only real winner, *Hill Street Blues,* into five different slots in its first twelve weeks). On the news side, the new nightly news team of Roger Mudd and Tom Bro-kaw drew 9 percent fewer homes than John Chancellor did a year ear-lier. But Reuven Frank stayed on as president of NBC News. After the hustle and flash of the Silverman years, what Tinker wanted was stabil-ity and that meant as few changes as possible in the management team.

Frank tried a newsmagazine again in 1983. This time it was called *Monitor* and it had Sy Pearlman as executive producer and Lloyd Dob-yns as host. No park bench this time, no visceral visuals, and no cartoons either. Frank and Pearlman managed some macho publicity mileage before the broadcast went on the air by saying that if it de-pended on them, *Monitor* would go head-on against *60 Minutes.* NBC was currently running *Small World,* a talent showcase for young people, and ABC was airing *Ripley's Believe It Or Not,* a kind of gee-whiz, Guinness Book of Records imitation show, on Sundays at seven. When

*Monitor* made its debut, however, it was on Saturdays at ten, opposite ABC's long-running *Fantasy Island* and *CBS Saturday Night Movie.*

Like Charles Kuralt on *Sunday Morning,* Dobyns was perched on a solitary high-tech chair in a bare, geometric decor as he introduced, in true magazine fashion, four segments dealing with human interests: humor pieces, photo essays, profiles, and investigative features. The hard pieces, Pearlman promised before the March 1983 debut, would be "without white hats vs. black hats" scenarios and, he added, "we won't chase people down the street with cameras." On the air, Dobyns said, "Our stories are about love, hate, greed—the spice of life." The first edition examined nonphysical harassment. Reported by Steve Delaney, *Get Out of My Life* showed a woman who had made abusive phone calls to the same man for forty-two years; a husband and wife, hounded from Hawaii to Texas by the husband's former girl friend; and a young woman in California, bothered constantly by a young man working in a grade school library, who kept saying, "I just want to be friends." For a giggle, *Monitor* looked at Tulelake, California, supposedly the horseradish capital of the world. *Black or White,* reported by Rebecca Sobel, told the story of a Louisiana woman who, on applying for a passport, discovered she was one-thirty-second black. *Trailing the Trailers,* narrated by Dobyns, focused on some 5,000 American gypsies of Scottish and Irish descent running home repair and mobile home swindles. "*Monitor,* the first program suggests, has not quite decided how it wants to put itself together," wrote *The New York Times'* critic. "It has made a promising start, however, as the newest television magazine."

The adrenalin flow improved with the second edition and a Delaney report on the Texas University hospital in Galveston where private area hospitals dumped the poor sick. "We're the real *St. Elsewhere,*" said a doctor in the chilling report on the 13 million Americans without health insurance and the cost squeeze that forced some private hospitals to turn away or transfer patients unable to pay.

The ratings remained modest. During its first season the best *Monitor* could manage was to rank sixty-second of sixty-five programs. Grant Tinker wanted a newsmagazine that worked, and gave Frank the network's commitment for a spruced-up new *Monitor,* a program that would have a fresh title, set, and format.

Reuven was ready with heavy ammunition. Marvin Kalb, Ken Bode, and Jack Reynolds would be visiting correspondents, NBC investigative ace Mark Nykanen would provide regular reports. "Without trying to translate into a hard news program," the news president said, "we will do subjects of greater currency, taping on Sundays and perhaps even go on live.'' Frank's real bombshell was that the new magazine would go head-on against *60 Minutes* on Sunday nights. The hope, said Pearlman, in announcing that Dobyns would continue as host, was that viewers were getting tired of *60 Minutes* and that the new NBC offering would be an alternative. Asked to comment on this new competition, Hewitt said *60 Minutes* had lived in the Sunday evening neighborhood for fifteen years. ''It is a nice neighborhood. Mr. Disney used to live across the street. Father Ripley lived down the block. I don't imagine a nice man like Mr. Reuven Frank would do anything to ruin our neighborhood. Whatever they do is fine with me.''

During the summer of 1983, NBC newsmagazine staffers scrawled suggestions for a new title on a blackboard across from Pearlman's office. *Ninth Try,* was one idea. *Seventh Son,* read another. Other title ideas were *Fifth of Scotch, Third Base, Eight Maids-a-milking,* and *Zero Affiliates.* The idea of putting the new program up against *60 Minutes* didn't sit well with NBC affiliates. As many as 10 percent of them threatened not to carry the new magazine, but to offer instead *Fame,* the weekly entertainment series about New York's School of Performing Arts that, ironically, was cancelled by NBC after two seasons. ''My reaction is one of regret,'' said Frank. ''It will make it harder for the show to succeed.'' Tinker admitted a few stations had been quite vocal about not clearing the new program, ''but I wouldn't call it a groundswell of antipathy.''

On its premier show, *First Camera* finished dead last in the ratings, and the rest of its 1983–84 season was not encouraging. The reporting was good to superb. There were tough, investigative stories about repeat offenders (Dobyns: ''Eighty percent of all crimes are committed by the same 20 percent of repeat criminals''), domestic violence, teenage drunk driving, Brazilian arms exports to Third World countries. A report on how little Las Vegas police and hotels care about what happens to visitors as compared to authorities in such tourist meccas as Disney World, featured Mark Nykanen, wired for sound carrying a hidden camera, eliciting from a Vegas cab driver which rich tourists' rooms he could burglarize. There were segments on the marketing of sports personalities, Asian immigrants, and underwater delivery of babies, and instead of Hoving-type celebrity fluff, there were portraits of a former Hollywood socialite, now a nun at a Mexican state penitentiary, a former Vietnam pilot practicing medicine in El Salvador.

But 7 percent of NBC's affiliates didn't carry *First Camera,* meaning that viewers in Boston, Detroit, San Francisco, Memphis, Charlotte,

North Carolina and, by early 1984, Philadelphia, couldn't sample the program. And Pearlman didn't have the clout to bump the network. Every other week through the football season, games crowded out up to half the newsmagazine.

*First Camera*'s pace was somewhat slower than *60 Minutes* and *20/20* and, critics noted, it often aired quirky, offbeat pieces that were unlikely to appear on most news programs. Dobyns was pronounced aloof, cold by a number of affiliates. "The affiliates are not right all the time," said Frank in defense of the magazine host. Still, it looked as if *First Camera* might become yet another failed attempt. "Grant Tinker has told me he wants a newsmagazine that works," Frank said. "If *First Camera* isn't the one, we'll yank it off and put on another until we get one that does work."

*First Camera* was consistently the lowest-rated broadcast on network television and in the spring of 1984 it was cancelled. The failure was the second major disappointment for Frank. Four months earlier he had axed *NBC News Overnight,* the acclaimed but low-rated late-hour newscast originally coanchored by Dobyns and Linda Ellerbee. Frank left the NBC news presidency and was succeeded by Lawrence Grossman, the former president of Public Broadcast Service. Chairman Tinker was committed to a newsmagazine and on the day *First Camera* died said NBC News was already developing "a new and competitive weekly program."

What *would* it take? By 1984, *60 Minutes* was ancient in terms of the lifespan of a television show. When Harry Reasoner introduced the first broadcast, LBJ was in the White House, *Hair* was running on Broadway, and Black Power was raising a clenched fist at the Olympic Games in Mexico City. Little had changed in personalities and format since. Morley Safer and Ed Bradley had joined, Dan Rather had come and gone, but Reasoner and Mike Wallace were still there, joining with the two junior men, in promising "those stories, and much more, tonight on *60 Minutes.*" The backstage crew was a mixture of old hands and new people, but there was no urge to outbid the competition for the services of a James Bellows. There was little talk of finding theme music, of adding computer graphics, of replacing the ticking stopwatch motif.

News is as competitive as prime time entertainment programming— the two are even cross-pollinating; *ET* is news in form, entertainment in content, the first TV hybrid. The combined annual budgets of the three network news division now exceed $500 million, but things are far from equal. Advertising miscalculations by top management forced Van Gordon Sauter to impose, for the first time in history, a personnel cutback at CBS News in 1983. At NBC, Reuven Frank was also told to hold the line, while a corporate fiscal squeeze at ABC delayed the launching of Roone Arledge's cherished prime time magazine being developed by James Bellows.

# 17

## Crossroads
### *"60 Minutes" future tense*

"Let's face it, we aren't the four best reporters in the world," said Morley Safer in a moment of hindsight. "There are a lot of good reporters around. What we have going for us is Don Hewitt."

*60 Minutes* was nearly three-quarters of the way toward *The Ed Sullivan Show* as the longest running television broadcast, but Don wasn't ready for aggregate introspection. It was another election year, and he was preparing for another of his quadrennial stints at control room swagger—a reduced role, to be sure, because the three commercial networks had decided 1984 was the year they wouldn't provide gavel-to-gavel coverage of the Democratic and Republican party conventions. Computers were providing graphic pyrotechnics and each presidential candidate had his own phalanx of image makers. So what was next for Don Hewitt? "This is what's next," he said, pointing to the electronic hardware in his offices on West 57th Street.

Longevity is subtle and exceedingly rare, but *60 Minutes* is the exception. Every Sunday, upwards of 40 million viewers find the stories that Bradley, Reasoner, Safer, and Wallace present important, exciting, controversial, or merely different enough from so much other television

225

fare to make the CBS program a continued national habit. Nearly everything in TV is imitative, a spin-off or a dust-off of something else, but
*60 Minutes* is curiously both a prototype and a one-of-a-kind phenomenon. While remaining originally, stubbornly, the same, it continues to
spawn imitations as ever newer recombinant satellite and cable entrants
announce newsmagazines.

Humility is not the chief character trait at *60 Minutes,* and Hewitt
and his angels see no reason to change anything, or to listen to any criticism. Inquiries into the program's journalistic ethics, when not conducted by CBS News itself, are dismissed out of hand. Hodding Carter,
the host and chief correspondent of *Inside Story,* the PBS series on the
media, may say *60 Minutes* is a fuzzy mix of journalism and showbiz
and that the blur affects its people's news judgment. At *60 Minutes,*
though, the former Carter administration's State Department spokesman
is rejected as "a professional flack." But CBS's own Bill Moyers was
Lyndon Johnson's State Department spokesman, and Diane Sawyer
"flacked" for the Nixon White House. Students at Columbia Graduate
School of Journalism may call Fred Friendly's seminars the most exciting at the school because of the gut questions he raises, but when he
berates *60 Minutes* for not addressing serious subjects confronting the
country, they call him an academic out of touch with the real world.
Criticism from Accuracy in Media's Reed Irvine is dismissed as the
yammering of a self-appointed TV guru. The party line at *60 Minutes* is
that *60 Minutes* is not the evening news; that *60 Minutes* doesn't have
to cover *anything;* that its criteria have to do with dramatic impact and
its ability to involve an audience, not with social obligations. Hewitt has
little patience with the print media's fascination with television journalism. He likes to remind print journalists who label TV news "showbiz"
that it is newspapers that carry gossip columns, advice to the lovelorn,
horoscopes, crossword puzzles, and bingo-style numbers games, and that
newspapers' and magazines' obsession with television isn't recipro-
cated. Television news doesn't evaluate newspaper coverage and doesn't
pretend to be the judge of whether *The Washington Post* or the *Chicago
Tribune* did the better job of covering the last Democratic convention.

CBS is very protective of *60 Minutes* and the program's star correspondents. Mike, Morley, Harry, and Ed can dish it out but they don't
have to take it. Hodding Carter's efforts to look into the reasons behind
General Westmoreland's $120 million suit against CBS and Mike Wal-
lace set off a revolt against the network's daddy-knows-best attitude.
Wallace was tired of being treated like a baby by the legal department
and of the network pretense that he was never available when others were

trying to interview him. He called for a "free the slaves" rebellion so he and his colleagues could speak up if they felt like it. Indeed, Wallace and Gary Paul Gates published *Close Encounters: Mike Wallace's Own Story*. Advance word had it that this 1984 book would be candid and forthright.

*60 Minutes'* own public relations are handled by Aristides Maravel, who will mail press kits to inquiring reporters so long as their investigating of the investigators remains in the lighter mode, but will say neither Hewitt nor other key members of the staff have the time or the inclination to explore the newsmagazine's deeper meanings and responsibilities.

People love to criticize a winner, of course, and after fifteen years the candy factory's "middle age spread" is a print journalists' theme, together with the Wallace Question. A *TV Guide* cover story in 1983 by John Weisman spoke of flat and uninteresting stories, of *60 Minutes* no longer being the show it used to be. Weisman quoted Reasoner as saying the percentage of hard-hitters had not diminished in recent years. Wallace would only talk about ambush journalism in the past tense. Bradley complained about the people who wouldn't talk to him, while Safer bewailed the "dreadful job" most people writing about television were doing. "Off-handed putdowns of their critics seem to be a habit of the *60 Minutes* staff," wrote Weisman.

The Wallace Question was laid to rest six months before Mike Wallace turned sixty-five and CBS offered him five more years. The contract, which he described as "generous," put his salary for the final year at $1 million, about the same as Hewitt's annual stipend. The contract takes Wallace through his seventieth birthday, May 8, 1988, and four months later, through *60 Minutes'* twentieth anniversary. Frank Stanton, Richard S. Salant, and Walter Cronkite were never offered such contracts, and to CBS watchers it only proved that Van Gordon Sauter and Hewitt believed Wallace indispensable to the continued success of the program.

There were those, like Morley, who were sure the broadcast could survive Mike's departure, or even that of Don himself, who saw superb replacement possibilities in Charles Kuralt and Diane Sawyer. And, a little further afield, there was Richard Threlkeld, lost to ABC but someone who, like Reasoner and Rooney, probably could be lured back. Dan Rather, on the other hand, belongs to the après Wallace le deluge school, calling Mike the broadcast's "nuclear engine" without which it would cease to generate power. Wallace brought up the question himself when he turned sixty-five, variously saying he would surely continue to do segments through 1985, although how many a year he couldn't tell, or that he'd better stay a full-fledged member of the team or he might be replaced by Sawyer. He kept going not so much because it was an obsession to continue, he said, but because it was fun. What both he and the various bodies of opinion tended to ignore was the numbers. *60 Minutes* ranked first in the ratings. An average of 40 percent of the television audience watched the weekly reports over the last two years.

Yet television was changing dramatically, and Thomas H. Wyman, CBS's president and chief executive officer, moved aggresively into the new technologies. Deregulation was the catchword, and the FCC had opened the process aimed at allowing the networks once more to own cable TV systems in 1981 when it granted CBS an exception to its network-cable cross-ownership ban. To make sure CBS wasn't perceived by Wall Street as standing pat in the midst of mutation, Wyman quickly started up CBS Cable as a cultural channel, only to kill the new service after a scant year and not tolerable amounts of red ink. Next, CBS joined the enemy and, with Time Inc.'s Home Box Office (HBO) and Columbia Pictures, created a new motion picture company to make fodder for all those insatiable new cable systems. The move came three months after MCA Inc., the parent company of Universal Pictures, Paramount, and Warner had, together with Viacom and Group W, formed Showtime and The Movie Channel.

Pay television wasn't just challenging the networks, it was thinning their lifeblood—the ratings. For the country's 35 million cable viewers—40 percent of the total television households—HBO and its cable competitors offered programming that until recently had been the exclusive province of ABC, CBS, and NBC: original, made-for-TV films, miniseries, and continuing comedy and drama series. HBO even planned to launch a series called *Stopwatch,* a parody of *60 Minutes.* The cablers were beginning to earn enough from their base of subscribers to spend dollars comparable to the networks. The dilution of the ratings began slowly, then accelerated. In terms of their share of the total viewing audience, ABC, CBS, and NBC slipped from 92 percent in 1975 to 78 percent in 1983. There were indications that by 1990, the networks' share might be down to 65 and possibly as low as 60 percent, but a somewhat self-serving CBS research report showed the networks' loss was perhaps being stemmed and that 70 percent of all viewers might still be tuned to the networks in 1990. ABC, CBS, and NBC didn't like to even think that viewers were deserting them because of ever-increasing numbers of commercials. Between 1967 and 1981, network commercials more than doubled and, led by CBS, the networks began experimenting with fifteen-second spots, so-called "split 30s," that added further to the mind-boggling commercial clutter.

HBO and the other cablers were taking the biggest chunk of viewers from the networks on weekend nights when they offered their most popular movies. *60 Minutes* was no longer competing with what ABC and NBC were offering, plus PBS and local stations in major markets, but was running against a whole alphabet soup offering commercial free, first-run movies—ART, HBO, MAX, MTV, NIK, PSM, SHO, TMC, and USA as Arts & Entertainment Network, Home Box Office, Cinemax, Music Television, Nickelodeon, PRISM, Showtime, The Movie Channel, and USA Network were listed in TV programs. The new competition made the networks even more fixated on instant winners. Norman Lear, the producer who created *All in the Family, The Jeffersons,* and a string of other hit shows in the 1970s and returned to network production in 1984, cited *60 Minutes* as proof that it was still possible to attract a wide audience to a weekly show, but that viewers over the last few years had learned there wasn't going to be anything different in prime time network television. "The adventure that once came with the new shows in the fall now comes from hopping around thirty channels on the dial," he said.

CBS needed a keen eye for long-term planning as William S. Paley finally faded from power after fifty-five years of being in charge. His resignation as chairman of the board left Wyman free to run the company, although Paley continued to cast an elder statesman's shadow, maintaining his office at Black Rock and insisting he was available for tough calls. By 1984, however, the day-to-day decision-making was in the hands of the fifty-five-year-old Wyman, who not only diversified into pay TV but also into the new software that the $15 billion a year home computer revolution spawned. Despite the early defeat of CBS Cable, he kept the corporate finger in the cable pie with MCS, a joint CBS-Contemporary Communications venture. After spending $10 million on interactive cable with AT&T as a partner, CBS joined IBM and Sears in a potentially major videotext venture. With an eye toward the 1990s it teamed up with Japan's NHK to push high-definition television that would offer spectacularly sharper picture reception.

Sauter moved up the corporate ladder in 1983, and Edward M. Joyce became the CBS News boss. Joyce had been news director and general manager of CBS's owned and operated New York and Los Angeles stations. The Broadcast Group continued to account for more than half the total revenues and pretax earnings of CBS Inc., but the expanding news cost money. Unable to persuade their affiliates to give up any of their lucrative local news time for hour-long network evening newscasts, ABC, followed by CBS and NBC, added late-night news. The cost was not directly proportional to the 80 percent increase in daily news programming, but it was still more expensive than running old movies. The numbers were not there at 3 A.M. and, after a year, the networks began to retrench on the early-morning news. ABC cut back *Nightline,* NBC dropped *Overnight,* and both went back to old films and reruns of vintage series while CBS tried to keep *Nightwatch* alive by cutting the 2 A.M. to 6 A.M. program to two hours of original material that was repeated during the subsequent two hours.

Television journalism was evolving a number of formats—breaking news, panel discussions, investigations, documentaries—each with its own feel and almost subliminal instinct and impact. The new overnight broadcasts deepened and broadened television coverage and gained a surprising, if numerically lightweight, following. This explosion of news, from CNN's round-the-clock news and INN midday editions to two- and even three-hour local newscasts, hourly newsbreaks, and all news radio, forced the three networks to reassess their seven o'clock broadcasts. Like Hewitt and Cronkite twenty years earlier, Stringer and Rather tried to measure the evening news in new terms. The news explosion, they reasoned, meant that the early evening viewers already knew the major stories of the day. The broadcast should therefore contain more "discretionary news," more reflection and perspective.

Celebrity journalism remained a fact of TV life. As Barbara Walters put it, the fame of television broadcasters is unavoidable because "you can't go on television and not be recognized." Attractive performers who command national attention and respect are rare and, to the networks, seem to be worth their weight in gold. Such a news anchor can not only give the product sheen and stature, but credibility and authority as well. The downside, for which Roone Arledge's bidding wars for top news-flesh bore a heavy responsibility, is that star anchors, earning five times as much as the president of the United States, tend to be equated with show business rather than legitimate, responsible journalism.

*60 Minutes,* Hewitt has said, with characteristic modesty, could go on forever, and from the perspective of dollars and cents the show seemed as secure as Fort Knox. Hewitt and his group could do no wrong when CBS's Sunday leadership role was mostly due to *60 Minutes'* hefty lead-in each week, year in and year out. Energy and inspiration were Hewitt's trademark as his authority continued to both reflect and impose itself upon the complexity of nonfiction television. He might go off half-cocked on occasion, as his intimates would admit, but his instinct for guessing what viewers want and for dishing it up in ways they couldn't think of wanting remained unerring.

For the news side, he scored one of his most sensational scoops when he obtained a purloined government videotape of John Z. DeLorean allegedly on the verge of completing a $24 million cocaine deal. The tape, aired by CBS two days before jury selection was to begin in the celebrity car maker's Los Angeles trial, showed DeLorean toasting an undercover FBI agent over a satchel said to be full of dope and then being arrested by the lawman. Judge Robert M. Takasugi decounced CBS and promptly postponed the trial, setting off another fair trial *vs.* free press conflict. Hewitt said he got the tapes from *Hustler* magazine publisher Larry Flynt, and that they merely corroborated what the prosecution had already disclosed to the press and in court papers. Flynt admitted he had freely passed the reels along as part of his one-man campaign against "government hypocrisy" and that he believed DeLorean had been entrapped. The new CBS News president backed Hewitt. Any question of whether Flynt had obtained the tapes legally was "between Mr. Flynt and the government," Joyce said, and had no bearing on the decision to broadcast parts of one of the tapes. *The New York Times* called Hewitt "an acquaintance of DeLorean."

Hewitt never forgets he is the creator of a broadcast with stars, that *60 Minutes'* credibility is in direct proportion to his four correspondents' trustworthiness, and that its responsibility is to make sense of things and to give us a visceral charge. "For God's sake, who wants to watch a documentary," he said in a telling remark. "Bill Moyers did a thing called *CBS Reports: Illegal Aliens.* It was great, but it should have been called *The Gonzales Brothers* and the ads should have shown the Immigration Service chasing two wetbacks through the back alleys of Los Angeles."

He called a Jeanne Solomon-Ed Bradley piece on forced labor on the Soviet natural gas pipeline *Gulag Gas.* An Esther Kartiganer-Harry Reasoner report on sulphites found in processed foods that could kill asthma sufferers was tagged *To Your Health;* a Grace Diekhaus-Mike Wallace segment on making older people feel good about themselves was titled *Over the Hill?* He told Harry Moses and Wallace to work up a report on the competition among the ABC, CBS, and NBC evening newscast. He had the title—*The Selling of the Anchor*—before he had the other networks' okay. Av Westin wasn't sure ABC News would cooperate. When *20/20* had tried to film the *CBS Evening News* as it was being produced, he was turned down.

But that was par for the *60 Minutes-20/20* rivalry. Geraldo Rivera put it best when he was asked whether his conscience would allow him to put a story on the air, even if all the facts weren't verified. He wouldn't, he replied, "unless Mike Wallace is about to go with it."

To give the newsmagazine a new twist, Hewitt signed on Jim Henson—who, with the Muppet characters had entertained children and grownups for fifteen years—to do an animated political cartoon for *60 Minutes*. The thirty-second to one-minute clip was to be an animated version of Mount Rushmore with Presidents Thomas Jefferson, Abraham Lincoln, George Washington, and Theodore Roosevelt talking to each other and commenting on current events. "It will be funny but dignified," said Don of the cartoon idea, which would be produced by Henson and use Henson, Frank Oz, and other Muppet animators as the presidential voices.

Was it time for reminiscing? Hewitt began working on *Minute by Minute,* a book collection of *60 Minutes'* anecdotes to be published in 1985. To fight the middle-aged image on the air, Don and crew spiced the show with exciting and disturbing hard-hitters on the Palestinian people, Americans learning the Japanese way in a Nissan Motor plant, and our society's contradictory views on drugs.

The William McClure-Reasoner piece on the Palestinians was about a people without a home, a mirror people of the Jews, living in the Diaspora in 100 countries, emphasizing education and always telling their children not to forget the homeland. The report concentrated on the 300,000 Palestinians living in Kuwait. Four out of every ten doctors in Kuwait were Palestinians, as were the upper echelon of the country's civil service, its bankers, lawyers, merchants, and university graduates, yet citizenship was denied them. The report ended with a 3 A.M. interview in Algiers with Yassir Arafat, portraying him as a man of conviction as he told of his people's deep roots.

The Suzanne St. Pierre-Safer story on Nissan Motor's assembly plant in Smyrna, Tennessee, was another seminal "packaged reality" moment that measured the epicenter of new social tremors. It had Martin R. Runyon, the president of Nissan's United States unit, explain that "we're transplanting Japanese techniques wherever we can, wherever they seem appropriate," and showed company-uniformed workers telling Safer they were grateful (more than 80,000 people had applied for the 2,000 available jobs) and were going to do their damndest to do the company proud and build trucks, "American trucks," that will stand up to the competition. One in six workers was sent to Japan to learn to build the "Tennessee Cadillacs," as they affectionately named the compact vehicles they would be building, and the segment showed them doing "whatever the Japanese did," including exercises on the shop floor. It showed a humbled Douglas Fraser, the outgoing United Auto Workers president, saying American car makers had better learn a few things, too. The segment reflected something of the new global insecurity and the brave face blue-collar American was trying to put on to conceal a deep resentment against too clever foreign competition and a government in Washington that might not understand the challenge.

Society's ambivalence toward drugs as both never-never solution to the control of heinous criminals and the curse of America's youth was illustrated in early 1984. On January 15, Allan Maraynes and Ed Bradley reported on Johns Hopkins University's research into the use of Depo-Provera, a contraceptive for women, as a sex drive suppressant for male sex offenders. The segment featured rapists saying that didn't mind the possible cancer side effects of the drug as long as it controlled their urge, and zeroed in on Larry Paoli—a sex offender serving eighteen consecutive life sentences for rape—and a victim of rape. To protect both rapist and victim from possible vengeful harm, both were disguised for the camera by makeup artists, a first for *60 Minutes*.

Two weeks later, Martin Phillips and Bradley presented the story of Straight Inc., a St. Petersburg, Florida based drug program that claims a 50 percent success rate in curing teenage drug addicts. Parents paid $2,000 to enroll their kids in the program, which worked somewhat like Alcoholic Anonymous on peer pressure, but also used isolation as a psychological weapon. The segment was less than overbearing. Bradley talked to Fred Collins, a young man who brought a $200,000 suit against Straight for subjecting him to ten-hour interview sessions and for holding him against his will. Bill Oliver, a Straight executive, defended the methods and said parents were grateful they had somewhere they could turn, a sentiment strongly echoed in letters to 555 West 57th Street in the following weeks, letters berating *60 Minutes* for daring to savage this one drug treatment program desperate parents could turn to.

There were difficult stories on health, disease, and cures. With Steve Glauber, Bradley examined the moral dilemma faced by parents who must decide whether children born with birth defects should live or die. With Joel Bernstein, he scrutinized a controversy over whether chemical spraying in Moundville, Alabama, killed a child and, with Esther Kartiganer (responsible for earlier pieces on nuclear reactor failures and the Love Canal), a story on cancer victims. Allan Maraynes and Wallace did controversial drug stories. Jim Jackson and Reasoner told of a suburban New York doctor who had become the pillar of an inner city neighborhood, and Joseph Wershba and Safer reported on the motion picture home for Hollywood's dues-paying retirees.

The power of *60 Minutes* as a public relations vehicle was severely questioned with *Man of Honor*, a two-part profile of reputed Mafia boss Joseph Bonanno, aired in the spring of 1983 and smelling of publicity hype as part two of the broadcast coincided with Simon and Schuster's launch of Bonanno's autobiography, intriguingly entitled *Man of Honor*. Produced by Ira Rosen, *Man of Honor I* and *II* featured Wallace interviewing the seventy-eight-year-old retired crime boss in his Tucson, Arizona, home, and tooling around Brooklyn in Bonanno Junior's car while father and son ridiculed all allegations and philosophized that what others might call conspiracy to murder was, to them, the settling of accounts among honorable men. To listen to them, the elder Bonanno's role at meetings of Mafia bosses was to spread peace and harmony, and his life in crime certainly never extended beyond the traditional crime family activities of extortion, gambling, and loan sharking to such unforgivable offenses as trafficking in prostitution, narcotics, and murder. The Mike Wallace plug was a PR agent's dream. *Man of Honor* never made it onto the best seller list, however.

The power to corrupt was illustrated in *From Pac-Man to Poker-Man*, a searing 1984 report on video poker machines invading bars and restaurants in big and small cities and leaving behind a trail of organized intimidation, bribery, and abuse. Produced by Paul Loewenwarter and reported by Wallace, the segment showed that each machine grossed bar owners $500 a week, or in many instances $100,000 a year. The estimated total for New York State alone was three-quarters of a billion dollars. With the exception of one lone lawman in the South, Wallace reported that state and local authorities "won't or can't put a stop to it." Besides ducking threats and bribes, prosecutors had a hard time having the machines declared slot machines, a definition that would make video poker illegal practically everywhere except Nevada and Atlantic City. High-powered defense lawyers for manufacturers, distributors, and owners of the twenty-five cents a throw machines persuaded more than one court that video poker was nothing more than an electronic card game. Two weeks after the *60 Minutes* report aired, the Montana Supreme Court overturned such a lower court decision and ruled that although poker was legal in the state, video machines were not because only one person could play the game and the machine was programmed to retain 22 to 25 percent of money deposited. "Poker is a game of skill and chance," the ruling said. "It is not a game programmed so no one wins a certain percentage of the time."

News and information were the exception to a generally negative viewer attitude toward network television. Americans were becoming increasingly dissatisfied with the entertainment they saw on the tube and spending less time watching than they had done before, a major trade association study revealed. Commissioned by the National Association of Broadcasters, the 1983 survey found viewers had become more critical and more judgmental of the programming offered by the three commercial networks and that they considered television a less important force in their lives. John Bowen, one of the authors of the study, said viewers thought there was too much violence and sex, that situation comedies had become sillier, and that there was not enough family programming. The survey came as network executives acknowledged new prime time programs had a higher failure rate than ever and as the networks' share of the audience continued to slip. Said Bowen, "The hardest attitude for the television industry to overcome is the belief that the public out there loves them."

The one bright spot was greater viewer satisfaction with news and information programs and an increase in network news watching as opposed to a fall-off in local news viewing. This, said Bowen, reflected "a pervasive concern and interest in the economy at all levels of society." News as the exception was confirmed by a Roper poll. Television was the main source of news by the widest margin in the twenty-four years of the Roper survey, and television was by far the most credible news source, enjoying a better than 2 to 1 margin over newspapers.

"We have been guilty of putting our audience to sleep too often," said NBC Chairman Grant Tinker in reaction to the National Association of Broadcasters study. Such self-criticism was not the corporate style at Black Rock. In the face of the survey findings that the public was jilting its TV love, CBS Broadcast Group President Gene Jankowski said he thought people continued their love affair with the tube. As proof he cited *60 Minutes* and such multipart miniseries as *Roots, Shogun, The Winds of War,* and *The Thorn Birds.*

The average American is now spending about four hours a week watching news and information. The onrush of high-tech development is unrelenting. Today it is helicopter mobile units and electronic news gathering (ENG) cameras, married to microwave transmission that permit live reports from practically anywhere, computer generated graphics that allow visual explanations of complex issues that a Hewitt couldn't even have dreamed of when he bought that coffee shop sandwich board. Tomorrow promises to stress videotext, allowing two-way interactivity. But the future seems less a matter of technology than of imagination.

New technology doesn't guarantee quality journalism. Choppers and ENG cameras increase competitive pressures and compress the time available for preparing the facts, including the time to get the facts right. Graphics generators might cause oversimplification and distortions, and videotext might mean more intrusiveness.

In this perspective, *60 Minutes* can take the future in stride. "We're already the best, the most watchable," says Hewitt. The kind of television *60 Minutes* confects is supposed to be out of sync with popular demands. It should be too speculative, risky, potentially litigious and, finally, unmarketable because it requires a degree of attention that supposedly bored, sated, and indifferent viewers won't bother with. Hewitt still has no grand theory as to why, in spite of this, people continue to consider his show the most watchable program, but the public apparently is putting its dial where its mouth is, as he once said it should do. And this is what the networks are supposed to want anyway—a more even split between news and entertainment to even out the high cost of prime time programming.

The newsmagazines seems to be softening their posture of perennial mistrust, but so is the American public. Activism as a historical phase may be ebbing. Political radicals of both extremes may regret that and find the new era unexciting, but for survivalists and pacifists this is reassuring.

Is the public's wish to be informed catching up with the wish to be entertained? Dan Rather, who is emerging as the favorite dispenser of the nightly news roundup, thinks public understanding of the news process is increasing. "I think the public has become very knowledgeable about news, newspeople, and how news is done. I think they understand a great deal about what it is journalists do and how they do it."

Disclosure in courts and in media of the news process has a salutory effect as we all develop a more sophisticated understanding of how it is all put together for us. A lawyer's contention that parts of a *60 Minutes* segments were staged can result in wide publicity, but the example of a powerful network vigorously defending and explaining a number of its news practices also shows newspeople believing in themselves and in their work.

"The show is excellent, the best thing on television," says Fred Friendly, *60 Minutes'* most perceptive critic. "It could be so much more. It's got a lock now on one hour of prime time. No one in news has had that kind of franchise before, not even Ed Murrow. They could do so much more with it. You see that when they're at their best." Hewitt himself knows that his program's success could also cause its death by institutionalizing its shortcomings and by simplifying complex issues into a world populated almost exclusively by heroes and villains. But he also knows he tried something new by making his reporters report from the field, by making them protagonists in the stories instead of hosts on studio swivel chairs. In the thirty-year evolution of television news, there is something revolutionary in the idea of taking us along, of letting us in on the story up front, of giving it transparency.

Too many stories are still manipulative, going for the easy "wow" instead of illumination. The most interesting reports are not the ones trying to pull strings, but the ones giving us a glimpse of an unsuspecting side of ourselves and, better still, bearing witness to what we are to each other. What we want from *60 Minutes* is to be able to tune into our society as it is here and now. The program became a habit when it told us who we were, and what kind of world we lived in.

The show is put together by professional people, most of whom have been around for a while and have earned our acceptance and their place in our awareness. As long as they take us along on their journalistic adventures, they can count on a very sizable audience keeping the appointment for the now familiar, "We will be back next week with another edition of *60 Minutes.*"

# Notes

The primary source of the factual material in this book is scores of hours of interviews—many of them tape-recorded—with executives and producers at all three networks, individuals who have been featured in *60 Minutes* stories, and the reviewing of video and printed transcripts of over a hundred newsmagazine transcripts. The author attended the Princeton University sessions and sat in on the *Galloway v. CBS* trial in Superior Court in Los Angeles, where he lived until 1983.

The sources and documentation supporting certain portions of the narratives are cited below.

1. *Afterburn:* The author visited Polo, Illinois, in the spring of 1983 and kept abreast of developing legal ramifications through correspondence with Eric Gubelman of the *Tri-County Press.* While in Polo, the author interviewed all the prinicpals involved in the Stitzel case.

2. *From There to Here:* Details of Don Hewitt's startup of the newsmagazine in 1968 are contained in interviews given by him, Harry Reasoner, and Mike Wallace and in *Air Time: The Inside Story of CBS News* by Gary Paul Gates (see Bibliography). Hewitt wrote the "My Turn" column in *Newsweek,* Aug. 1, 1983, on groups and individuals critical of *60 Minutes,* from the World Jewish Congress to the Palestine Liberation Organization, the National Council of Churches, and the National Rifle Association. The author spoke to Jorge O'Leary, a rallying point in the Phelps Dodge strike in Arizona, about striking copper miners staging violence in a bid for *60 Minutes* attention in 1984. The Jan. 21, 1983, issue of *U.S. News & World Report* gave the findings of news media authority Lawrence Lichty on "news seekers." *TV Guide* rated newscasters Sept. 25, 1983. Channel 9, Sidney's Los Angeles office, furnished details of the "down under" *60 Minutes.* Ratings statistics were culled from Hollywood trade papers and the *Los Angeles Herald Examiner;* points and ad revenues from *The New York Times.*

3. *Newsflesh:* Besides personal interviews, the author has relied on the abundant print documentation on Ed Bradley, Harry Reasoner, Morley Safer, Dan Rather, Mike Wallace, and Andy Rooney. Rod Townley in "Slow down, Ed Bradley, Slow down!" in *TV Guide* Feb. 20, 1982, and Kristin McMurran, in "Can a Whole Life Fit into *60 Minutes?*" in *People,* 1983 outlined Bradley's background, his Vietnam years, and his difficulty in adapting to the *60 Minutes* pace and excellence. *Time,* Nov. 29, 1982, reported on the obstacles faced by minority journalists, and a Jan. 22, 1983, *TV Guide* piece compared Bradley with other investigative reporters. A number of newspaper articles in *W* and the *New York Post* have added to Reasoner's autobiography, *Before the Colors Fade,* since its 1981 publication (see Bibliography). Don Hewitt's dissatisfaction with Reasoner's work was detailed in *The Los Angeles Times,* June 11, 1980. Articles on Safer have appeared in *People,* Jan. 15, 1979, and the *Toronto Globe & Mail,* Nov. 17, 1979. His Vietnam years are described in *Air Time op. cit.* News articles on Wallace go back to *Newsweek,* Sept. 16, 1957, detailing the Mike Wallace interview show with Mickey Cohen and scandal sheet private eye Fred Otash. Mike and Lorraine Wallace's marriage is detailed in *Women's Wear Daily,* Dec. 10, 1974 and *Good Housekeeping,* May 1978. *Playboy's Guide to Electronic Entertainment,* fall-winter 1981, featured a candid conversation with him; *Mother Jones* published "Semi-Tough, the Politics Behind 60 Minutes" as a Q and A and an interview with Wallace in Sept.–Oct. 1979, and *Newsweek,* Dec. 27, 1982, provided details of his 1983–88 contract. Andy Rooney's background and ascent were covered by *New York,* March 17, 1980. The *Chicago Tribune* magazine, Aug. 31, 1981, featured Rooney, as did *The Los Angeles Times* Dec. 4, 1970, and *Time,* July 11, 1969. Richard Leibner was featured in *People,* July 17, 1982.

4. *Getting the Story:* The author was associate producer on the shooting of a feature film in Lordsburg, New Mexico. His connections with KCET, Los Angeles, led to the Community Informational Project. The *Arson for Profit* story was researched by the author in Chicago and received polemic attention in *Broadcast Journalism; The Eighth Alfred I. Dupont/Columbia University Survey,* ed: Marvin Barrett. The author interviewed Roman Polanski and Anjelica Houston before his 1978 trial in Los Angeles. Barbara Leaming, *Polanski: A Biography* contains details of Mike Wallace filming Polanski in Normandy. Stanley Rader detailed his *God and Mammon* clashes in his autobiography, *Against the Gates of Hell.*

5. *Hewitt* and 6. *The Back of the Book:* The formative years of CBS television are covered in a number of volumes, including William S. Paley, *As It Happened;* Eric Barnouw, *A History of Broadcasting in the United States;* Fred Friendly, *Due to Circumstances Beyond Our Control,* and David Halberstam, *The Powers That Be.* CBS News has its own literature: Robert Metz, *CBS: Reflections in a Bloodshot Eye* and, especially important, Gates, *Air Time.* Herbert J. Gans wrote *Deciding What's News, A Study of CBS Evening News, NBC*

*Nightly News, Newsweek, and Time,* and Av Westin mentioned his years at CBS with and under Don Hewitt in *Newswatch.* Hewitt's role in the 1960 Kennedy-Nixon debates is documented in the volumes by Gates and Barnouw. The *Encyclopedia Britannica Yearbooks* are especially instructive on the year-by-year progress of television in the late 1950s and early 1960s. UPI covered the death of Mike Wallace's son in Greece; Gates and Friendly discuss Hewitt's fall from grace at the Cronkite evening news. *The New York Times,* Nov. 11, 1970, *Variety,* Dec. 29, 1965, *American Film,* April 1982, and Barnouw examined the decline of documentaries in television. The leadup to *60 Minutes'* debut is described in William Leonard's foreword to *60 Minutes Verbatim, Who Said What to Whom.*

7. *Developing Muscle: Daily Variety,* Sept. 26, 1968, reviewed the first edition of *60 Minutes,* as did *The New York Times,* Sept. 25, 1968. In *Before the Colors Fade,* Reasoner describes how Hewitt approached him to become the newsmagazine's correspondent. Barnouw and Joe McGinniss, *The Selling of the President,* detail the 1968 Chicago convention riots; Dan Rather, with Mickey Herskowitz, in *The Camera Never Blinks,* tells of Rather's personal adventures in the 1968 politics. *The New York Times,* Sept. 11, 1970, discusses Palmer Williams' role in the early *60 Minutes,* and Sept. 18, 1970, *60 Minutes'* first glimpse at cable television. On Nov. 12, 1970, the *Times* speculated on Reasoner's successor and, a week later, announced Safer's appointment. The Nixon administration's feud with the networks is documented by Halberstam and Les Brown in *Television, The Business Behind the Boss.* Stephan Lesher, *Media Unbound: The Impact of Television Journalism on the Public,* details Barry Lando's attempt to sell Hewitt on a segment on Colonel Anthony Herbert. The author supplemented this information with accounts from Herbert's lawyer, Johnathan Lubell, and Ret. General Paul Harkins.

8. *Getting the Politicos:* The Cluster Bomb Units controversy was covered by the *New Republic,* July 21, 1973. Details of *60 Minutes'* coverage of the Clifford Irving hoax were described in *The New York Times,* Jan. 24, 1972, and Hewitt getting to Dita Beard in Denver in the same newspaper April 3, 1971. CBS publicity releases have the background of *60 Minutes* time slot shifts. *Newsweek,* April 9, 1973, reviewed *60 Minutes* as did *The New York Times'* John J. O'Connor, Nov. 11, 1973. *Life's* review of *60 Minutes* appeared May 12, 1972. *Accuracy in Media* is published every other week in Washington. *TV Guide,* April 16, 1983, reported Defense Department's standing policy of noncooperation, confirmed by Hewitt in *Newsweek,* Aug. 1, 1983. *The New York Times,* Jan. 25, 1981, documented *60 Minutes'* producer Harry Moses' filming the James Thornwell story.

9. *Scams and Hustles:* The author interviewed Lawrence Kessler on *The Criminal Mind* and Dr. Stan Samenov's theories. Paley's tribute to *60 Minutes* appears in *As It Happened. Rolling Stone* published Donovan Moore's "60

Minutes," January 12, 1978: *The New York Times* cover story "How '60 Minutes' Makes News" by Harry Stein, May 6, 1979 and Laura Cunningham's article in *Cosmopolitan,* June 1980. *The Los Angeles Times* published David Shaw's two-part story on *60 Minutes* June 10 and 11, 1980, and *The Christian Science Monitor* its interview with Hewitt Nov. 21, 1981. The Clarence Medlin scam was a media event in North Carolina in November and December 1975. The *Greensboro Record* followed up on the arrest and restitution of some of the money to *60 Minutes* Dec. 9, 1975, and the Associated Press carried the story of Medlin's arrest in New Orleans Dec. 13, 1975. Dan Rather mentions the impact of the Kepone controversy in *The Camera Never Blinks; The Wall Street Journal* covered the Illinois Power contretemps June 27, 1980, a chapter on credibility in *Broadcast Journalism* examined the response to IP's *60 Minutes/Our Reply.* The author researched the continued construction delays in Illinois since the broadcast. *New York,* Feb. 4, 1980, detailed the Franklin Mint "meltdown" by *60 Minutes.*

10. *The Business of Religion:* Garn Baum confirmed the basics of his lawsuit against the Mormon Church to the author; *The New York Times,* March 23, 1976, detailed *60 Minutes'* return to film the Syrian Jews; the Scientology inquiry held press attention through 1983 as the fate of founder L. Ron Hubbard remained a mystery. *Time* covered the subject Jan. 31, 1983; Baghwan Shree Rajneesh held national attention during deportation proceedings against him, notably in *The New York Times,* March 18, 1983 feature and in *Newsweek* "Update" April 11, 1983. *60 Minutes'* reliance on evidence supplied by neoconservative groups attacking mainline Protestant churches was detailed in *Time,* March 28, 1983. National Council of Churches president James Armstrong told *Newsweek,* Feb. 7, 1983, that the *60 Minutes* program could do the NCC great damage. *Variety,* March 23, 1983, reported the FCC had asked CBS to respond to a complaint about the segment.

11. *Honorable Mention:* Events leading to the release of convicted Texas engineer Lenell Geter following the Dec. 4, 1983 airing of his story were covered in *The New York Times,* December 11, 15, and 19. The author researched the Mims Hackett story in New Jersey and conferred with the office of Florida Governor Robert Graham on the developments of the Stanley Jaffe case, as well as with Dr. Robert Nejdl and Los Angeles prosecutors on *Charged with Murder.* The author interviewed Pearl S. Buck Foundation director Don Shade, Jr., in Perkasie, Pennsylvania, and, by telephone, Dr. Jerry Jampolsky in Tiburon, California, on the effects of *60 Minutes* exposure in *Honor Thy Children* and *Helping. Newsweek,* Oct. 18, 1982, featured Dr. Jerrold Petrofsky of Wright University in Dayton. The author interviewed Marva Collins in Chicago and relied on background reports in *Saturday Review,* April 14, 1979, *Ebony,* Feb. 18, 1981, *Essence,* Oct. 1981, and Collins and Civia Tamarkin, *Marva Collins' Way.*

12. *Affairs of State:* The White House attempts to bar *The Iran File* segment were revealed at Press Secretary Jody Powell's March 6, 1980 press briefing and reported the next day in *The New York Times.* White House Chief of Staff Hamilton Jordan dwelt on his day-to-day maneuvers to offset media attention from his meetings with Sadegh Ghotbzadeh in *Crisis: The Last Year of the Carter Presidency.* Stephan Lesher quotes Hewitt's response to Jody Powell's appeal for patriotism in *Media Unbound.* William Leonard confirmed to the author the White House attempt to suppress *The Iran File.* Checkbook journalism was a public issue after Wallace's interview with H. R. Haldeman and is discussed in a number of books, including Metz, *CBS Reflections in a Bloodshot Eye.* Wallace himself discussed the Haldeman encounter on *CBS Morning News,* May 18, 1983. The Frank E. Terpil and George Gregory Korkala convictions in absentia in New York were carried in *The New York Times,* June 9, 1981, and the prosecution's attempt to obtain *60 Minutes'* outtakes with the fugitives from justice, Sept. 22, 1983. The post-Grenada invasion antimedia attitude and a quick analysis of *60 Minutes'* Lone Ranger journalism were part of the *Time,* Dec. 12, 1983, cover story, ''Accusing the Press.''

13. *Shaping It: The New York Times* brought up the Writers Guild of America fight for accreditation for anonymous *60 Minutes* collaborator on May 15, 1981. The author interviewed WGA attorney Mona Mangan. Daniel Schorr's autobiography, *Clearing the Air,* details the Wallace interview during the Pike commission hearings, and Schorr's views on editing. Hewitt is quoted on editing in *The New Yorker,* July 26, 1982; Paley mentions reverse shots and his objections to them in *As It Happened.* Dr. Paul Shriver of the Indiana State Prison for Women described the Joyce DeVillez case and the Safer filming at the prison in correspondence with the author. The national media and the author himself covered the five-week trial of Dr. Carl Galloway's suit against CBS and the *It's No Accident* segment during the summer of 1983. *The Los Angeles Times* and *Daily Variety* covered the proceedings at Dept 58A, Los Angeles Superior Court on a day-to-day basis, starting with the court's March 20, 1983, decision not to release outtakes of the *60 Minutes* segment to the June 6 verdict, and the July 11, request for a new trial.

14. *Hanging versus Lynching: The New York Times* reported Dec. 8, 1983, on the tension on the frontiers of libel and courts wrestling with major First Amendment questions. The newspaper covered the Long Island appeals court decision in the *Dr. Joseph Greenberg vs. CBS* libel suit resulting from the *Over the Speed Limit* segment, Aug. 10, 1979. *The Uncounted Enemy,* broadcast Jan. 23, 1982, received intense coverage during the 1983 pretrial phase when CBS lost a number of court decisions in General William C. Westmoreland's $120 million libel suit. The author interviewed a number of the principals and attended news conferences at which both plaintiff and defendant disclosed sworn testimony. *The New York Times* April 25 and May 15 reported the dispute over

the Don Kowet book, *A Matter of Honor,* as did *The Los Angeles Times,* April 27 and May 24, and *Time,* May 7, 1984. *The Wall Street Journal, Los Angeles Herald Examiner,* and *The New York Times* covered the Jan. 14, 1983, attempts by U. S. District Judge Adrian Duplantier to block the *60 Minutes* broadcast on seven New Orleans police officers charged with violating the civil rights of blacks during a police murder investigation.

15. *A Judgmental Business:* The author attended the Columbia Graduate School of Journalism/CBS conferences at Princeton University. *The New York Times,* Sept. 28, 1981, reviewed *60 Minutes* looking at itself.

16. *Imitations: The New York Times,* May 2, 1978, and June 18, 1978, and *Newsweek,* June 26, 1978, reported the troubled debut of *20/20. TV Guide,* Feb. 18, 1978, detailed the birth of *Weekend. The New York Times* critic John J. O'Connor reviewed David Brinkley and his *NBC Magazine,* Aug. 5, 1980; *TV Guide* rated TV's investigative reporters, Jan. 22, 1983. *The Wall Street Journal* profiled Grant Tinker Dec. 6, 1982; *Newsweek,* May 16, 1983, did NBC programmer Brandon Tartikoff. *Variety,* May 18, 1983, reported NBC affiliate resistance to Sunday night scheduling of *First Camera. Esquire* profiled Van Gordon Sauter, Nov. 1982. Barbara Matusow, *The Evening Stars* dwelt extensively on ABC's wooing of Dan Rather and CBS's countermoves to retain him. *Variety* reported Oct. 5, 1983, on Roger Mudd's uncertain future at NBC and *The New York Times* Feb. 12, 1984, on his election year duties at NBC. *The New York Times* reported on affiliates dropping *First Camera* Aug. 16, 1983, and on the NBC newsmagazine's poor ratings Oct. 20, 1983.

17. *Crossroads:* The National Association of Broadcasters and Roper surveys were publicized by the trade press in April 1983. Van Gordon Sauter announced the Charles Kuralt-Bill Moyers *CBS Reports* programming Jan. 6, 1983. *The New York Times,* May 14, 1983, and *The Wall Street Journal,* May 16, 1983, reported the CBS News hiring freeze. *The New York Times* detailed Paley's retirement and Wyman's future Sept. 9, 1982, and *Channels* the corporate CBS play in cable, Nov.–Dec. 1982. *Forbes,* Jan. 2, 1984, detailed broadcasting economics outlook and news operating costs. *The New York Times,* reported Oct. 25 and Oct. 30, 1983, how Hewitt acquired videotapes of John Z. DeLorean, *Newsweek* Nov. 7, 1983, on airing of tapes. The slippage and possible arrest of network percentages of viewing audience were continued trade press stories in 1983 and 1984.

# Bibliography

ARLEN, MICHAEL. *The Livingroom War*. New York: Viking, 1979.

BARNOUW, ERIK. *A History of Broadcasting in the United States; The Golden Web; A Tower of Babel;* and *The Image Empire*. New York: Oxford University Press, 1966, 1975.

BARRETT, MARVIN (ed.). *Broadcast Journalism,* the Eighth Alfred I. Dupont/Columbia University Survey. New York: Everest House, 1982.

BRADY, JOHN. *The Craft of Interviewing*. New York: Vintage Books, 1976.

CARTER, JIMMY. *Keeping Faith: Memoirs of a President*. New York: Simon & Schuster, 1982.

COLLINS, MARVA and TAMARKIN, CIVIA. *Marva Collins' Way*. Los Angeles: J. P. Tarcher, 1982.

DIAMOND, EDWIN. *The Tin Kazoo: TV, Politics and the News*. Cambridge: MIT Press, 1975.

EPSTEIN, EDWARD J. *News from Nowhere: TV and the News*. New York: Random House, 1973.

FRIENDLY, FRED. *Due to Circumstances Beyond Our Control*. New York: Random House, 1967.

GATES, GARY PAUL. *Air Time: The Inside Story of CBS News*. New York: Harper & Row, 1978.

GELFMAN, JUDITH S. *Women in Television News*. New York: Columbia University Press, 1976.

GLAD, BETTY, *Jimmy Carter: In Search of the Great White House*. New York: Norton, 1980.

GREEN, TIMOTHY. *The Universal Eye: The World of Television*. New York: Stein & Day, 1972.

245

HILTON, JACK and KNOBLAUCH, MARY. *On Television! A Survival Guide for Media Interviews*. New York: Amacom, 1980.

KENDRICK, ALEXANDER. *Prime Time: The Life of Ed Murrow*. Boston: Little, Brown. 1969.

KOWET, DON. *A Matter of Honor: General William C. Westmoreland vs. CBS*. New York: Macmillan, 1984.

LEAMING, BARBARA. *Polanski: A Biography*. New York: Simon & Schuster, 1981.

LESHER, STEPHEN. *Media Unbound: The Impact of Television Journalism on the Public*. Boston: Houghton Mifflin, 1982.

MCNEAL, ROBERT. *The People Machine*. New York: Harper and Row, 1968.

MATUSOW, BARBARA. *The Evening Stars: The Making of the Network News Anchor*. Boston: Houghton Mifflin, 1983.

METZ, ROBERT. *CBS: Reflections in a Bloodshot Eye*. Chicago: Playhouse Press, 1975.

MICKELSON, SIG. *Electronic Mirror: Politics in an Age of TV*. New York: Dodd, Mead, 1972.

PALEY, WILLIAM S. *As It Happened: A Memoir*. New York: Doubleday, 1979.

RATHER, DAN with HERSKOWITZ, MICKEY. *The Camera Never Blinks*. New York: William Morrow, 1977.

REASONER, HARRY. *Before the Colors Fade*. New York: Knopf, 1981.

ROONEY, ANDREW A. *A Few Minutes with Andy Rooney*. New York: Atheneum, 1981.

———. *And More by Andy Rooney*. New York: Atheneum, 1982.

———. *Conqueror's Peace: A Report to the American Stockholders*. New York: Doubleday, 1947.

ROONEY, ANDREW A. and HARTWELL, DICKSON JAY. *Off the Record: The Best Stories of Foreign Correspondents*. New York: Doubleday, 1952.

ROONEY, ANDREW A. and HUTTON, BUD. *The Story of the Stars and Stripes*. New York: Rinehard, 1944.

SCHORR, DANIEL. *Clearing the Air*. Boston: Houghton Mifflin, 1977.

VANCE, CYRUS. *Hard Choices: Four Years in America's Foreign Policy*. New York: Simon & Schuster, 1983.

WESTIN, AV. *Newswatch: How TV Decides the News.* New York: Simon & Schuster, 1982.

WHITE, THEODORE. *Breach of Faith, The Fall of Richard Nixon.* New York: Atheneum, 1975.

ZENKER, ARNOLD. *Mastering the Public Spotlight.* New York: Dodd, Mead, 1983.

# Index

249